Peter Steigerwald
Renae Geerlings
—collected editions editors
Jason Medley
—graphic designer/goddess lover
Marco 'Madman' Galli
Victor Llamas
Team Tron•
Andy Kim • Marcia Chen •Jose Guillen
Jeff de los Santos • Viet Truong
—ink assists
Nick Chun
Raul Arroyo
—production crew

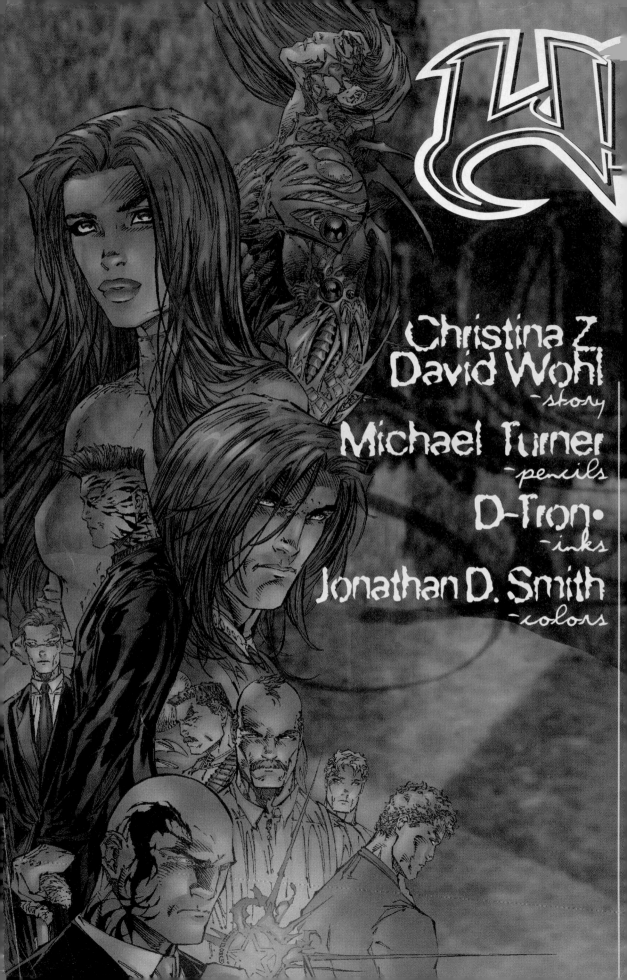

Christina Z
David Wohl
-story

Michael Turner
-pencils

D-Tron·
-inks

Jonathan D. Smith
-colors

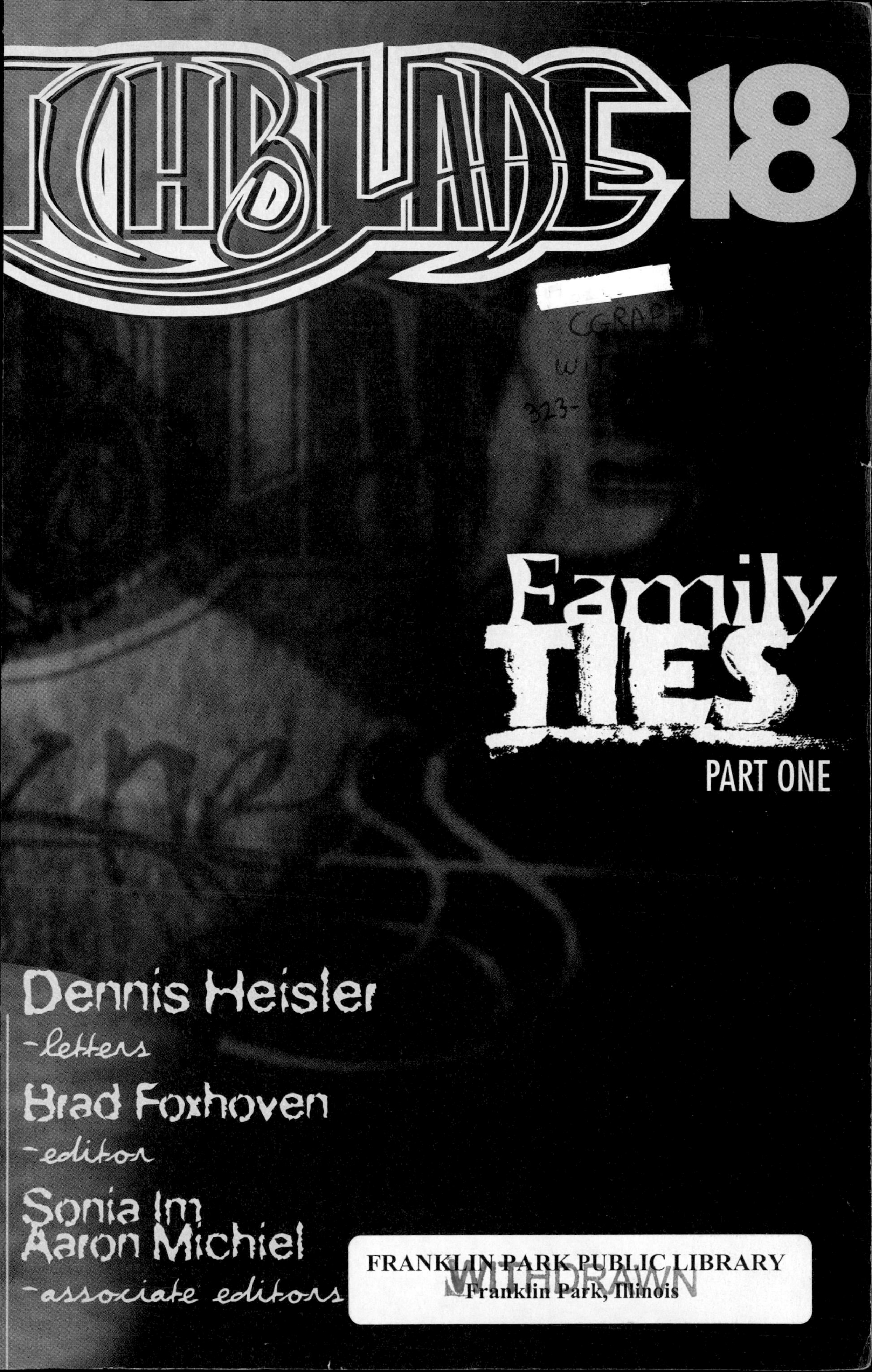
WITCHBLADE 18
Family TIES
PART ONE
Dennis Heisler
-letters
Brad Foxhoven
-editor
Sonia Im
Aaron Michiel
-associate editors

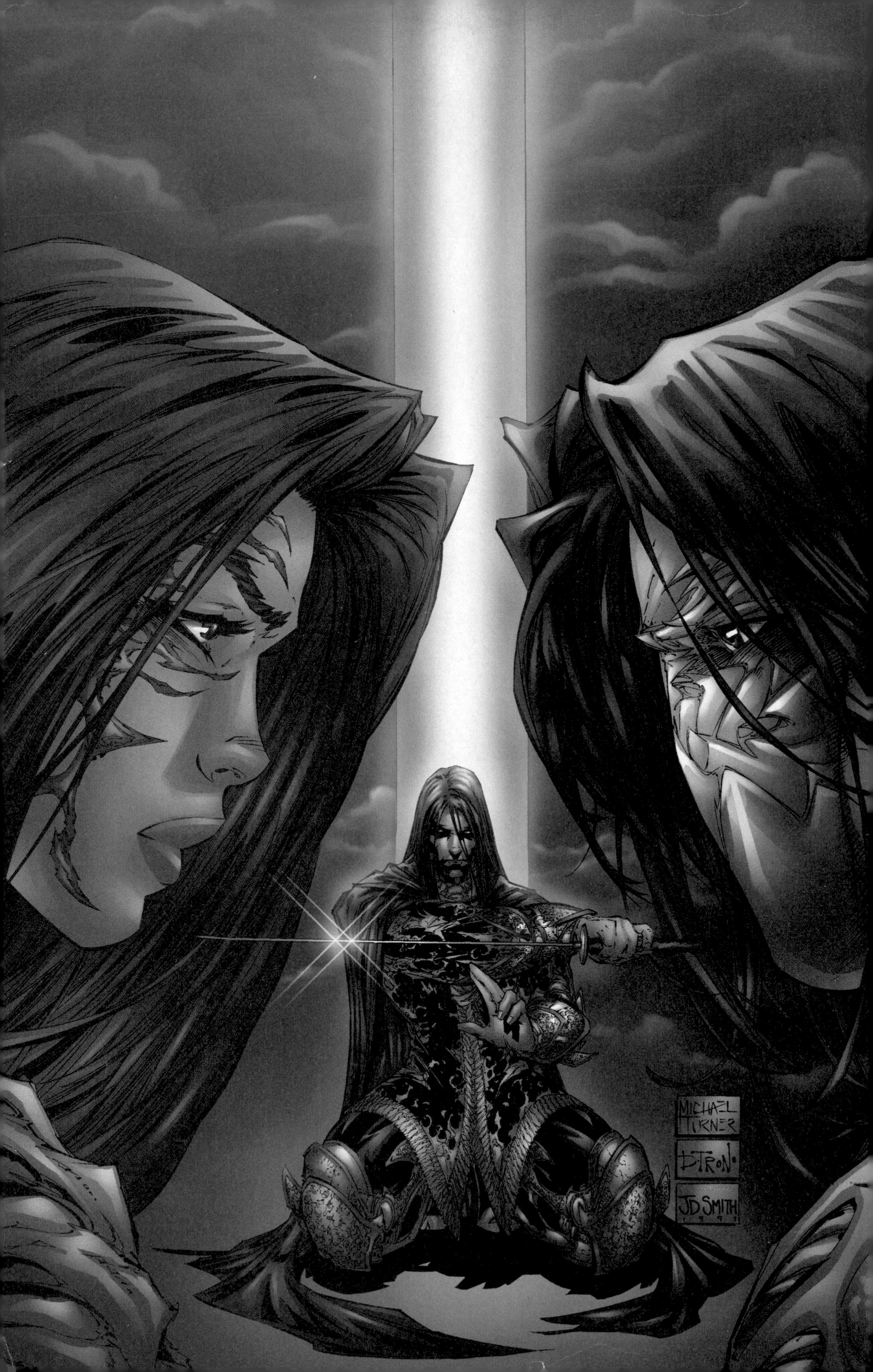
MICHAEL TURNER
D.TRON
JD SMITH

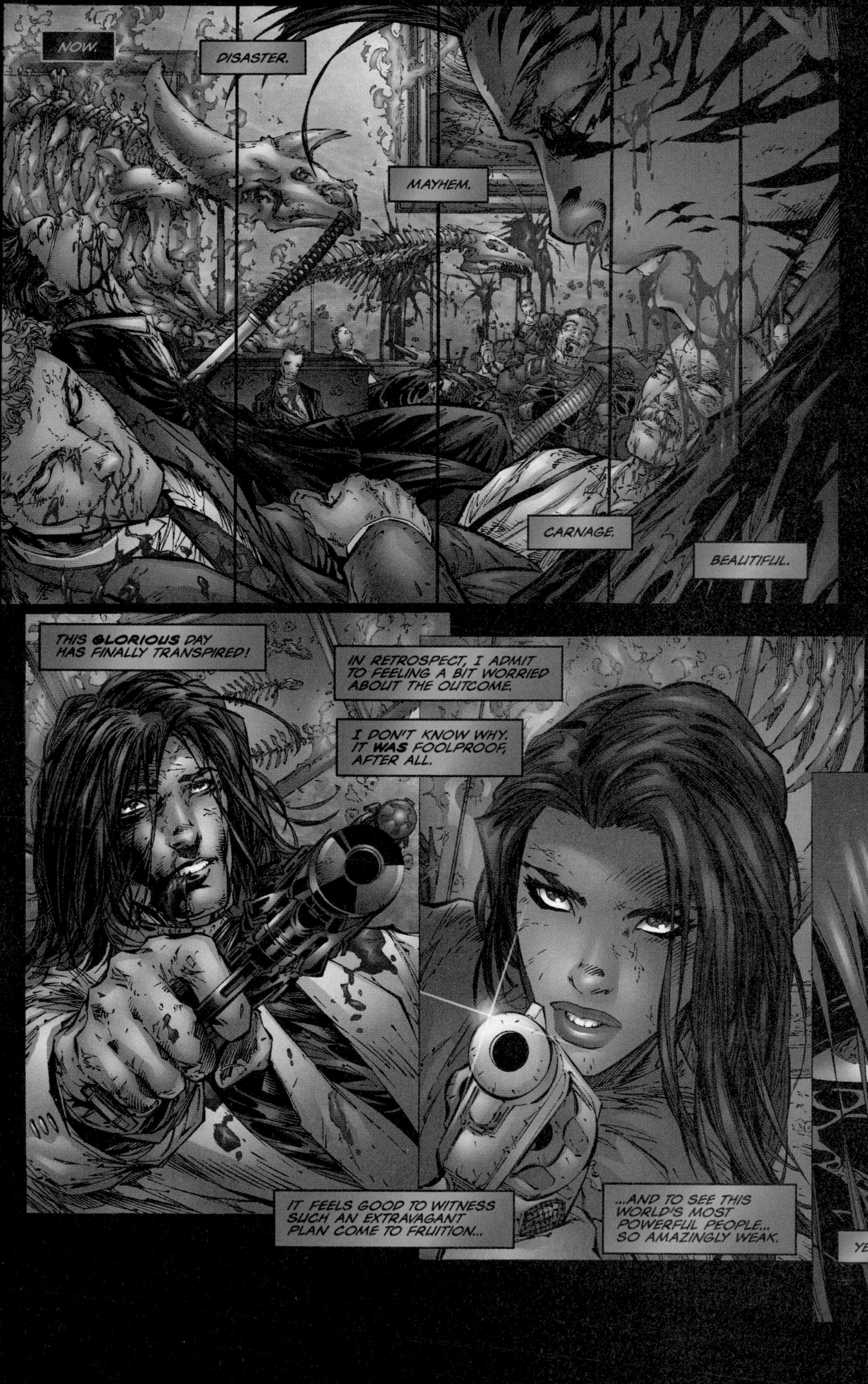
NOW.
DISASTER.
MAYHEM.
CARNAGE.
BEAUTIFUL.
THIS GLORIOUS DAY HAS FINALLY TRANSPIRED!
IN RETROSPECT, I ADMIT TO FEELING A BIT WORRIED ABOUT THE OUTCOME.
I DON'T KNOW WHY. IT WAS FOOLPROOF, AFTER ALL.
IT FEELS GOOD TO WITNESS SUCH AN EXTRAVAGANT PLAN COME TO FRUITION...
...AND TO SEE THIS WORLD'S MOST POWERFUL PEOPLE... SO AMAZINGLY WEAK.
YES...

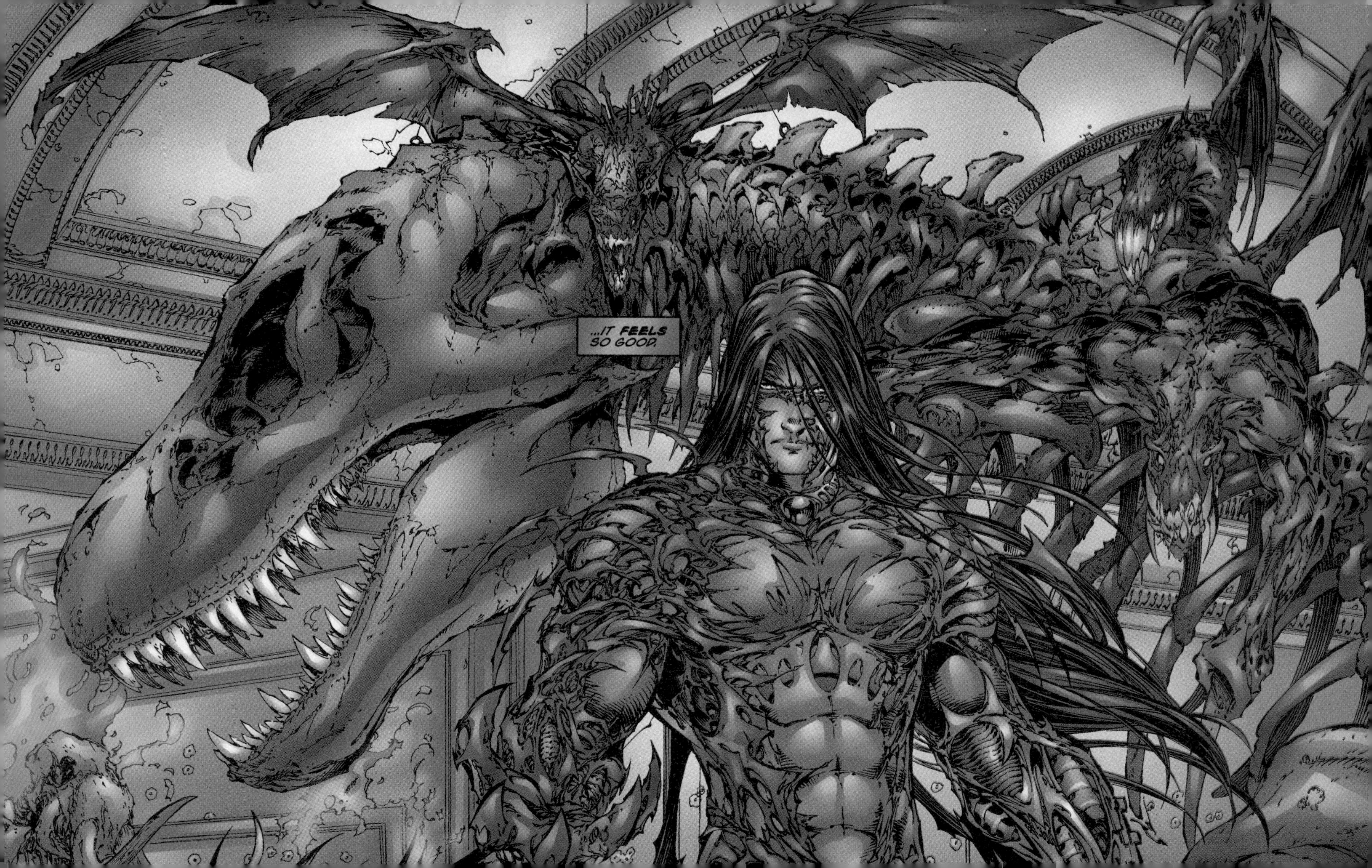
...IT FEELS
SO GOOD.

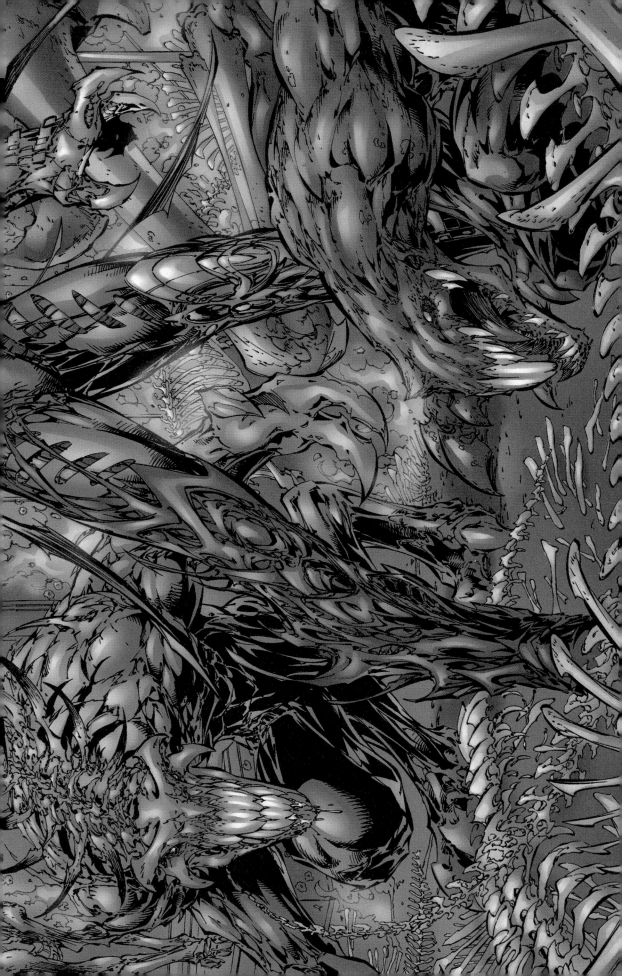

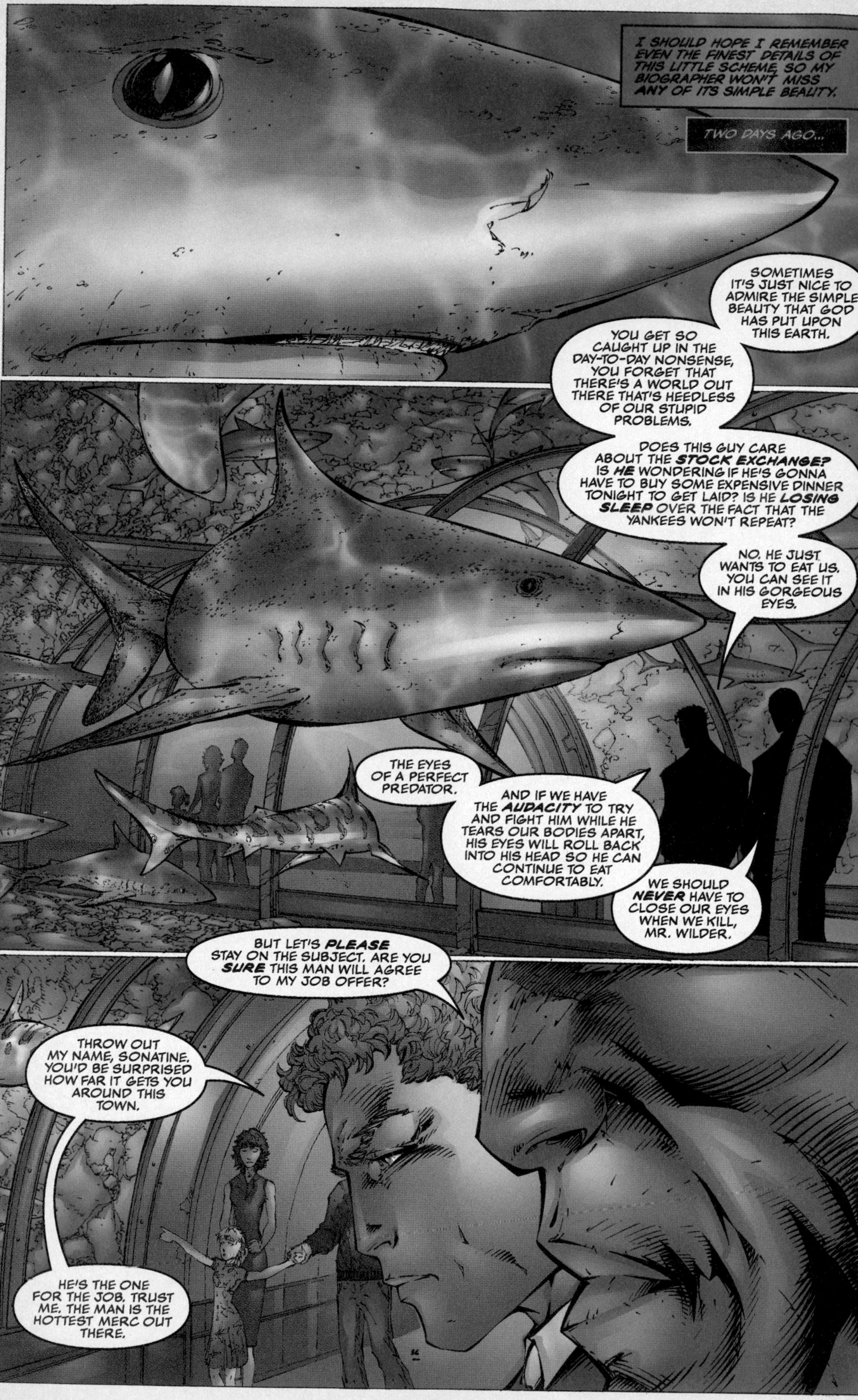
I SHOULD HOPE I REMEMBER EVEN THE FINEST DETAILS OF THIS LITTLE SCHEME, SO MY BIOGRAPHER WON'T MISS ANY OF ITS SIMPLE BEAUTY.
TWO DAYS AGO...
SOMETIMES IT'S JUST NICE TO ADMIRE THE SIMPLE BEAUTY THAT GOD HAS PUT UPON THIS EARTH.
YOU GET SO CAUGHT UP IN THE DAY-TO-DAY NONSENSE, YOU FORGET THAT THERE'S A WORLD OUT THERE THAT'S HEEDLESS OF OUR STUPID PROBLEMS.
DOES THIS GUY CARE ABOUT THE STOCK EXCHANGE? IS HE WONDERING IF HE'S GONNA HAVE TO BUY SOME EXPENSIVE DINNER TONIGHT TO GET LAID? IS HE LOSING SLEEP OVER THE FACT THAT THE YANKEES WON'T REPEAT?
NO. HE JUST WANTS TO EAT US. YOU CAN SEE IT IN HIS GORGEOUS EYES.
THE EYES OF A PERFECT PREDATOR.
AND IF WE HAVE THE AUDACITY TO TRY AND FIGHT HIM WHILE HE TEARS OUR BODIES APART, HIS EYES WILL ROLL BACK INTO HIS HEAD SO HE CAN CONTINUE TO EAT COMFORTABLY.
WE SHOULD NEVER HAVE TO CLOSE OUR EYES WHEN WE KILL, MR. WILDER.
BUT LET'S PLEASE STAY ON THE SUBJECT. ARE YOU SURE THIS MAN WILL AGREE TO MY JOB OFFER?
THROW OUT MY NAME, SONATINE. YOU'D BE SURPRISED HOW FAR IT GETS YOU AROUND THIS TOWN.
HE'S THE ONE FOR THE JOB. TRUST ME. THE MAN IS THE HOTTEST MERC OUT THERE.

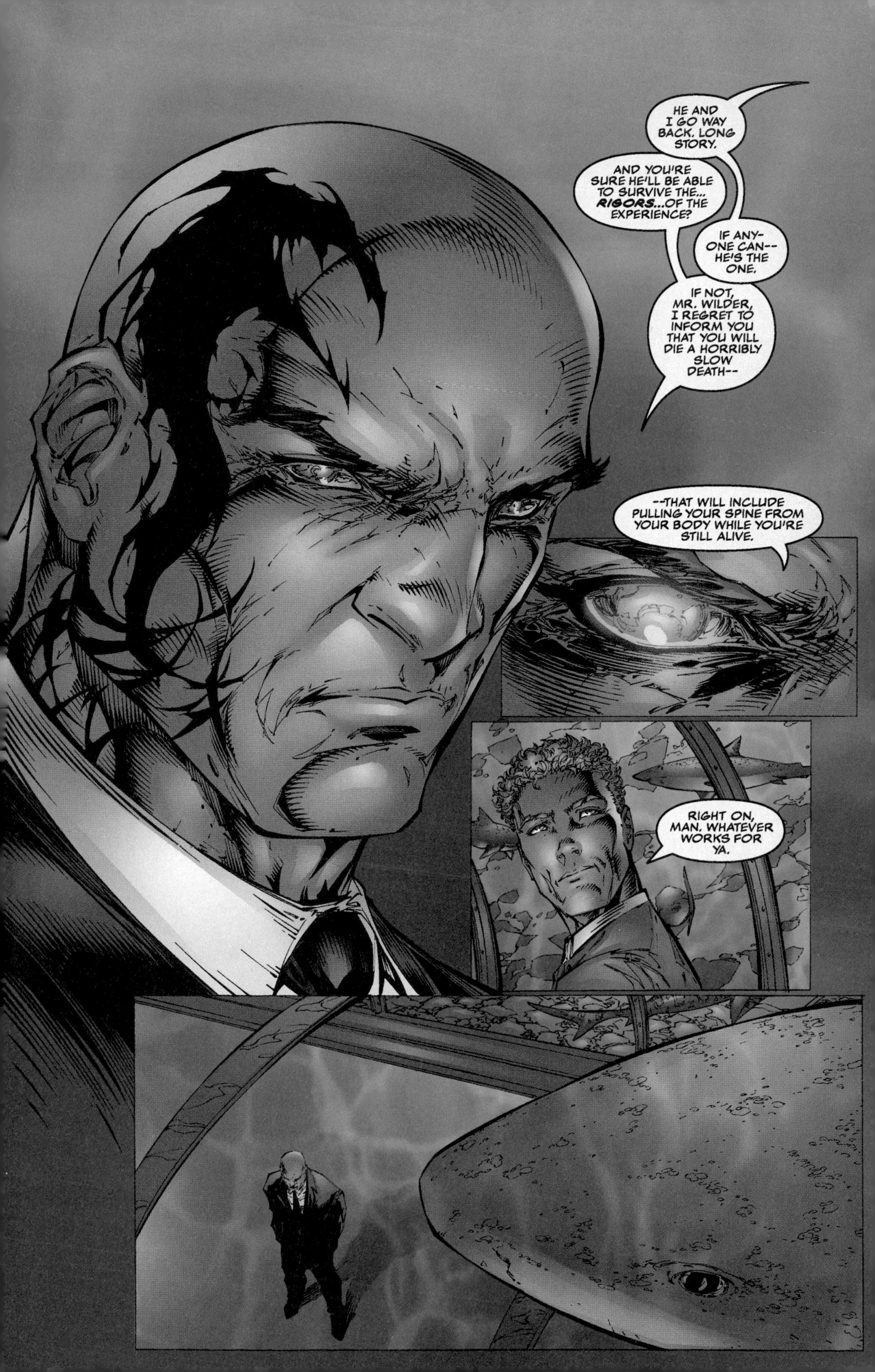
HE AND I GO WAY BACK. LONG STORY.
AND YOU'RE SURE HE'LL BE ABLE TO SURVIVE THE... RIGORS...OF THE EXPERIENCE?
IF ANY-ONE CAN--HE'S THE ONE.
IF NOT, MR. WILDER, I REGRET TO INFORM YOU THAT YOU WILL DIE A HORRIBLY SLOW DEATH--
--THAT WILL INCLUDE PULLING YOUR SPINE FROM YOUR BODY WHILE YOU'RE STILL ALIVE.
RIGHT ON, MAN. WHATEVER WORKS FOR YA.

STATEN ISLAND.

MY FIRST HOMICIDE CASE IN WEEKS, AND WE'VE GOT OURSELVES A REAL **BUTCHER**.

A BUTCHER WHO GETS AROUND.

JAKE SAYS HE FOUND THE SAME M.O. ON SOME YAKUZA HOMICIDES IN MANHATTAN.

IT SEEMS OUR KILLER HAS NO PREFERENCE FOR WHO HE WHACKS, AS LONG AS IT'S **FAMILY**.

MAFIA, THIS TIME. BUCCELLATO FAMILY.

IT'S FUNNY--SO MANY OF THOSE GUYS WHO COME TO MASSAGE PARLORS FOR A LITTLE "RELAXATION" END UP ANYTHING **BUT** RELAXED.

MARCO CESARO ENDED UP WAY MORE RELAXED THAN HE BARGAINED FOR.

ANOTHER VICTIM IN THIS **DAMNED** GANG WAR.

A WAR THAT IS BEING FOUGHT TOO CLOSE TO HOME.

THEY ATTACKED **THE STATION** WHILE I WAS GONE. I STILL CAN'T BELIEVE THAT.

THEY KILLED **DOZENS** OF COPS. SO MANY THAT LOFRUMENTO HAD TO BRING BACK US SUSPENDED DETECTIVES.

I MEAN, THEY CAN KILL EACH OTHER ALL THEY WANT, BUT WHY THE HELL SHOULD THEY PUT THE **COPS** IN THE MIDDLE OF IT?

THEY ALMOST KILLED JOE SIRY, FOR GOD'S SAKE, AND I WASN'T EVEN HERE TO **DO SOMETHING**.

I WAS OFF GETTING MY **OWN** ASS PULLED OUT OF THE FIRE...

...BY IAN **NOTTINGHAM**.

WHY, THOUGH?

WHY HIM?

HOW IS HE EVEN **ALIVE**?

AND WHERE IS HE NOW...?

PEZ?

GIRLS GIRLS GIRLS

POLICE LINE DO NOT CROSS

POLICE LINE DO NOT CROSS

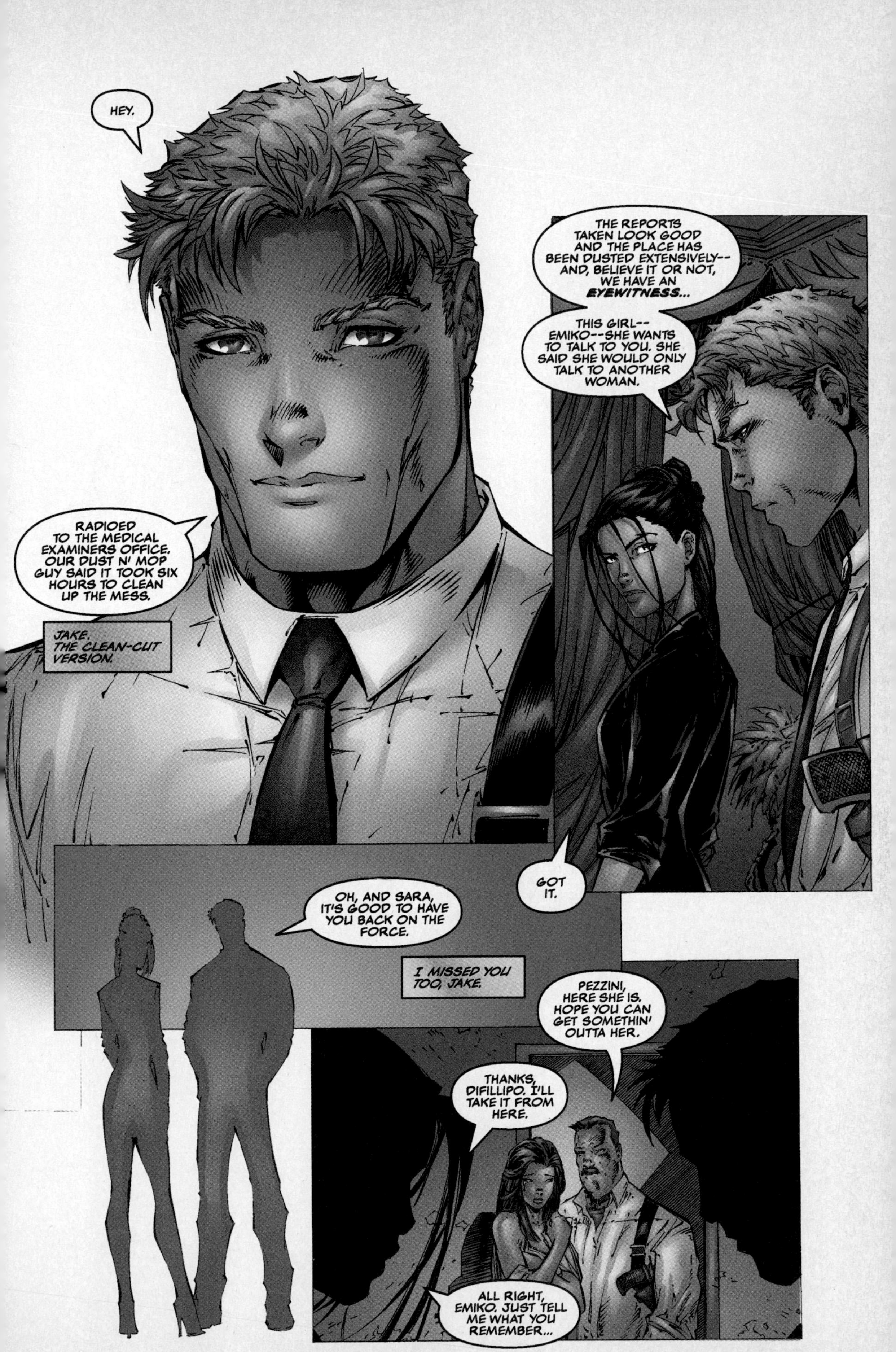
HEY.
RADIOED TO THE MEDICAL EXAMINERS OFFICE. OUR DUST N' MOP GUY SAID IT TOOK SIX HOURS TO CLEAN UP THE MESS.
JAKE. THE CLEAN-CUT VERSION.
THE REPORTS TAKEN LOOK GOOD AND THE PLACE HAS BEEN DUSTED EXTENSIVELY-- AND, BELIEVE IT OR NOT, WE HAVE AN EYEWITNESS...
THIS GIRL-- EMIKO--SHE WANTS TO TALK TO YOU. SHE SAID SHE WOULD ONLY TALK TO ANOTHER WOMAN.
GOT IT.
OH, AND SARA, IT'S GOOD TO HAVE YOU BACK ON THE FORCE.
I MISSED YOU TOO, JAKE.
PEZZINI, HERE SHE IS. HOPE YOU CAN GET SOMETHIN' OUTTA HER.
THANKS, DIFILLIPO. I'LL TAKE IT FROM HERE.
ALL RIGHT, EMIKO. JUST TELL ME WHAT YOU REMEMBER...

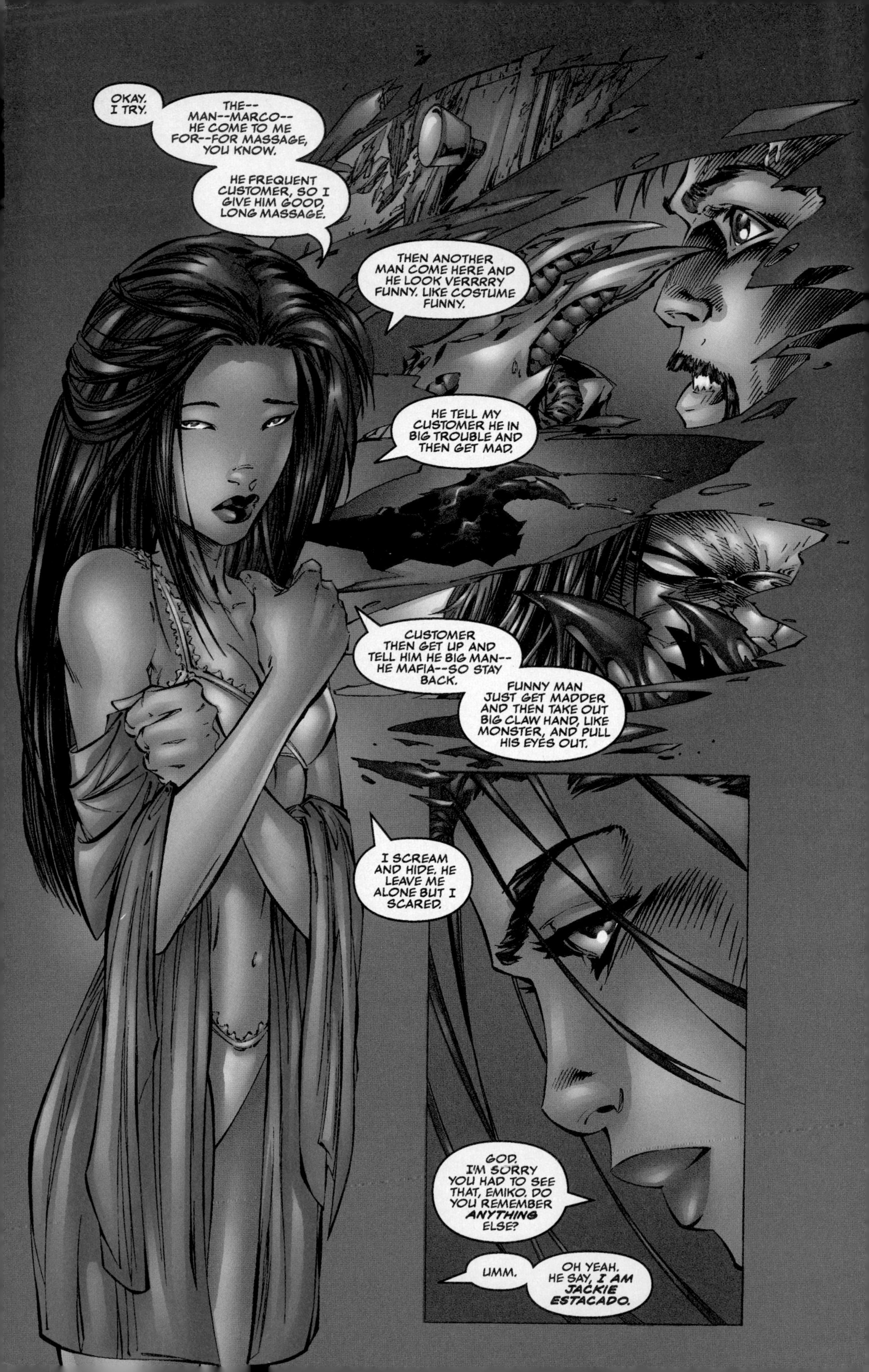
OKAY. I TRY.
THE-- MAN--MARCO-- HE COME TO ME FOR--FOR MASSAGE, YOU KNOW.
HE FREQUENT CUSTOMER, SO I GIVE HIM GOOD, LONG MASSAGE.
THEN ANOTHER MAN COME HERE AND HE LOOK VERRRRY FUNNY. LIKE COSTUME FUNNY.
HE TELL MY CUSTOMER HE IN BIG TROUBLE AND THEN GET MAD.
CUSTOMER THEN GET UP AND TELL HIM HE BIG MAN-- HE MAFIA--SO STAY BACK.
FUNNY MAN JUST GET MADDER AND THEN TAKE OUT BIG CLAW HAND, LIKE MONSTER, AND PULL HIS EYES OUT.
I SCREAM AND HIDE. HE LEAVE ME ALONE BUT I SCARED.
GOD. I'M SORRY YOU HAD TO SEE THAT, EMIKO. DO YOU REMEMBER ANYTHING ELSE?
UMM.
OH YEAH. HE SAY, I AM JACKIE ESTACADO.

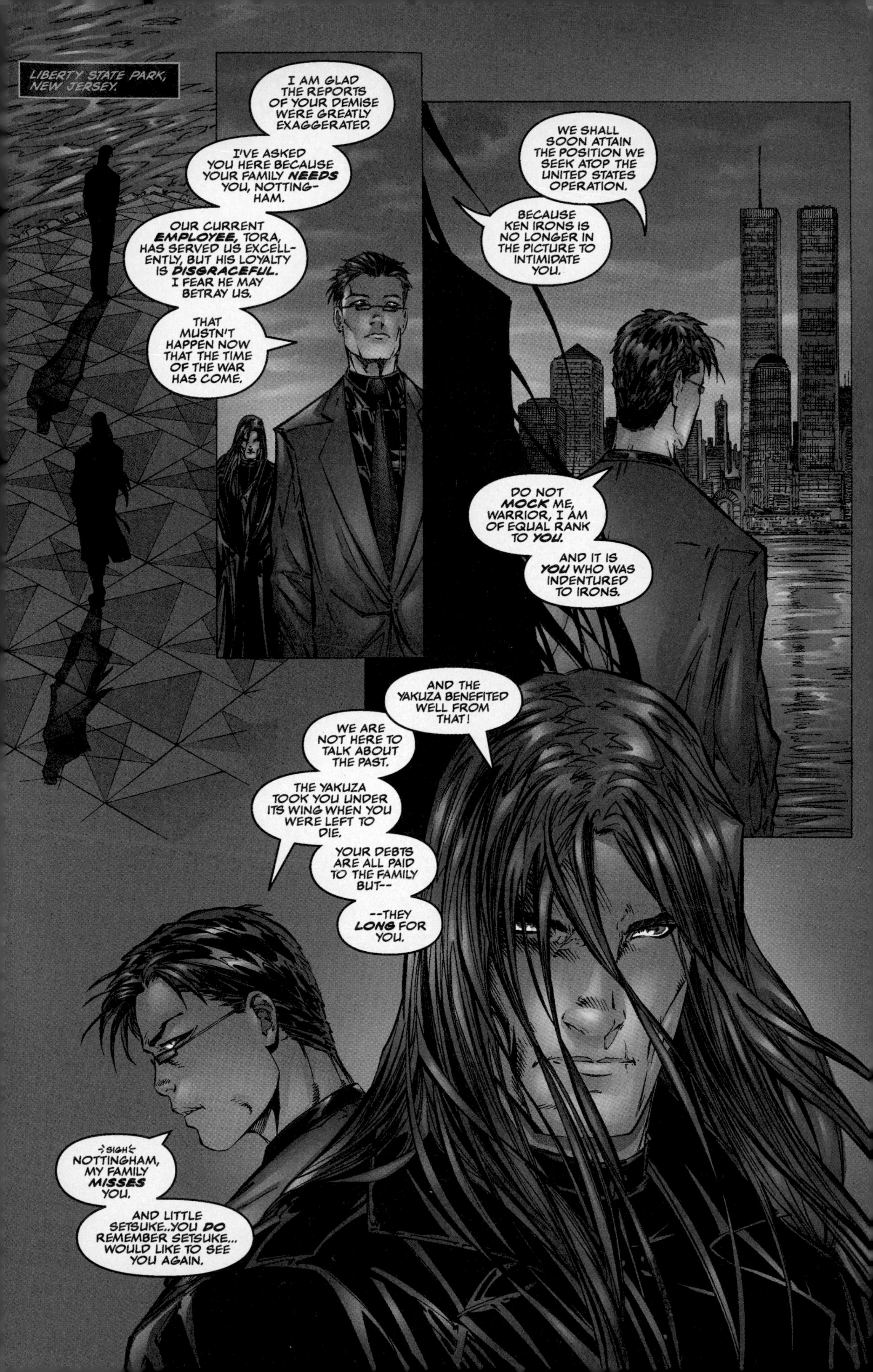
LIBERTY STATE PARK, NEW JERSEY.
I AM GLAD THE REPORTS OF YOUR DEMISE WERE GREATLY EXAGGERATED.
I'VE ASKED YOU HERE BECAUSE YOUR FAMILY NEEDS YOU, NOTTING-HAM.
OUR CURRENT EMPLOYEE, TORA, HAS SERVED US EXCELL-ENTLY, BUT HIS LOYALTY IS DISGRACEFUL. I FEAR HE MAY BETRAY US.
THAT MUSTN'T HAPPEN NOW THAT THE TIME OF THE WAR HAS COME.
WE SHALL SOON ATTAIN THE POSITION WE SEEK ATOP THE UNITED STATES OPERATION.
BECAUSE KEN IRONS IS NO LONGER IN THE PICTURE TO INTIMIDATE YOU.
DO NOT MOCK ME, WARRIOR, I AM OF EQUAL RANK TO YOU.
AND IT IS YOU WHO WAS INDENTURED TO IRONS.
AND THE YAKUZA BENEFITED WELL FROM THAT!
WE ARE NOT HERE TO TALK ABOUT THE PAST.
THE YAKUZA TOOK YOU UNDER ITS WING WHEN YOU WERE LEFT TO DIE.
YOUR DEBTS ARE ALL PAID TO THE FAMILY BUT--
--THEY LONG FOR YOU.
SIGH
NOTTINGHAM, MY FAMILY MISSES YOU.
AND LITTLE SETSUKE...YOU DO REMEMBER SETSUKE... WOULD LIKE TO SEE YOU AGAIN.

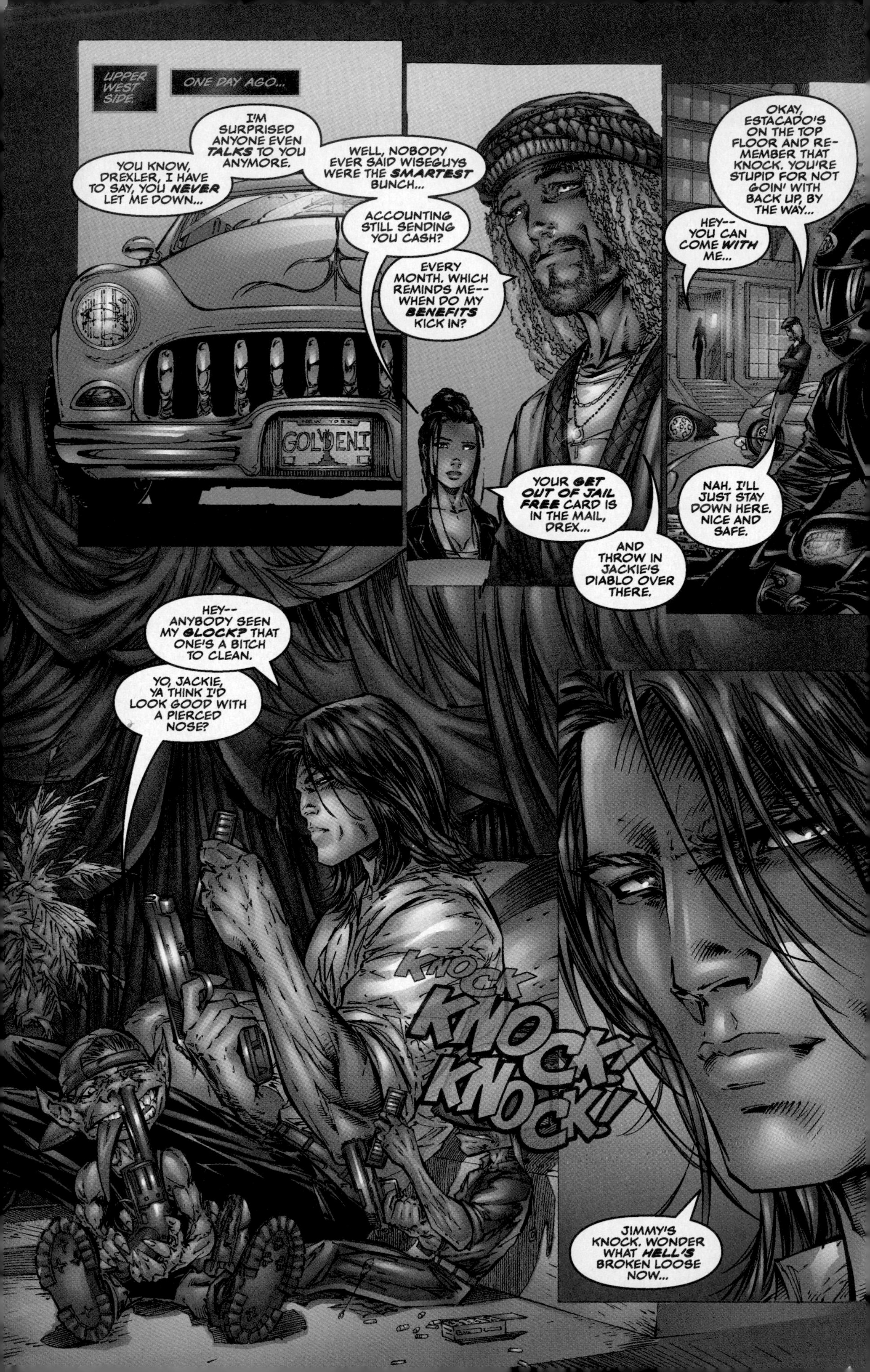
UPPER WEST SIDE.
ONE DAY AGO...
YOU KNOW, DREXLER, I HAVE TO SAY, YOU NEVER LET ME DOWN...
I'M SURPRISED ANYONE EVEN TALKS TO YOU ANYMORE.
WELL, NOBODY EVER SAID WISEGUYS WERE THE SMARTEST BUNCH...
ACCOUNTING STILL SENDING YOU CASH?
EVERY MONTH. WHICH REMINDS ME-- WHEN DO MY BENEFITS KICK IN?
GOLDEN.I
YOUR GET OUT OF JAIL FREE CARD IS IN THE MAIL, DREX...
AND THROW IN JACKIE'S DIABLO OVER THERE.
OKAY, ESTACADO'S ON THE TOP FLOOR AND RE-MEMBER THAT KNOCK. YOU'RE STUPID FOR NOT GOIN' WITH BACK UP, BY THE WAY...
HEY-- YOU CAN COME WITH ME...
NAH. I'LL JUST STAY DOWN HERE. NICE AND SAFE.
HEY-- ANYBODY SEEN MY GLOCK? THAT ONE'S A BITCH TO CLEAN.
YO, JACKIE, YA THINK I'D LOOK GOOD WITH A PIERCED NOSE?
KNOCK KNOCK! KNOCK!
JIMMY'S KNOCK. WONDER WHAT HELL'S BROKEN LOOSE NOW...

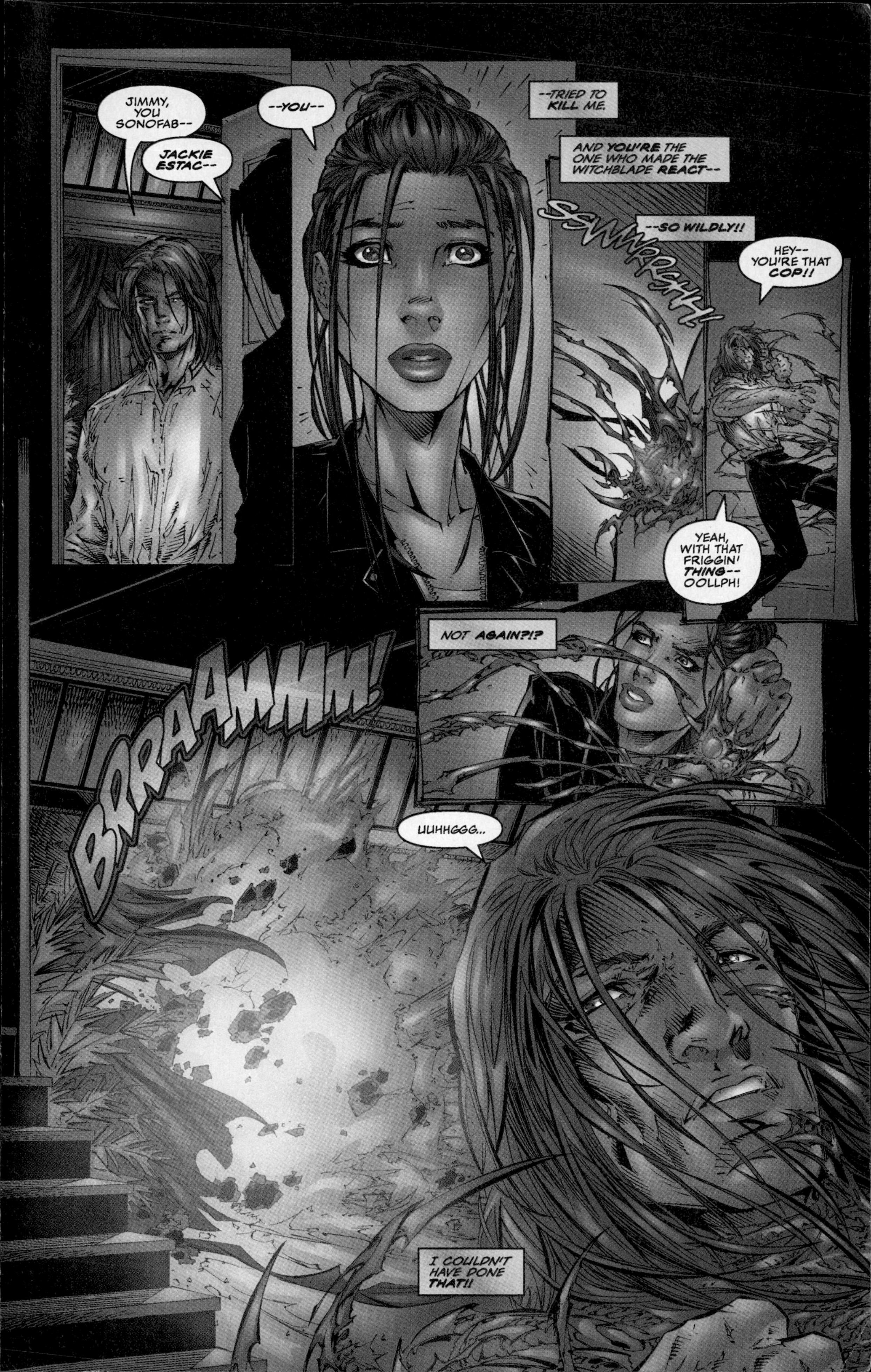

JIMMY, YOU SONOFAB--
JACKIE ESTAC--
--YOU--
--TRIED TO KILL ME.
AND YOU'RE THE ONE WHO MADE THE WITCHBLADE REACT--
SSWWRRSHH!
--SO WILDLY!!
HEY-- YOU'RE THAT COP!!
YEAH, WITH THAT FRIGGIN' THING-- OOLLPH!
NOT AGAIN?!?
BRRAAMMM!
UUHHGGG...
I COULDN'T HAVE DONE THAT!!

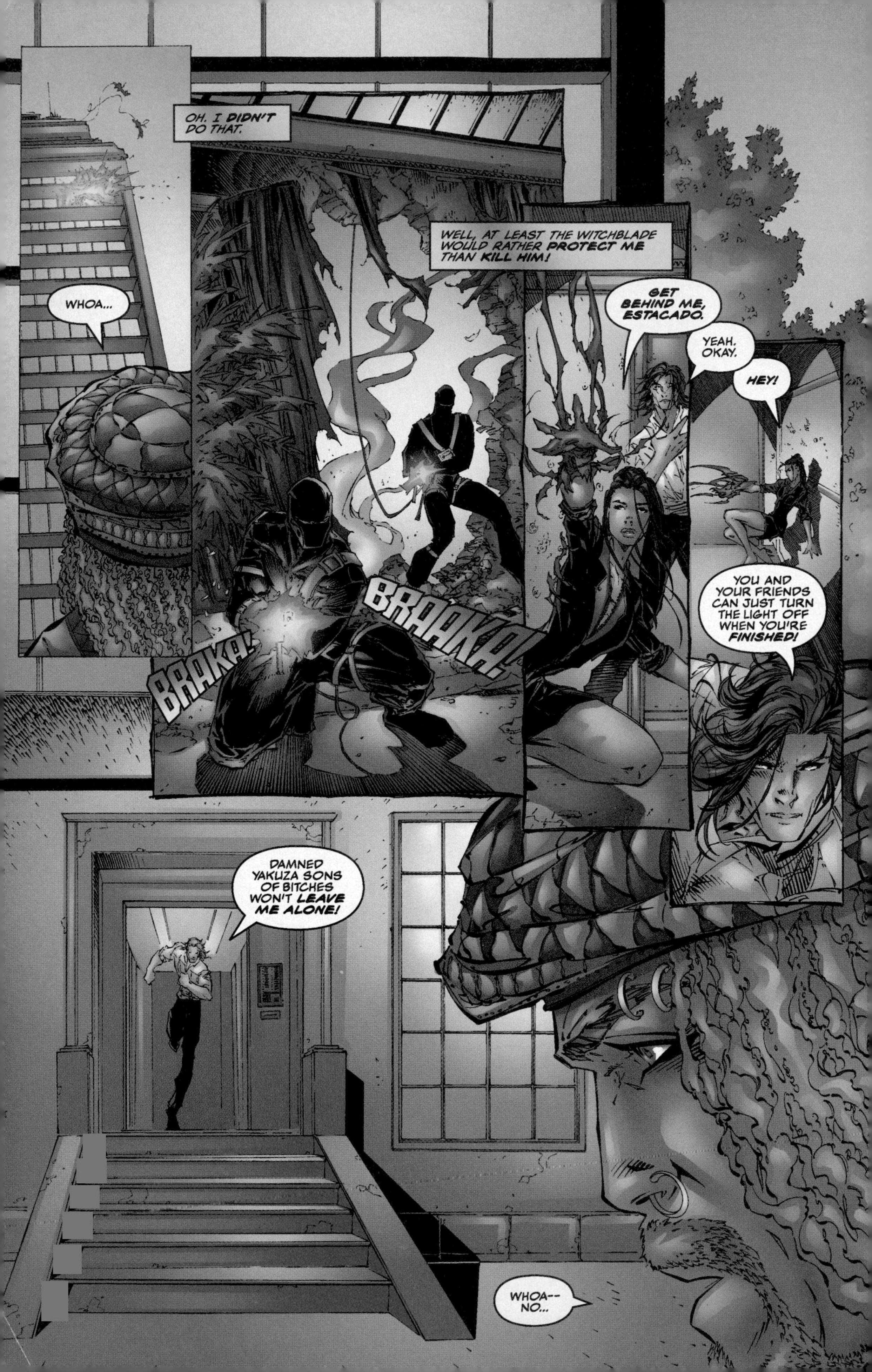

WHOA...
OH. I DIDN'T DO THAT.
WELL, AT LEAST THE WITCHBLADE WOULD RATHER PROTECT ME THAN KILL HIM!
BRAAKA!
BRAKA!
GET BEHIND ME, ESTACADO.
YEAH. OKAY.
HEY!
YOU AND YOUR FRIENDS CAN JUST TURN THE LIGHT OFF WHEN YOU'RE FINISHED!
DAMNED YAKUZA SONS OF BITCHES WON'T LEAVE ME ALONE!
WHOA-- NO...

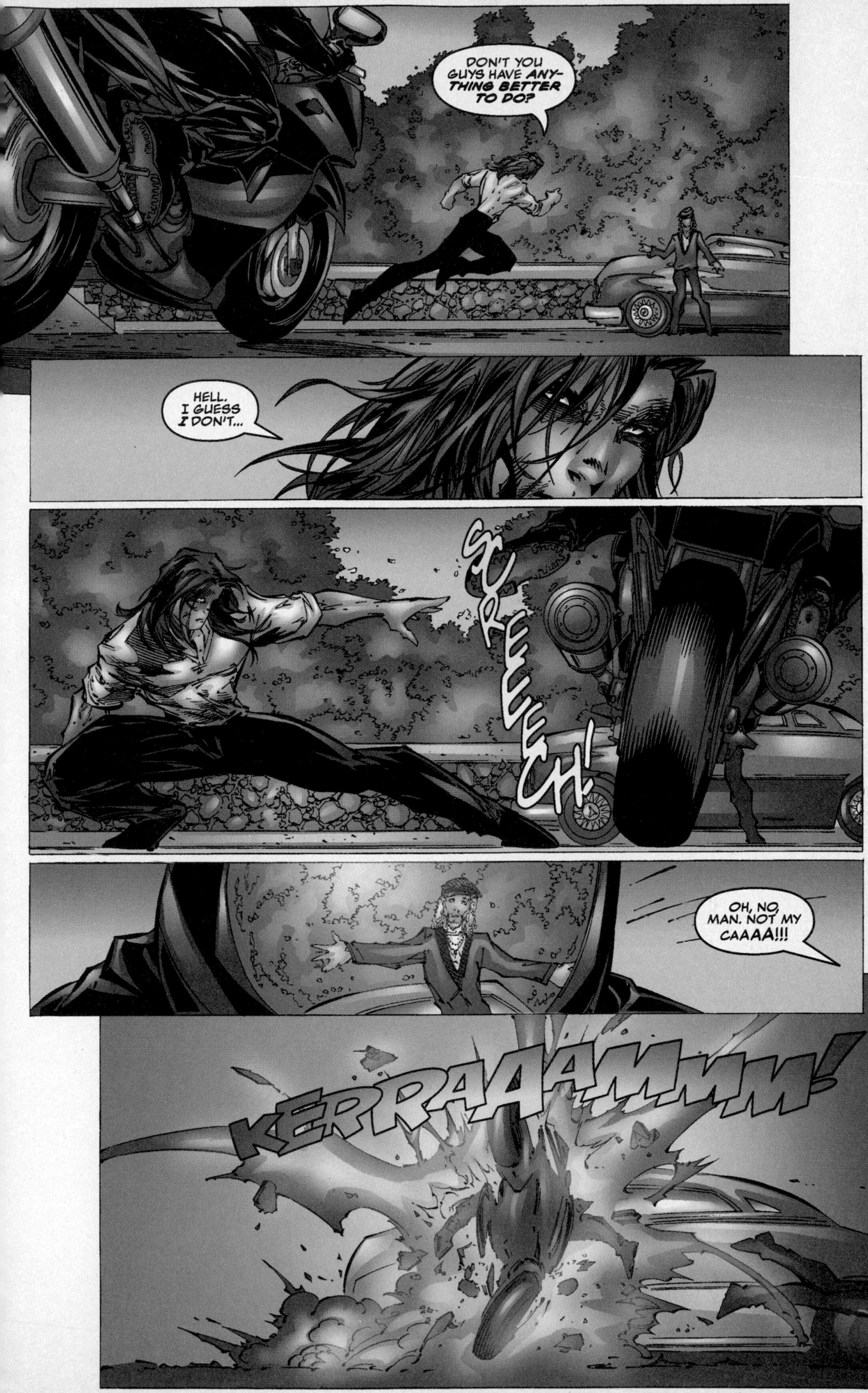
DON'T YOU GUYS HAVE ANYTHING BETTER TO DO?
HELL. I GUESS I DON'T...
SCREEEECH!
OH, NO, MAN. NOT MY CAAAA!!!
KERRAAAMMMM!

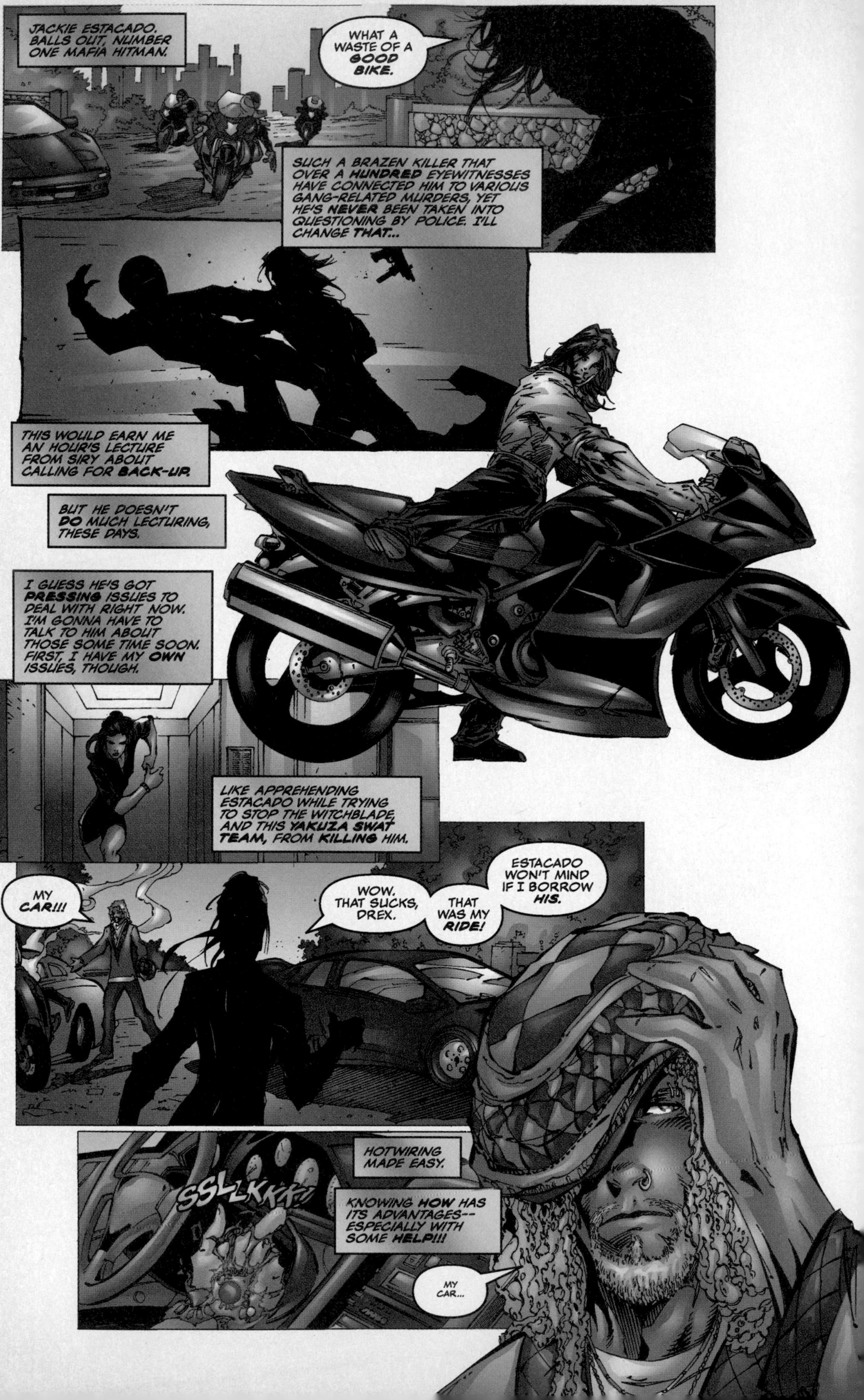
JACKIE ESTACADO. BALLS OUT, NUMBER ONE MAFIA HITMAN.
WHAT A WASTE OF A GOOD BIKE.
SUCH A BRAZEN KILLER THAT OVER A HUNDRED EYEWITNESSES HAVE CONNECTED HIM TO VARIOUS GANG-RELATED MURDERS, YET HE'S NEVER BEEN TAKEN INTO QUESTIONING BY POLICE. I'LL CHANGE THAT...
THIS WOULD EARN ME AN HOUR'S LECTURE FROM SIRY ABOUT CALLING FOR BACK-UP.
BUT HE DOESN'T DO MUCH LECTURING, THESE DAYS.
I GUESS HE'S GOT PRESSING ISSUES TO DEAL WITH RIGHT NOW. I'M GONNA HAVE TO TALK TO HIM ABOUT THOSE SOME TIME SOON. FIRST, I HAVE MY OWN ISSUES, THOUGH.
LIKE APPREHENDING ESTACADO WHILE TRYING TO STOP THE WITCHBLADE, AND THIS YAKUZA SWAT TEAM, FROM KILLING HIM.
MY CAR!!!
WOW. THAT SUCKS, DREX.
THAT WAS MY RIDE!
ESTACADO WON'T MIND IF I BORROW HIS.
HOTWIRING MADE EASY.
SSLLKKK!
KNOWING HOW HAS ITS ADVANTAGES-- ESPECIALLY WITH SOME HELP!!!
MY CAR...

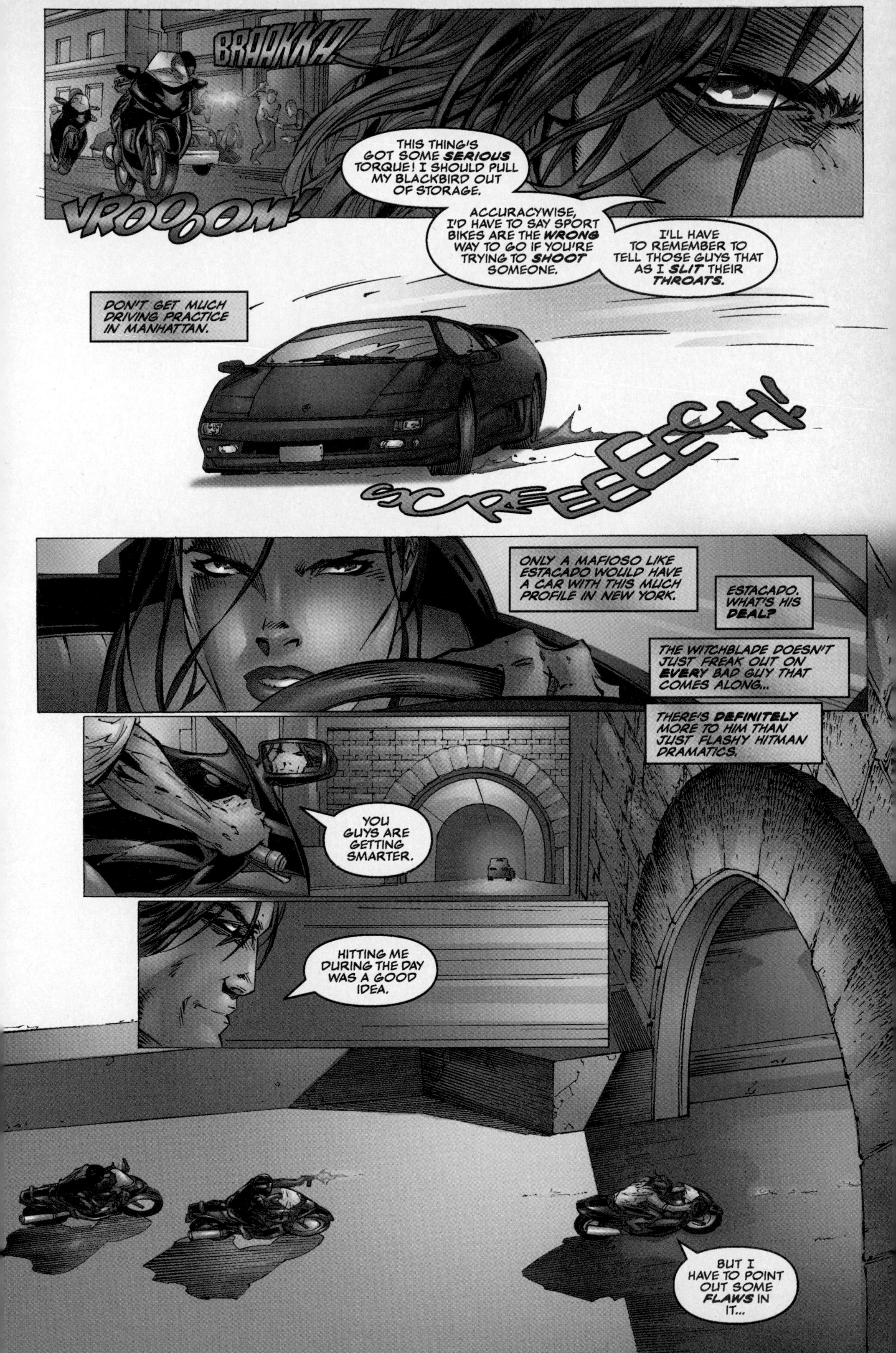
BRAKKA!
THIS THING'S GOT SOME SERIOUS TORQUE! I SHOULD PULL MY BLACKBIRD OUT OF STORAGE.
VROOoOOM
ACCURACYWISE, I'D HAVE TO SAY SPORT BIKES ARE THE WRONG WAY TO GO IF YOU'RE TRYING TO SHOOT SOMEONE.
I'LL HAVE TO REMEMBER TO TELL THOSE GUYS THAT AS I SLIT THEIR THROATS.
DON'T GET MUCH DRIVING PRACTICE IN MANHATTAN.
SCREEEEEECH!
ONLY A MAFIOSO LIKE ESTACADO WOULD HAVE A CAR WITH THIS MUCH PROFILE IN NEW YORK.
ESTACADO. WHAT'S HIS DEAL?
THE WITCHBLADE DOESN'T JUST FREAK OUT ON EVERY BAD GUY THAT COMES ALONG...
THERE'S DEFINITELY MORE TO HIM THAN JUST FLASHY HITMAN DRAMATICS.
YOU GUYS ARE GETTING SMARTER.
HITTING ME DURING THE DAY WAS A GOOD IDEA.
BUT I HAVE TO POINT OUT SOME FLAWS IN IT...

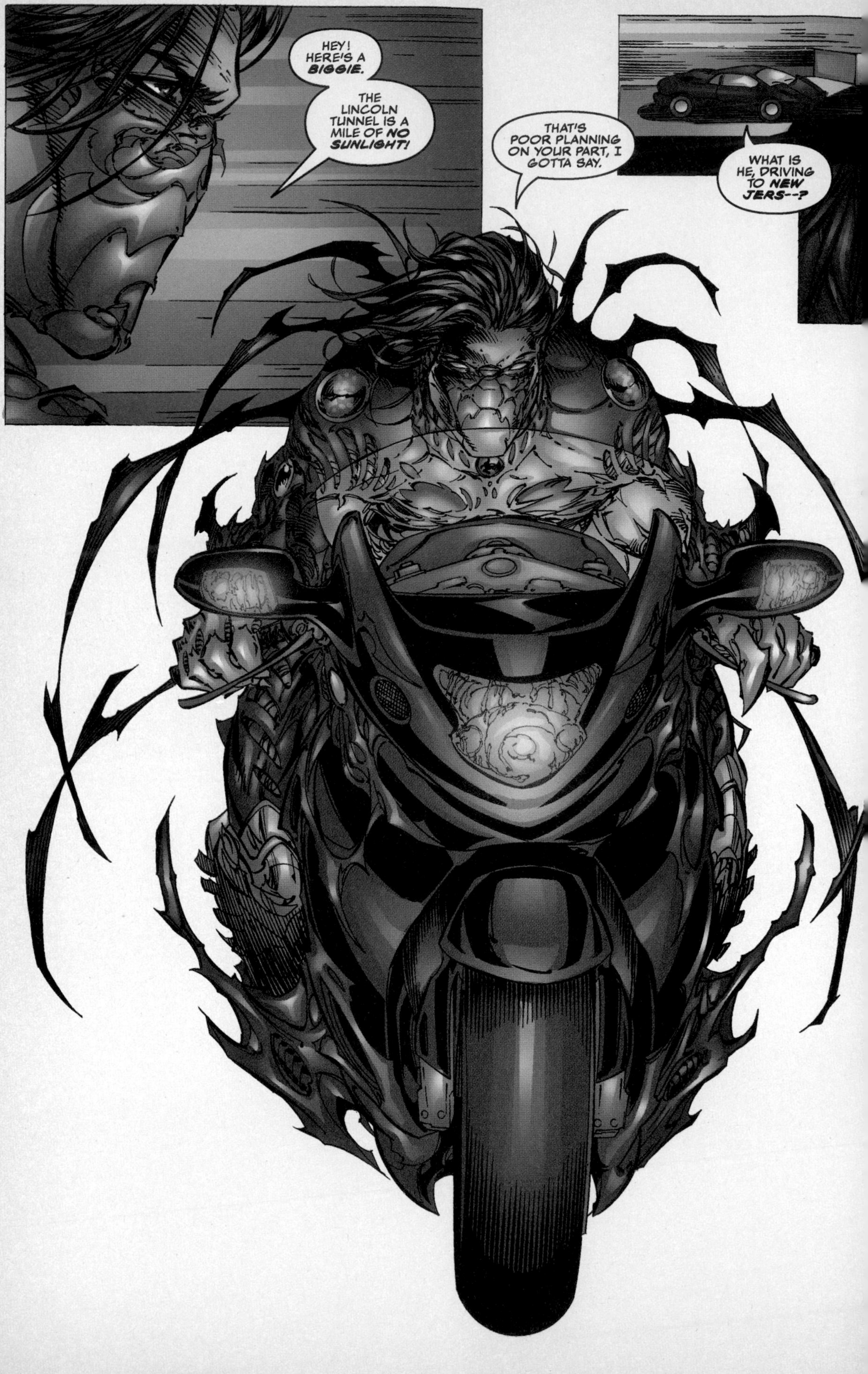
HEY! HERE'S A BIGGIE.
THE LINCOLN TUNNEL IS A MILE OF NO SUNLIGHT!
THAT'S POOR PLANNING ON YOUR PART, I GOTTA SAY.
WHAT IS HE, DRIVING TO NEW JERS--?

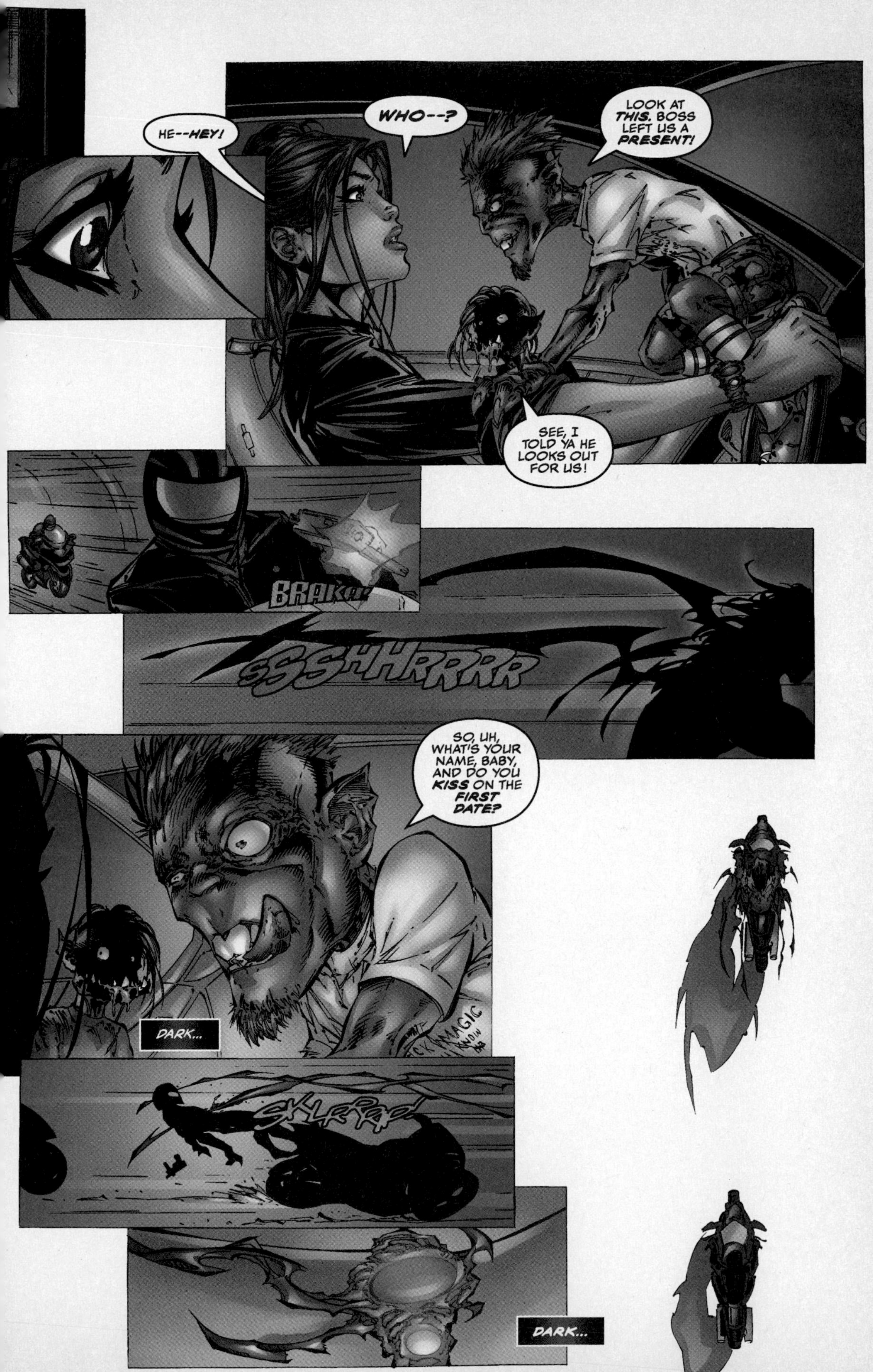
HE--HEY!
WHO--?
LOOK AT THIS. BOSS LEFT US A PRESENT!
SEE, I TOLD YA HE LOOKS OUT FOR US!
BRAKA!
SSSHHRRRRR
SO, UH, WHAT'S YOUR NAME, BABY, AND DO YOU KISS ON THE FIRST DATE?
DARK...
DARK...

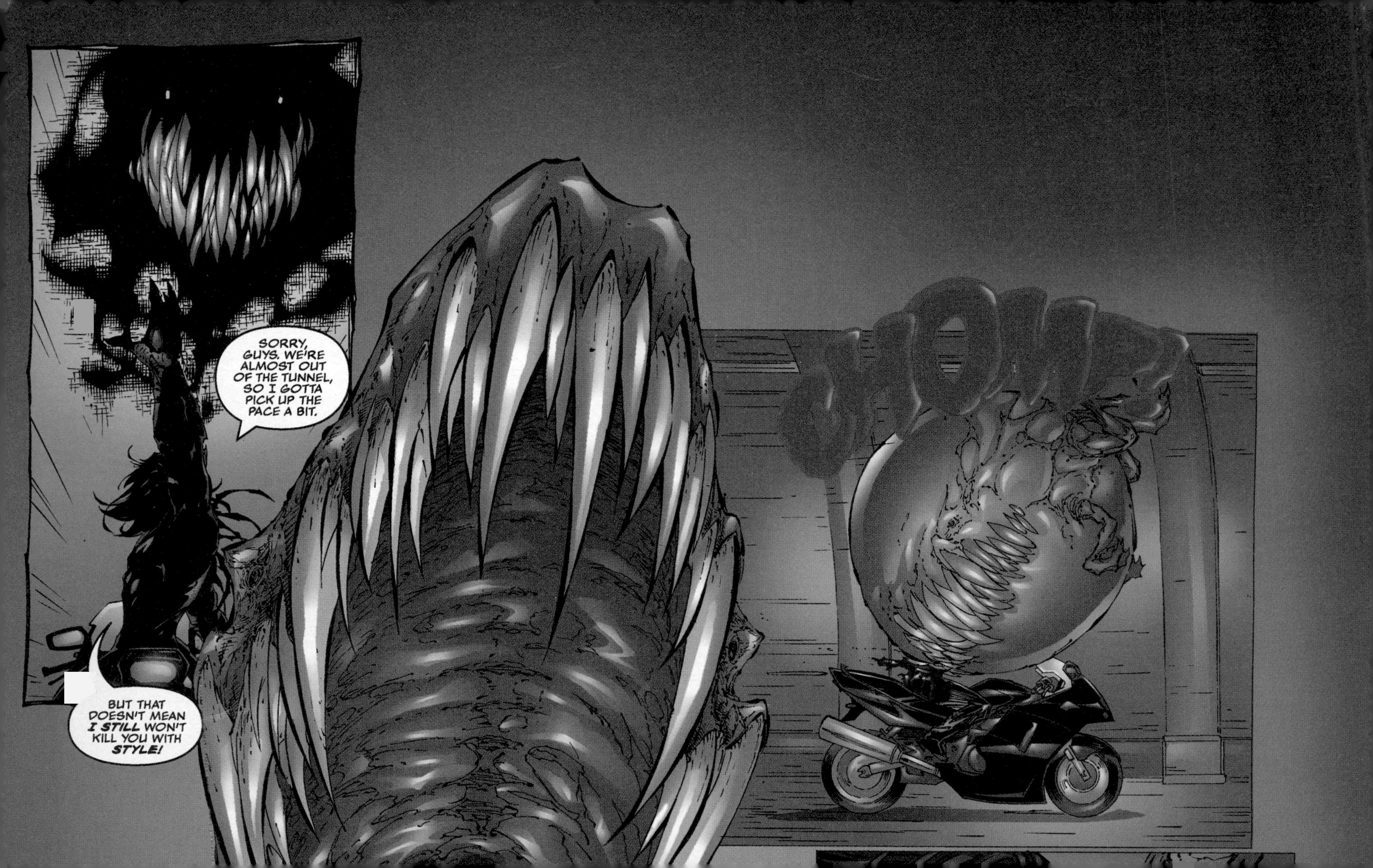
SORRY, GUYS, WE'RE ALMOST OUT OF THE TUNNEL, SO I GOTTA PICK UP THE PACE A BIT.
BUT THAT DOESN'T MEAN *I STILL* WON'T KILL YOU WITH *STYLE!*
WOW

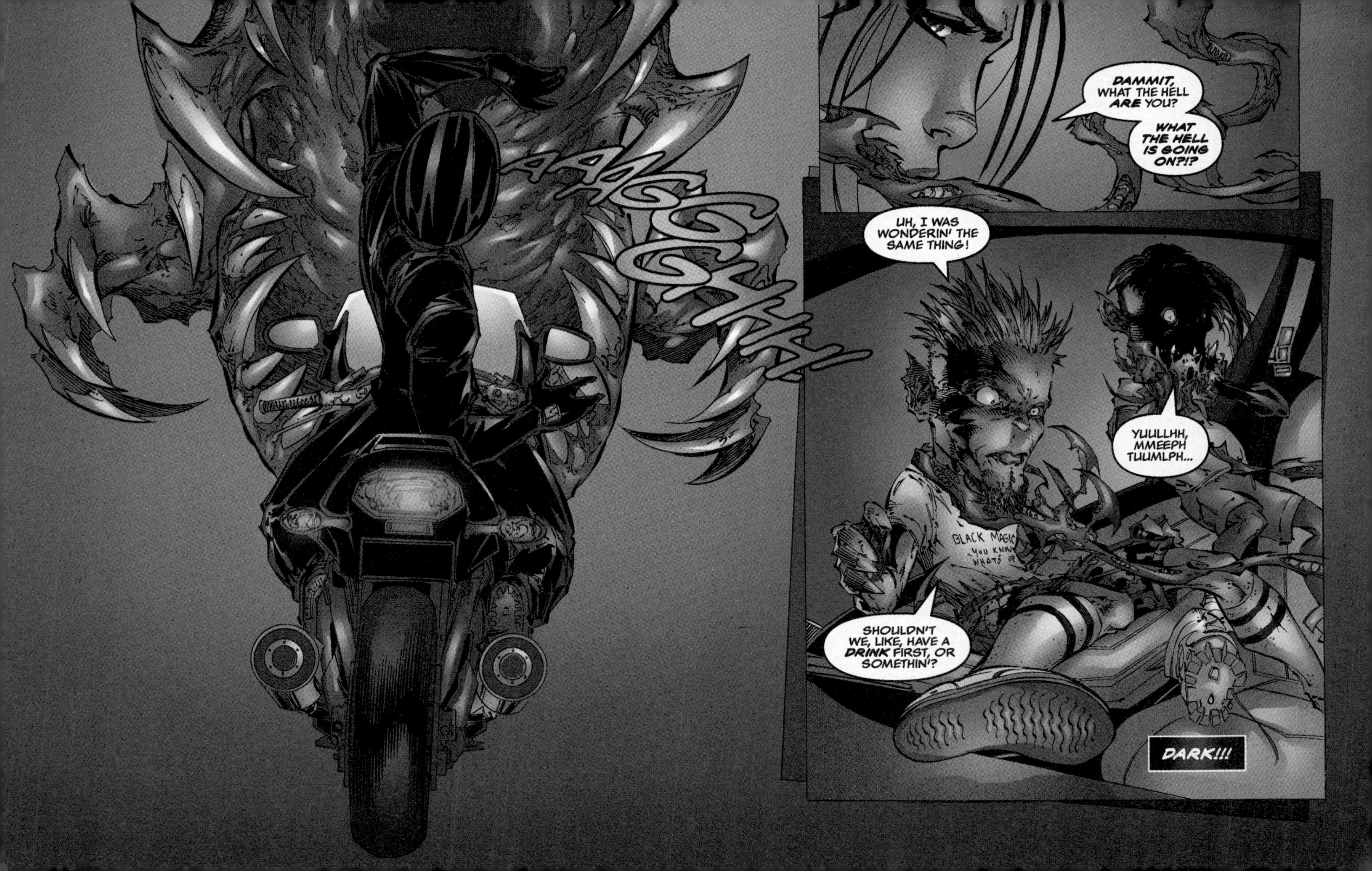
AAAGGGHHH!!
DAMMIT, WHAT THE HELL ARE YOU?
WHAT THE HELL IS GOING ON?!?
UH, I WAS WONDERIN' THE SAME THING!
YUULLHH, MMEEPH TUUMLPH...
BLACK MAGIC YOU KNOW WHAT'S UP
SHOULDN'T WE, LIKE, HAVE A DRINK FIRST, OR SOMETHIN'?
DARK!!!

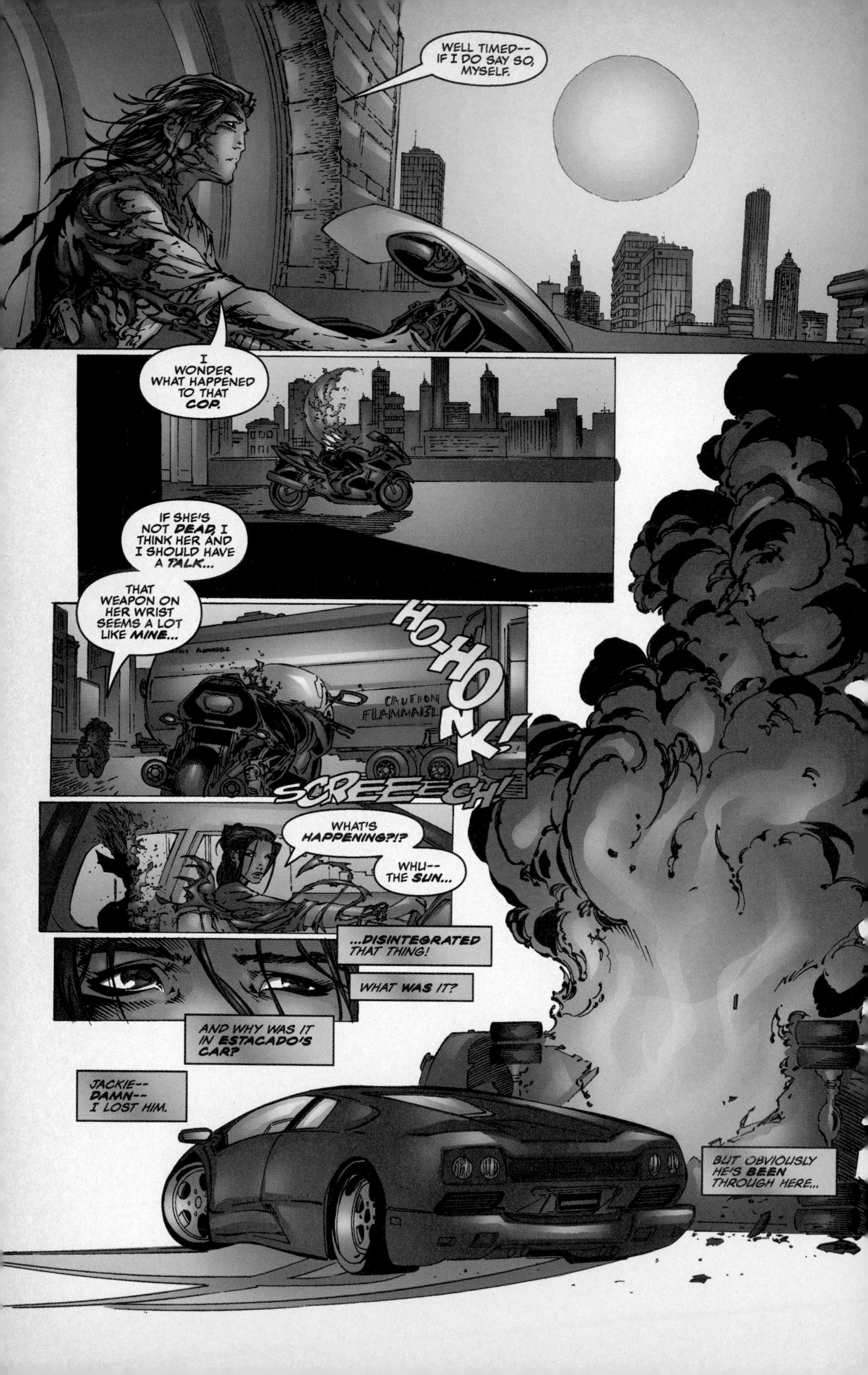
WELL TIMED-- IF I DO SAY SO, MYSELF.
I WONDER WHAT HAPPENED TO THAT COP.
IF SHE'S NOT DEAD, I THINK HER AND I SHOULD HAVE A TALK...
THAT WEAPON ON HER WRIST SEEMS A LOT LIKE MINE...
HO-HONK!
CAUTION FLAMMABL
SCREEECH!
WHAT'S HAPPENING?!?
WHU-- THE SUN...
...DISINTEGRATED THAT THING!
WHAT WAS IT?
AND WHY WAS IT IN ESTACADO'S CAR?
JACKIE-- DAMN-- I LOST HIM.
BUT OBVIOUSLY HE'S BEEN THROUGH HERE...

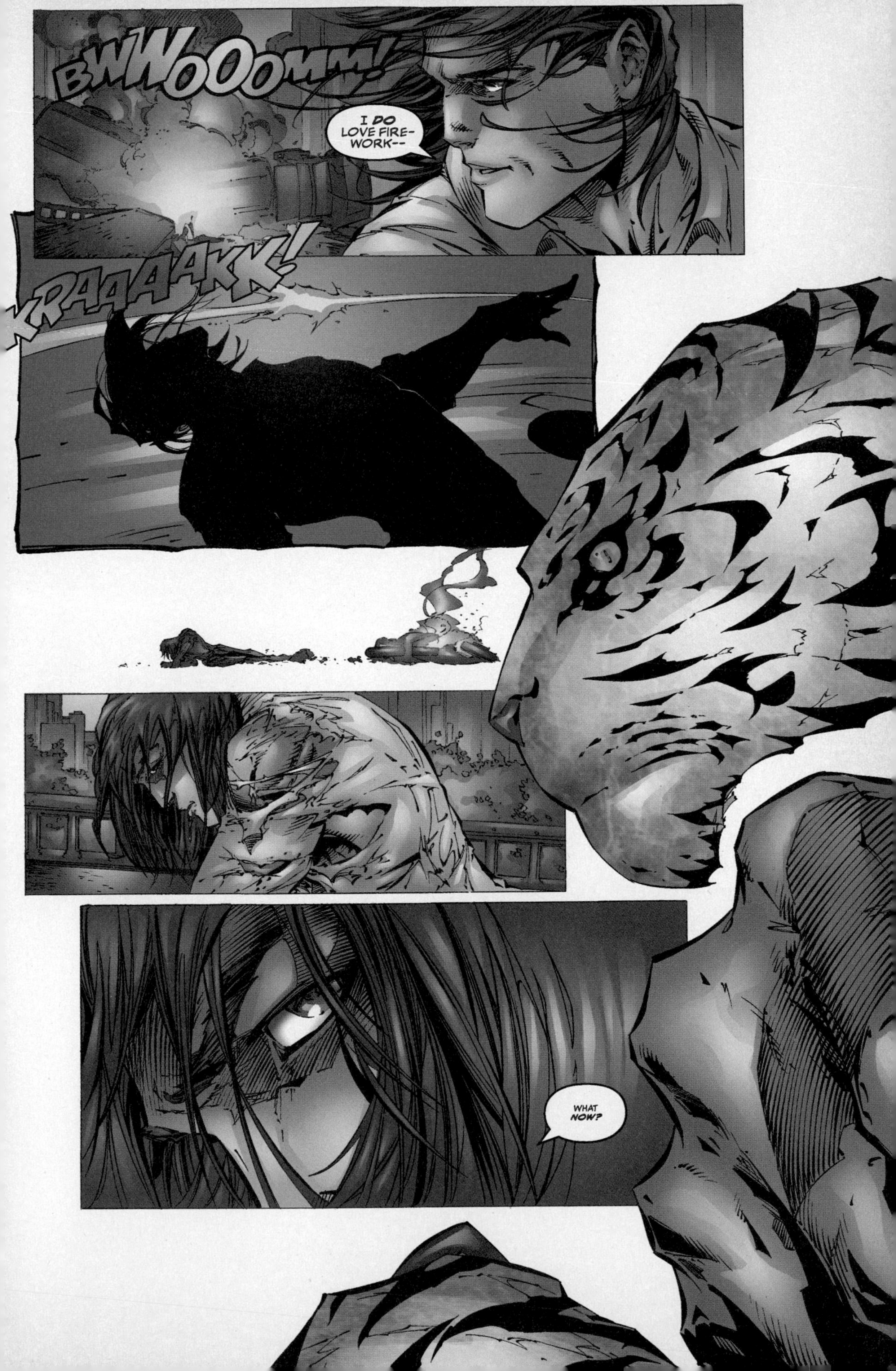
BWWOOOOMM!
I DO LOVE FIRE-WORK--
KRAAAAKK!
WHAT NOW?

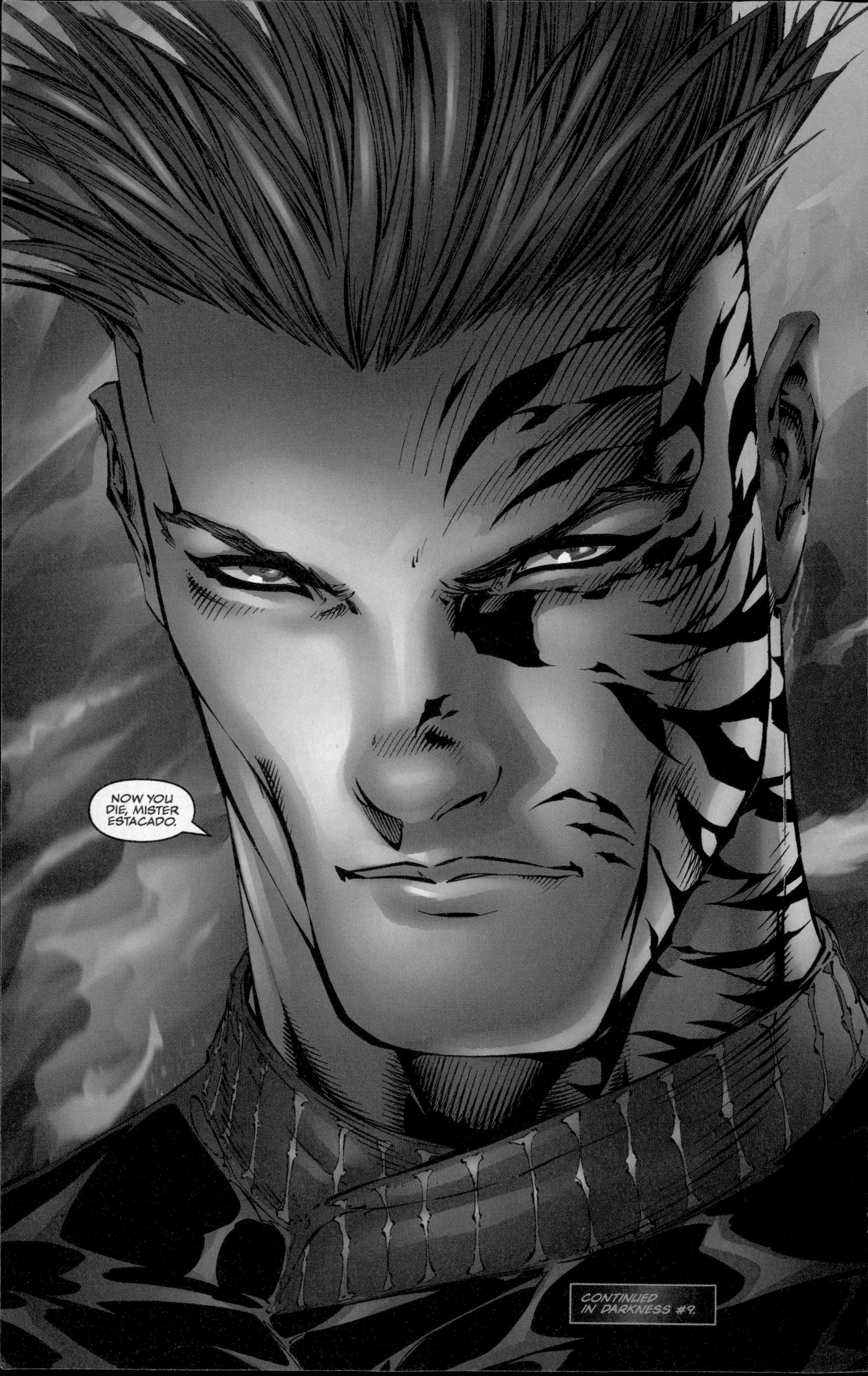
NOW YOU DIE, MISTER ESTACADO.
CONTINUED IN DARKNESS #9.

THE DARKNESS 9

David Wohl
Christina Z.
—story

Marc Silvestri
—pencils

Batt
Marc Silvestri
—inks

Richard Bennett
—finishes pg 8-12

Richard Isanove
Jonathan D. Smith
Matt Nelson
—colors

Family TIES

PART TWO

Dennis Heisler
—letters

Marc Silvestri
—editor

Sonia Im
—associate editor

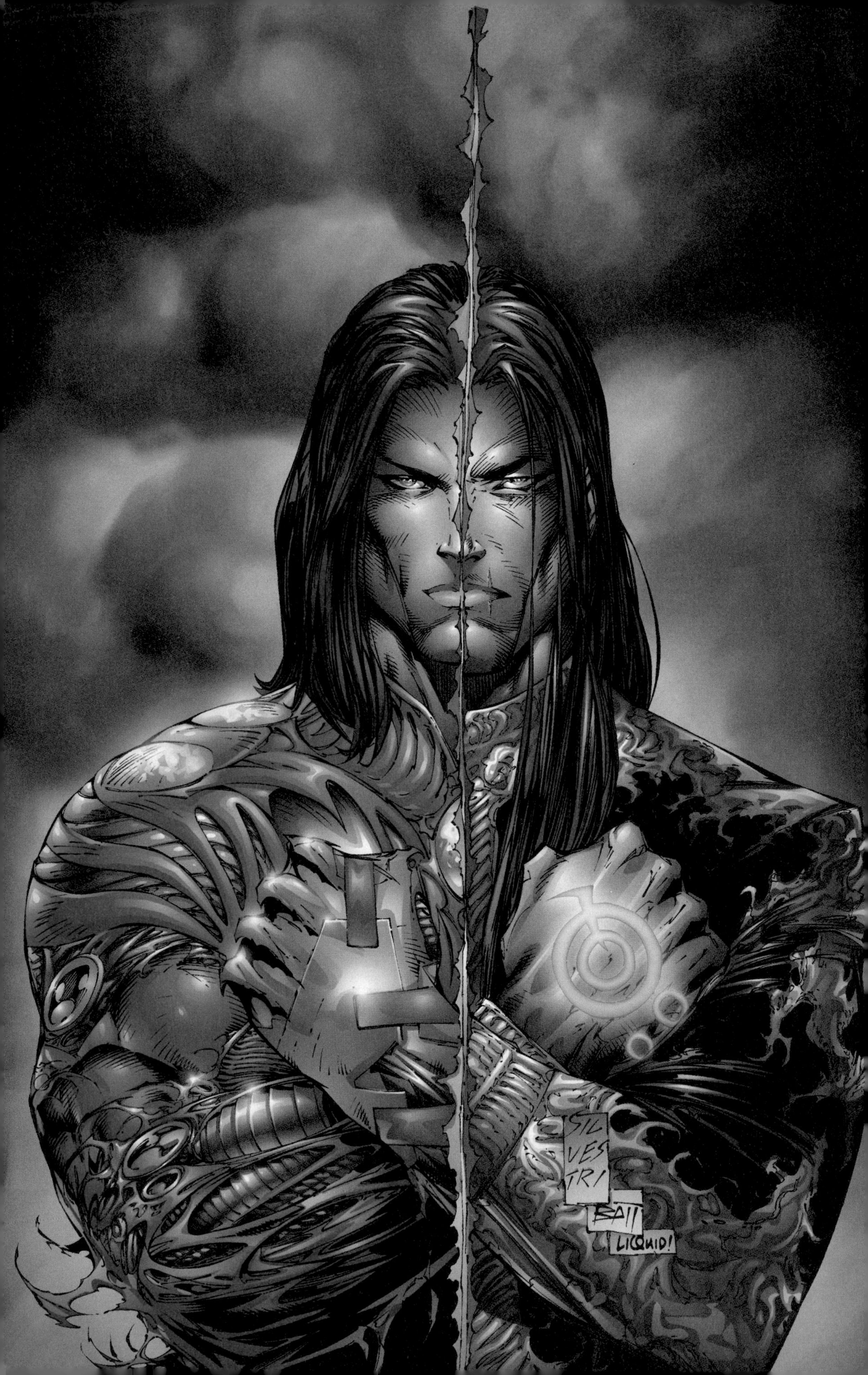
SIL VES TRI
BATT
LIQUID!

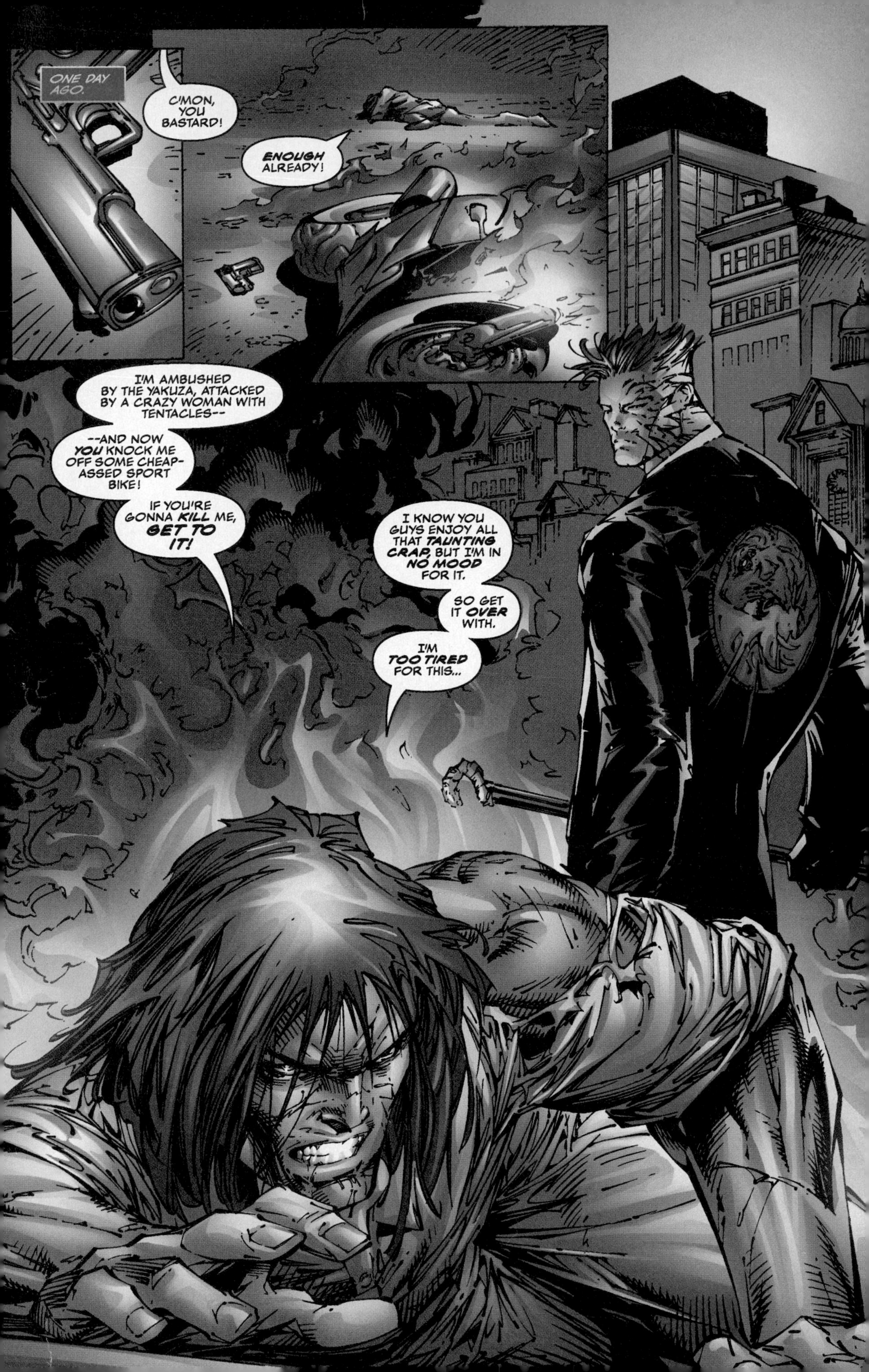
ONE DAY AGO.
C'MON, YOU BASTARD!
ENOUGH ALREADY!
I'M AMBUSHED BY THE YAKUZA, ATTACKED BY A CRAZY WOMAN WITH TENTACLES--
--AND NOW YOU KNOCK ME OFF SOME CHEAP-ASSED SPORT BIKE!
IF YOU'RE GONNA KILL ME, GET TO IT!
I KNOW YOU GUYS ENJOY ALL THAT TAUNTING CRAP, BUT I'M IN NO MOOD FOR IT.
SO GET IT OVER WITH.
I'M TOO TIRED FOR THIS...

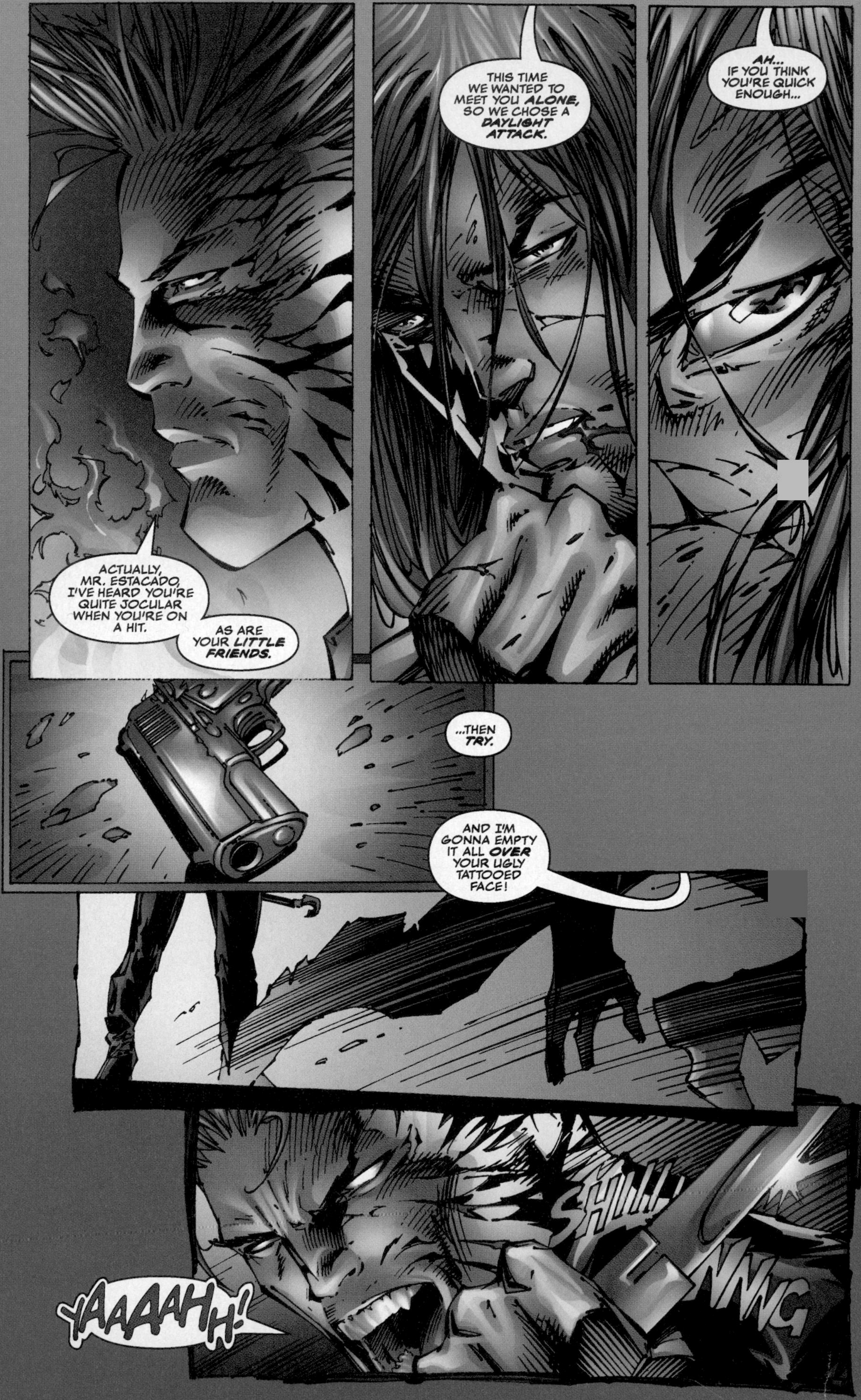
ACTUALLY, MR. ESTACADO, I'VE HEARD YOU'RE QUITE JOCULAR WHEN YOU'RE ON A HIT.
AS ARE YOUR LITTLE FRIENDS.
THIS TIME WE WANTED TO MEET YOU ALONE, SO WE CHOSE A DAYLIGHT ATTACK.
AH... IF YOU THINK YOU'RE QUICK ENOUGH...
...THEN TRY.
AND I'M GONNA EMPTY IT ALL OVER YOUR UGLY TATTOOED FACE!
SHLLLLNNNG
YAAAAHH!

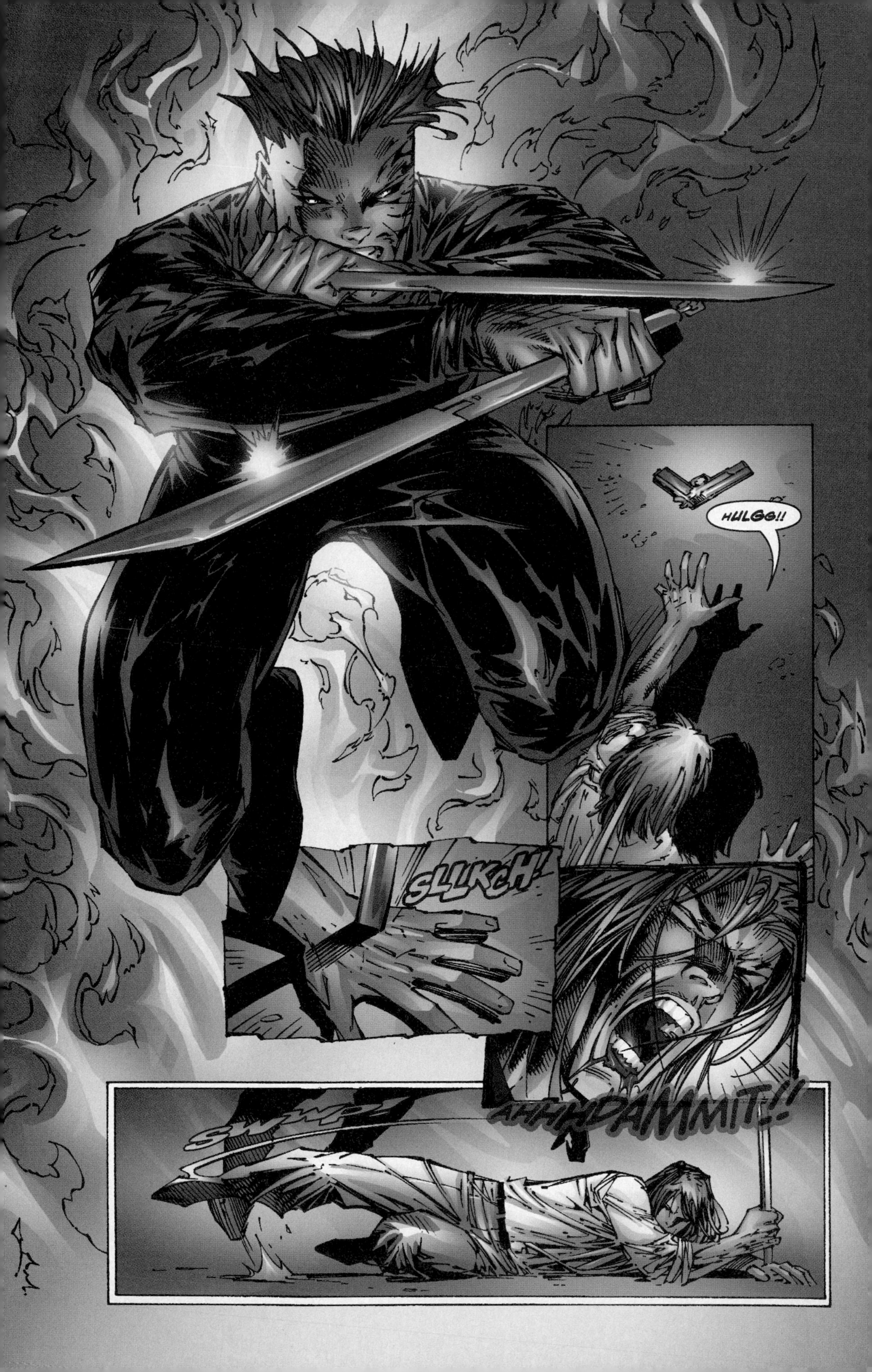
HULGG!!
SLLKCH!
AHHHDAMMIT!!

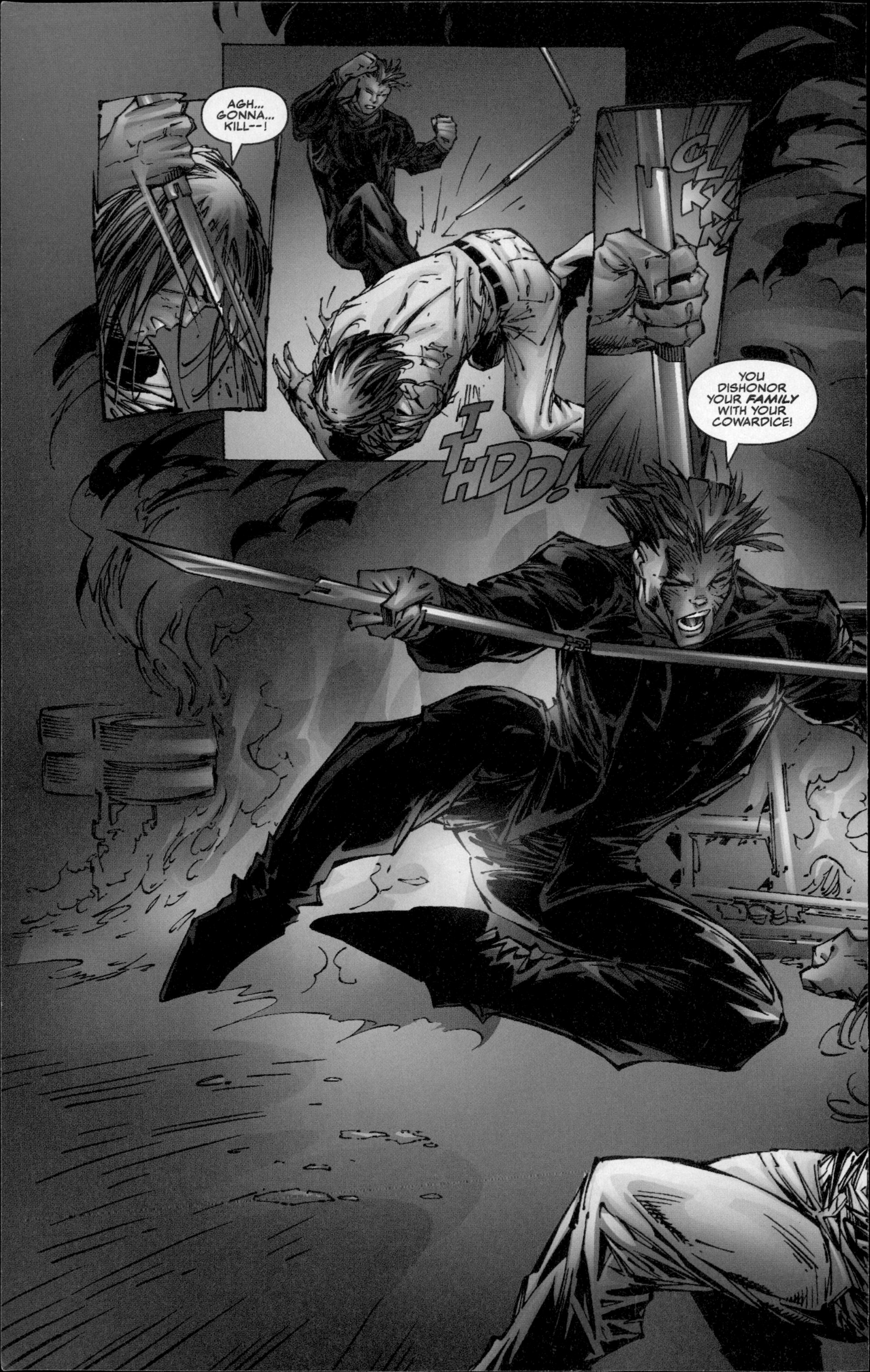
AGH... GONNA... KILL--!
THDD!
CLIKK
YOU DISHONOR YOUR FAMILY WITH YOUR COWARDICE!

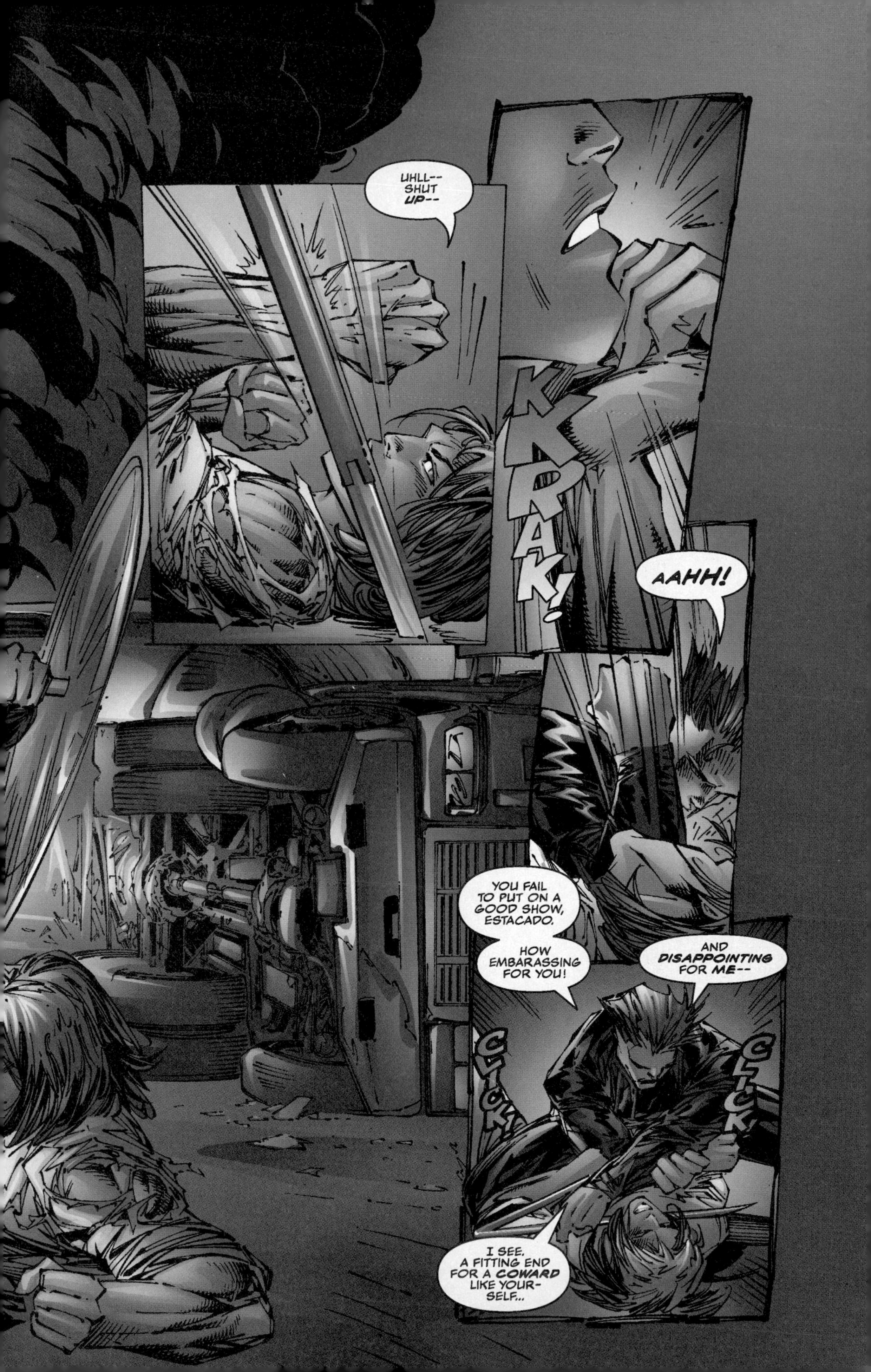
UHLL--
SHUT
UP--
KKRAK!
AAHH!
YOU FAIL TO PUT ON A GOOD SHOW, ESTACADO.
HOW EMBARASSING FOR YOU!
AND DISAPPOINTING FOR ME--
CLICK
CLICK
I SEE. A FITTING END FOR A COWARD LIKE YOUR-SELF...

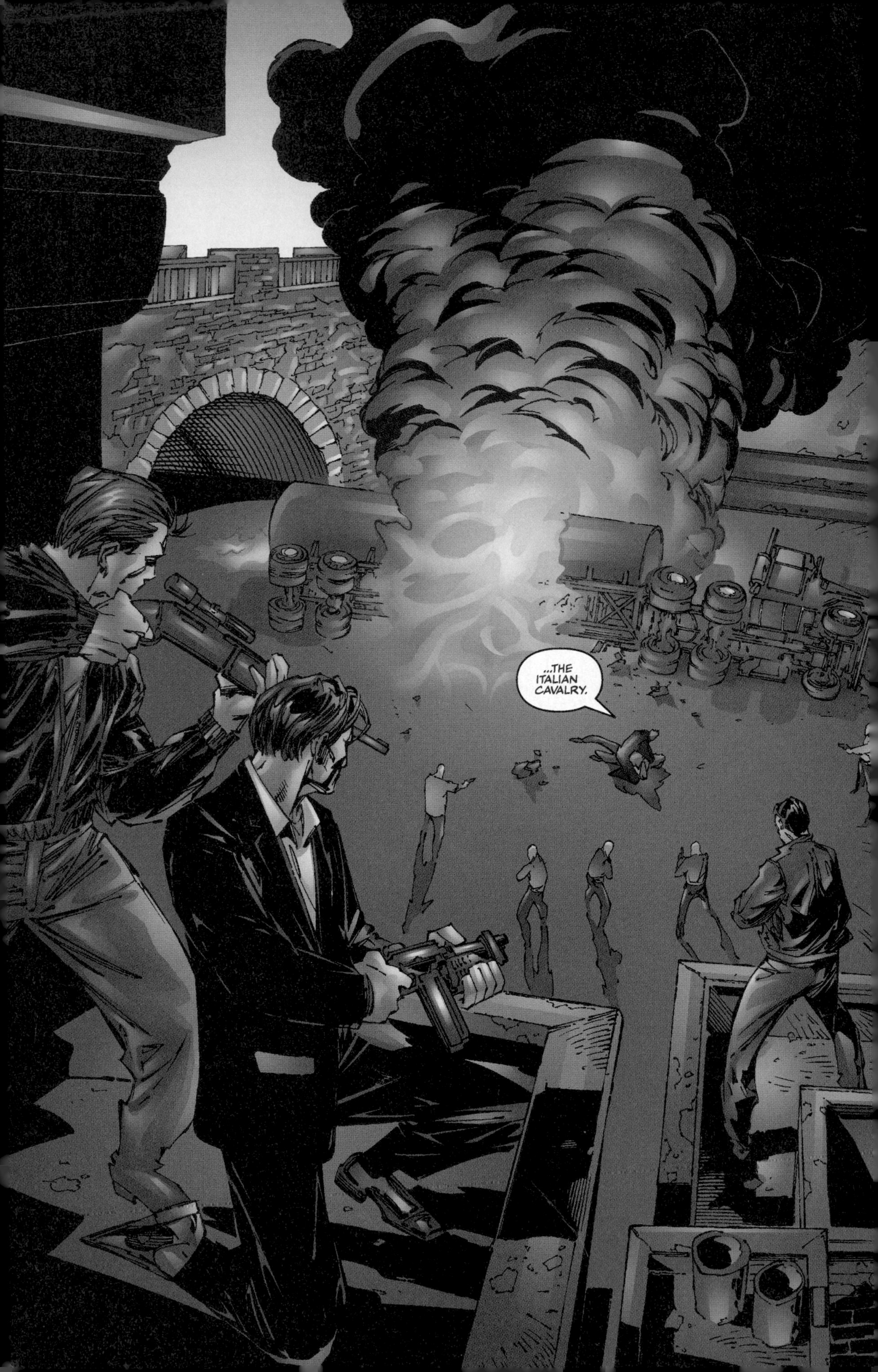
...THE ITALIAN CAVALRY.

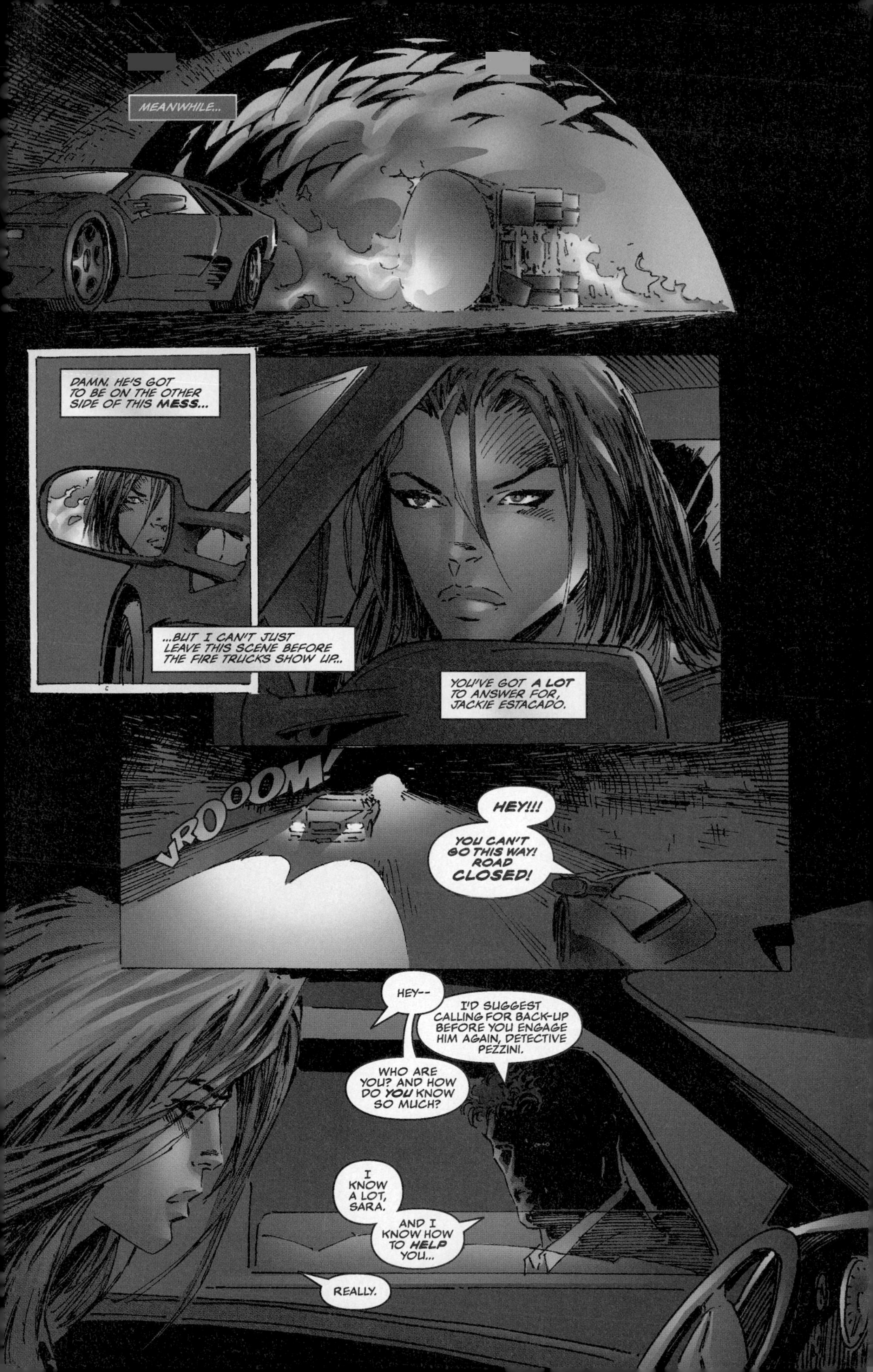
MEANWHILE...
DAMN. HE'S GOT TO BE ON THE OTHER SIDE OF THIS MESS...
...BUT I CAN'T JUST LEAVE THIS SCENE BEFORE THE FIRE TRUCKS SHOW UP...
YOU'VE GOT A LOT TO ANSWER FOR, JACKIE ESTACADO.
VROOOM!
HEY!!!
YOU CAN'T GO THIS WAY! ROAD CLOSED!
HEY--
I'D SUGGEST CALLING FOR BACK-UP BEFORE YOU ENGAGE HIM AGAIN, DETECTIVE PEZZINI.
WHO ARE YOU? AND HOW DO YOU KNOW SO MUCH?
I KNOW A LOT, SARA.
AND I KNOW HOW TO HELP YOU...
REALLY.

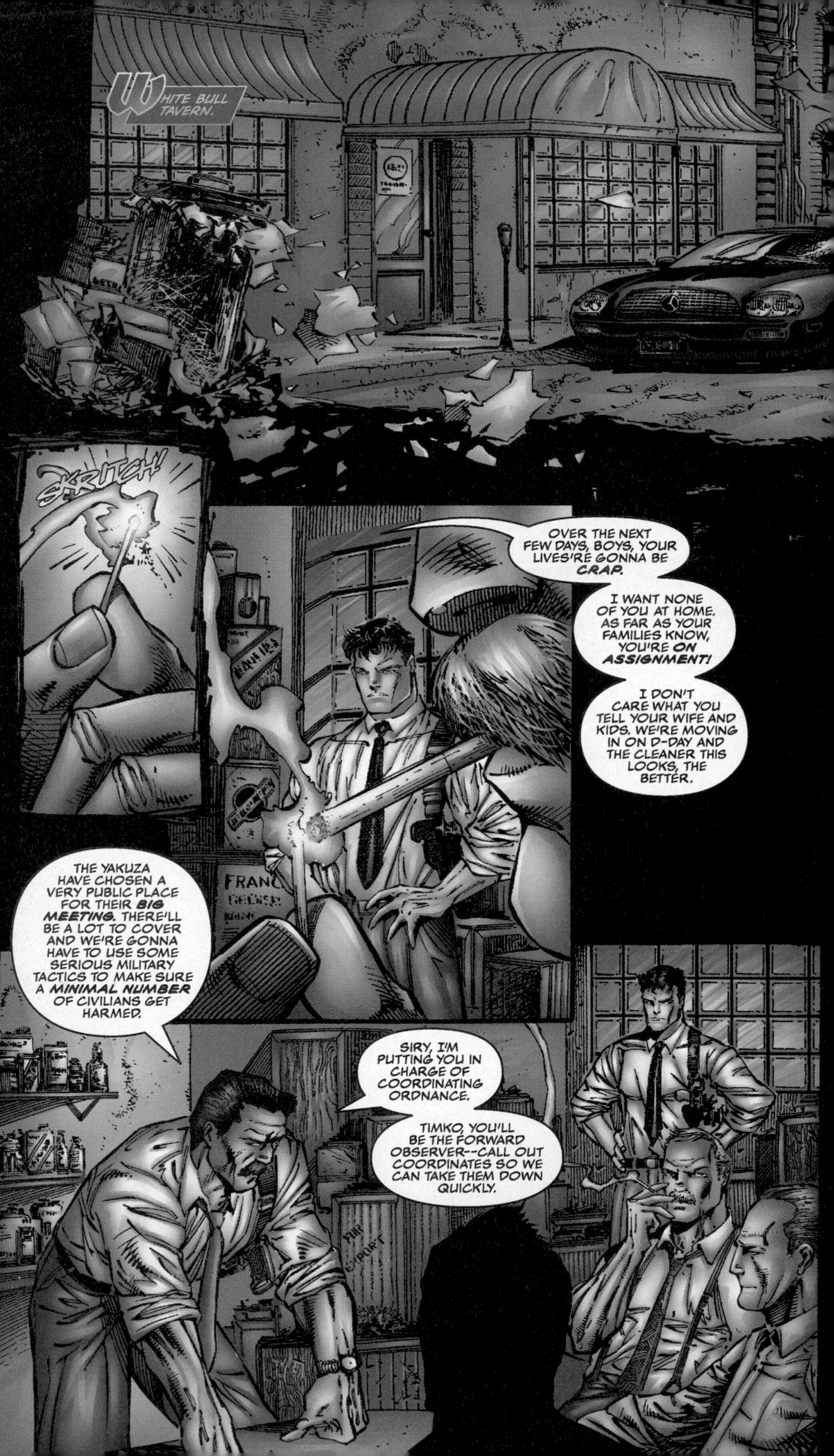
WHITE BULL TAVERN.
SKRITCH!
OVER THE NEXT FEW DAYS, BOYS, YOUR LIVES'RE GONNA BE CRAP.
I WANT NONE OF YOU AT HOME. AS FAR AS YOUR FAMILIES KNOW, YOU'RE ON ASSIGNMENT!
I DON'T CARE WHAT YOU TELL YOUR WIFE AND KIDS. WE'RE MOVING IN ON D-DAY AND THE CLEANER THIS LOOKS, THE BETTER.
THE YAKUZA HAVE CHOSEN A VERY PUBLIC PLACE FOR THEIR BIG MEETING. THERE'LL BE A LOT TO COVER AND WE'RE GONNA HAVE TO USE SOME SERIOUS MILITARY TACTICS TO MAKE SURE A MINIMAL NUMBER OF CIVILIANS GET HARMED.
SIRY, I'M PUTTING YOU IN CHARGE OF COORDINATING ORDNANCE.
TIMKO, YOU'LL BE THE FORWARD OBSERVER--CALL OUT COORDINATES SO WE CAN TAKE THEM DOWN QUICKLY.

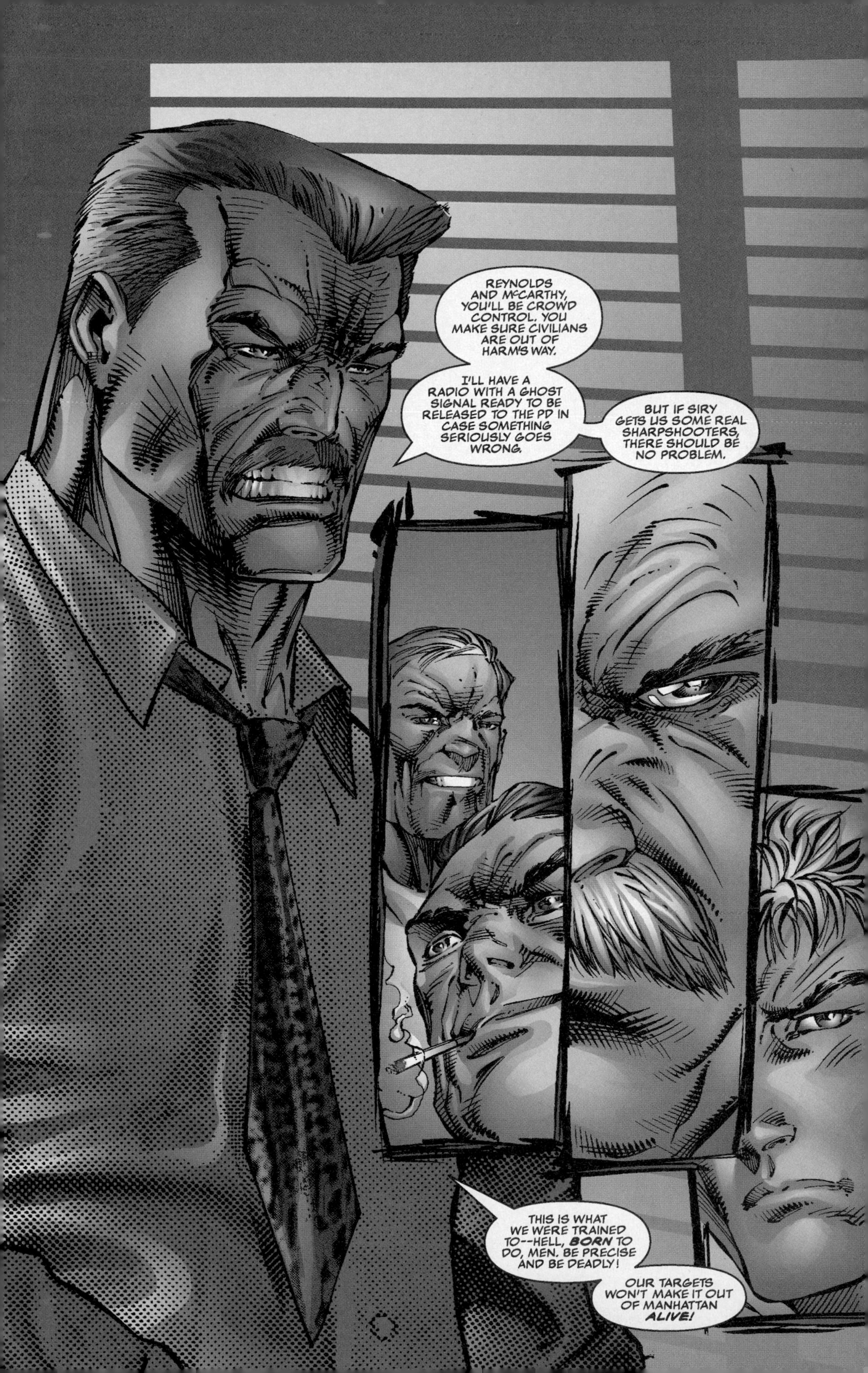
REYNOLDS AND McCARTHY, YOU'LL BE CROWD CONTROL. YOU MAKE SURE CIVILIANS ARE OUT OF HARM'S WAY.
I'LL HAVE A RADIO WITH A GHOST SIGNAL READY TO BE RELEASED TO THE PD IN CASE SOMETHING SERIOUSLY GOES WRONG.
BUT IF SIRY GETS US SOME REAL SHARPSHOOTERS, THERE SHOULD BE NO PROBLEM.
THIS IS WHAT WE WERE TRAINED TO--HELL, *BORN* TO DO, MEN. BE PRECISE AND BE DEADLY!
OUR TARGETS WON'T MAKE IT OUT OF MANHATTAN *ALIVE!*

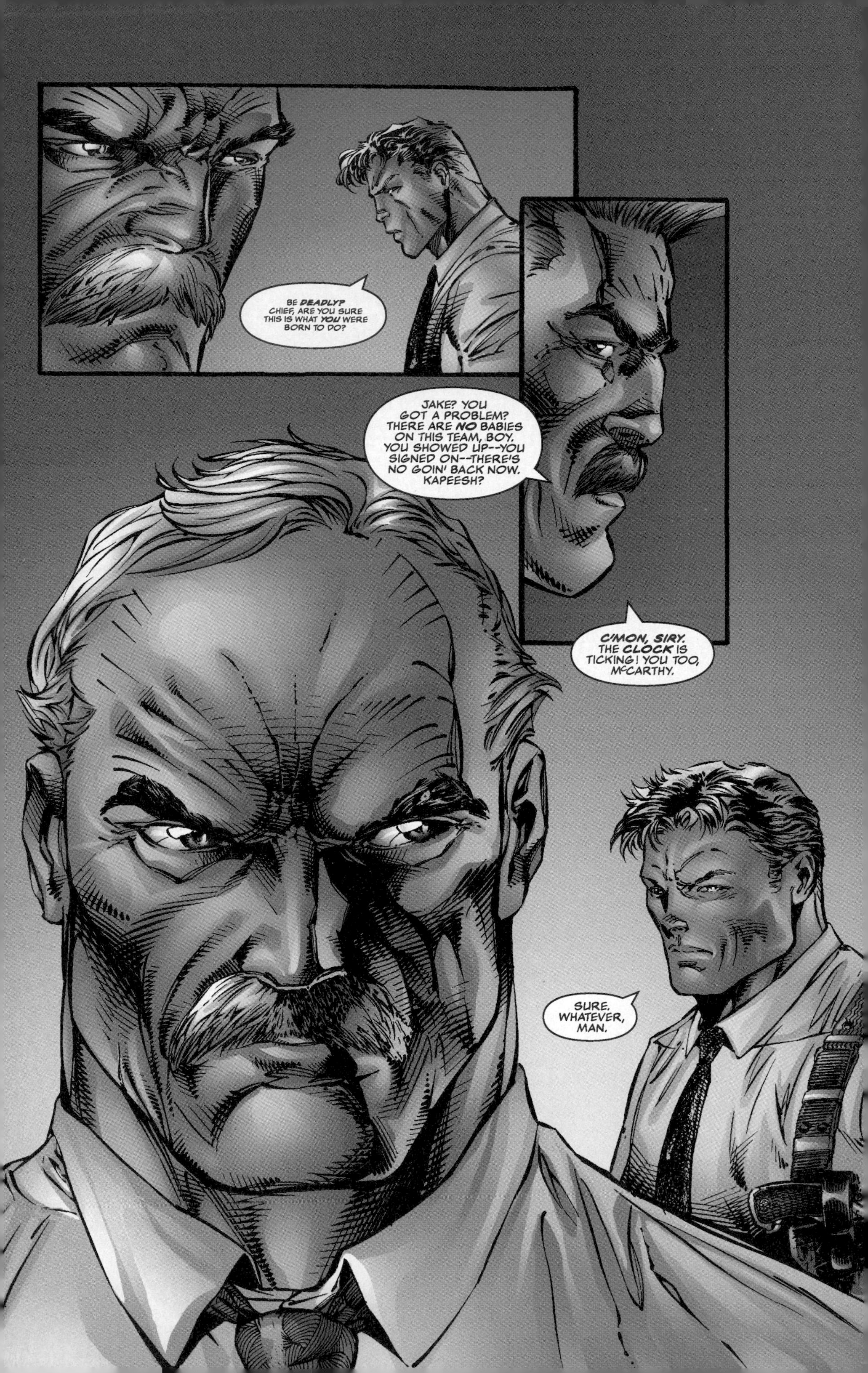
BE DEADLY? CHIEF, ARE YOU SURE THIS IS WHAT YOU WERE BORN TO DO?
JAKE? YOU GOT A PROBLEM? THERE ARE NO BABIES ON THIS TEAM, BOY. YOU SHOWED UP--YOU SIGNED ON--THERE'S NO GOIN' BACK NOW. KAPEESH?
C'MON, SIRY. THE CLOCK IS TICKING! YOU TOO, McCARTHY.
SURE. WHATEVER, MAN.

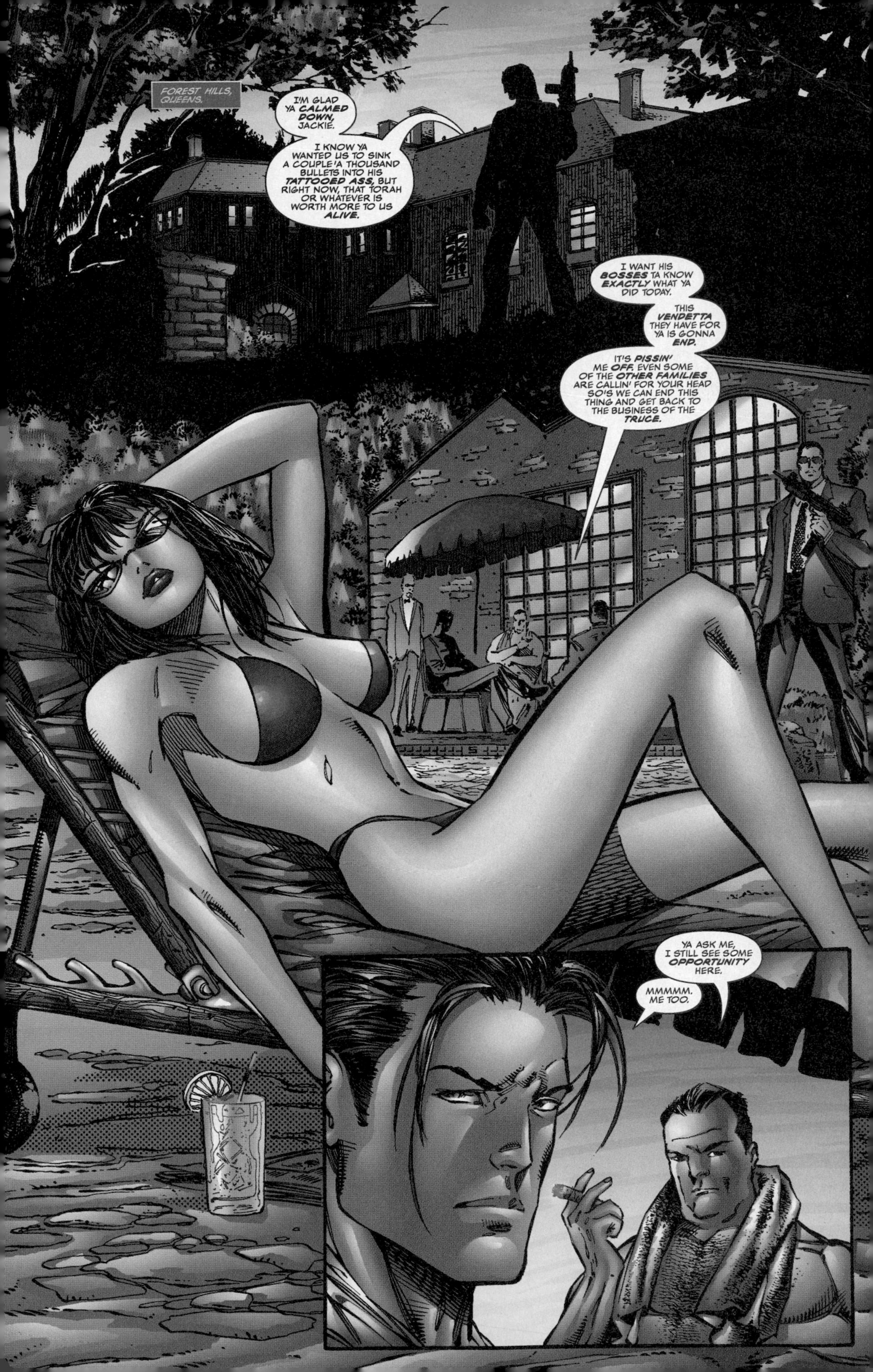
FOREST HILLS, QUEENS.
I'M GLAD YA CALMED DOWN, JACKIE.
I KNOW YA WANTED US TO SINK A COUPLE'A THOUSAND BULLETS INTO HIS TATTOOED ASS, BUT RIGHT NOW, THAT TORAH OR WHATEVER IS WORTH MORE TO US ALIVE.
I WANT HIS BOSSES TA KNOW EXACTLY WHAT YA DID TODAY.
THIS VENDETTA THEY HAVE FOR YA IS GONNA END.
IT'S PISSIN' ME OFF. EVEN SOME OF THE OTHER FAMILIES ARE CALLIN' FOR YOUR HEAD SO'S WE CAN END THIS THING AND GET BACK TO THE BUSINESS OF THE TRUCE.
YA ASK ME, I STILL SEE SOME OPPORTUNITY HERE.
MMMMM. ME TOO.

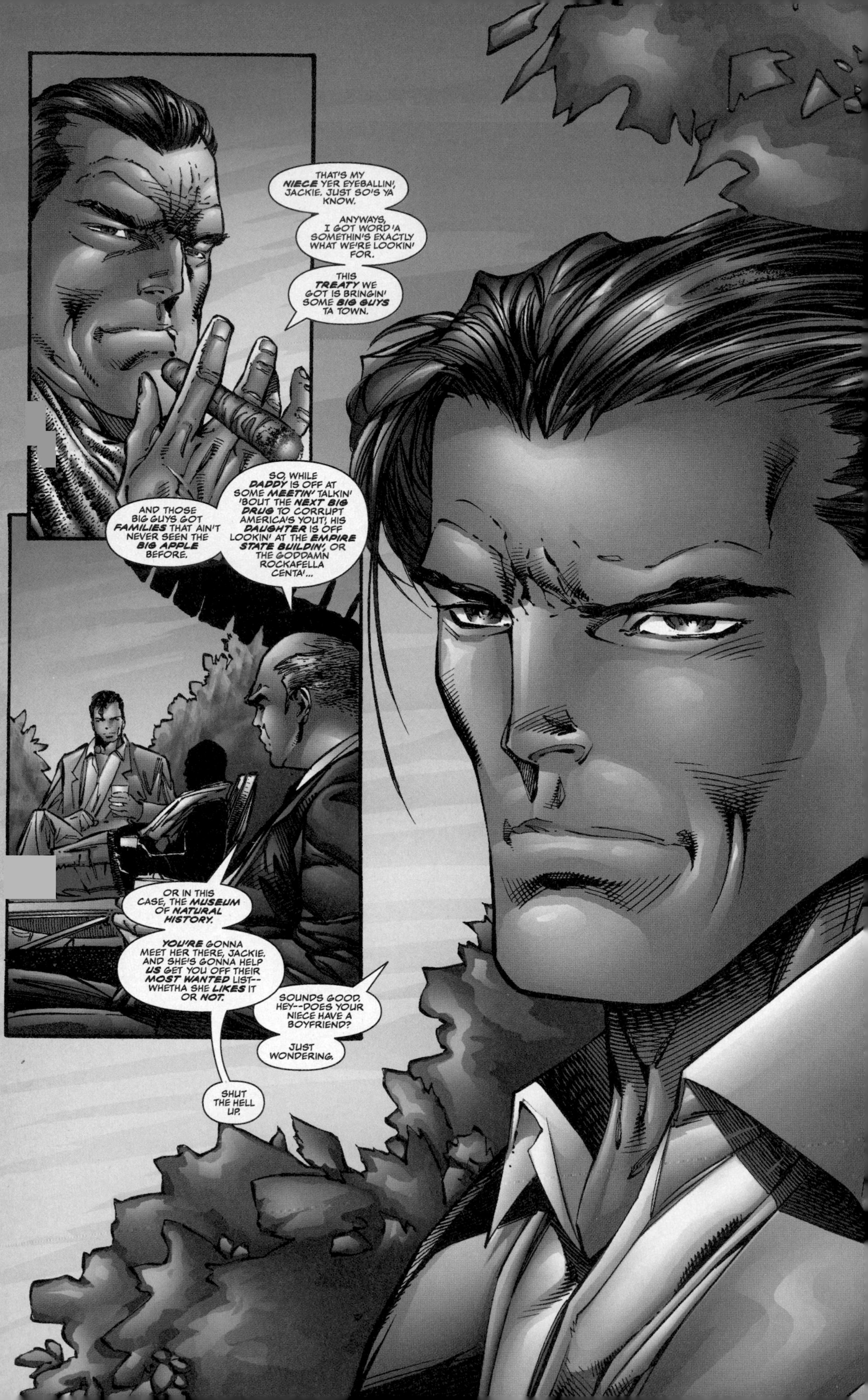
THAT'S MY NIECE YER EYEBALLIN', JACKIE, JUST SO'S YA KNOW.
ANYWAYS, I GOT WORD 'A SOMETHIN'S EXACTLY WHAT WE'RE LOOKIN' FOR.
THIS TREATY WE GOT IS BRINGIN' SOME BIG GUYS TA TOWN.
AND THOSE BIG GUYS GOT FAMILIES THAT AIN'T NEVER SEEN THE BIG APPLE BEFORE.
SO, WHILE DADDY IS OFF AT SOME MEETIN' TALKIN' 'BOUT THE NEXT BIG DRUG TO CORRUPT AMERICA'S YOUT', HIS DAUGHTER IS OFF LOOKIN' AT THE EMPIRE STATE BUILDIN', OR THE GODDAMN ROCKAFELLA CENTA'...
OR IN THIS CASE, THE MUSEUM OF NATURAL HISTORY.
YOU'RE GONNA MEET HER THERE, JACKIE. AND SHE'S GONNA HELP US GET YOU OFF THEIR MOST WANTED LIST-- WHETHA SHE LIKES IT OR NOT.
SOUNDS GOOD. HEY--DOES YOUR NIECE HAVE A BOYFRIEND?
JUST WONDERING.
SHUT THE HELL UP.

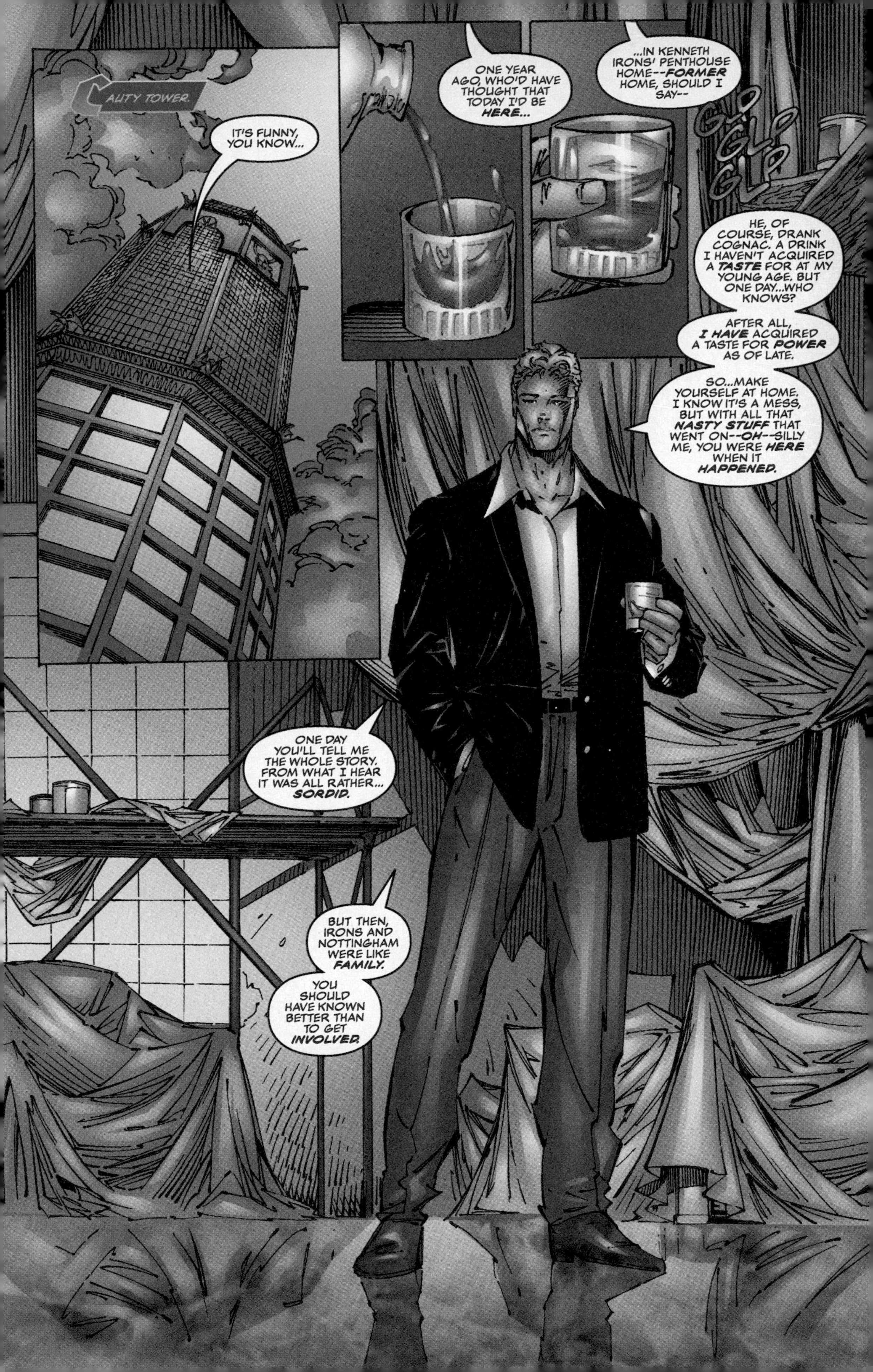
CAUTY TOWER.
IT'S FUNNY, YOU KNOW...
ONE YEAR AGO, WHO'D HAVE THOUGHT THAT TODAY I'D BE HERE...
...IN KENNETH IRONS' PENTHOUSE HOME--FORMER HOME, SHOULD I SAY--
GLP GLP GLP
HE, OF COURSE, DRANK COGNAC. A DRINK I HAVEN'T ACQUIRED A TASTE FOR AT MY YOUNG AGE. BUT ONE DAY...WHO KNOWS?
AFTER ALL, I HAVE ACQUIRED A TASTE FOR POWER AS OF LATE.
SO...MAKE YOURSELF AT HOME. I KNOW IT'S A MESS, BUT WITH ALL THAT NASTY STUFF THAT WENT ON--OH--SILLY ME, YOU WERE HERE WHEN IT HAPPENED.
ONE DAY YOU'LL TELL ME THE WHOLE STORY. FROM WHAT I HEAR IT WAS ALL RATHER... SORDID.
BUT THEN, IRONS AND NOTTINGHAM WERE LIKE FAMILY.
YOU SHOULD HAVE KNOWN BETTER THAN TO GET INVOLVED.

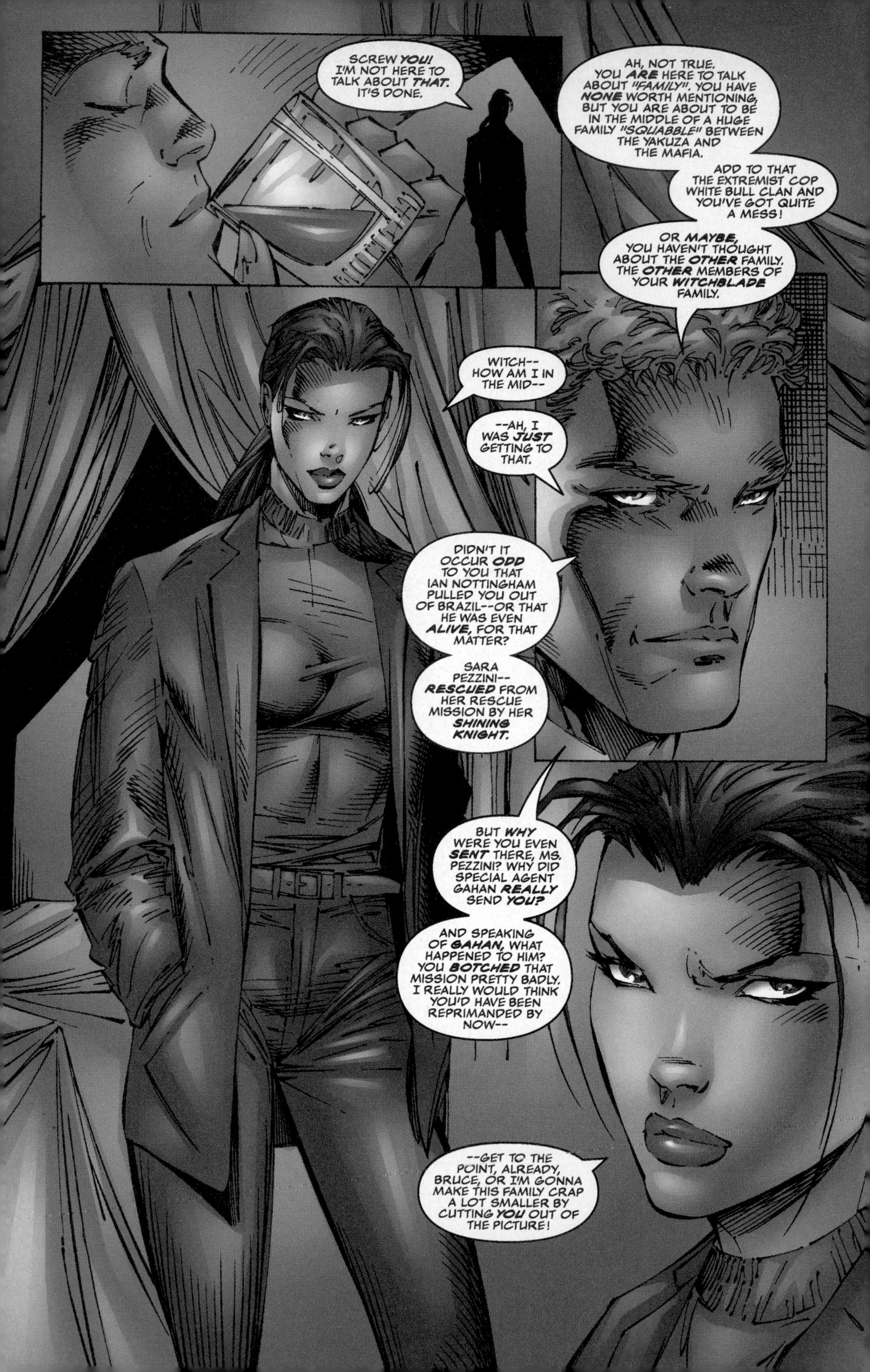
SCREW YOU! I'M NOT HERE TO TALK ABOUT THAT. IT'S DONE.
AH, NOT TRUE. YOU ARE HERE TO TALK ABOUT "FAMILY". YOU HAVE NONE WORTH MENTIONING, BUT YOU ARE ABOUT TO BE IN THE MIDDLE OF A HUGE FAMILY "SQUABBLE" BETWEEN THE YAKUZA AND THE MAFIA.
ADD TO THAT THE EXTREMIST COP WHITE BULL CLAN AND YOU'VE GOT QUITE A MESS!
OR MAYBE, YOU HAVEN'T THOUGHT ABOUT THE OTHER FAMILY. THE OTHER MEMBERS OF YOUR WITCHBLADE FAMILY.
WITCH-- HOW AM I IN THE MID--
--AH, I WAS JUST GETTING TO THAT.
DIDN'T IT OCCUR ODD TO YOU THAT IAN NOTTINGHAM PULLED YOU OUT OF BRAZIL--OR THAT HE WAS EVEN ALIVE, FOR THAT MATTER?
SARA PEZZINI-- RESCUED FROM HER RESCUE MISSION BY HER SHINING KNIGHT.
BUT WHY WERE YOU EVEN SENT THERE, MS. PEZZINI? WHY DID SPECIAL AGENT GAHAN REALLY SEND YOU?
AND SPEAKING OF GAHAN, WHAT HAPPENED TO HIM? YOU BOTCHED THAT MISSION PRETTY BADLY. I REALLY WOULD THINK YOU'D HAVE BEEN REPRIMANDED BY NOW--
--GET TO THE POINT, ALREADY, BRUCE, OR I'M GONNA MAKE THIS FAMILY CRAP A LOT SMALLER BY CUTTING YOU OUT OF THE PICTURE!

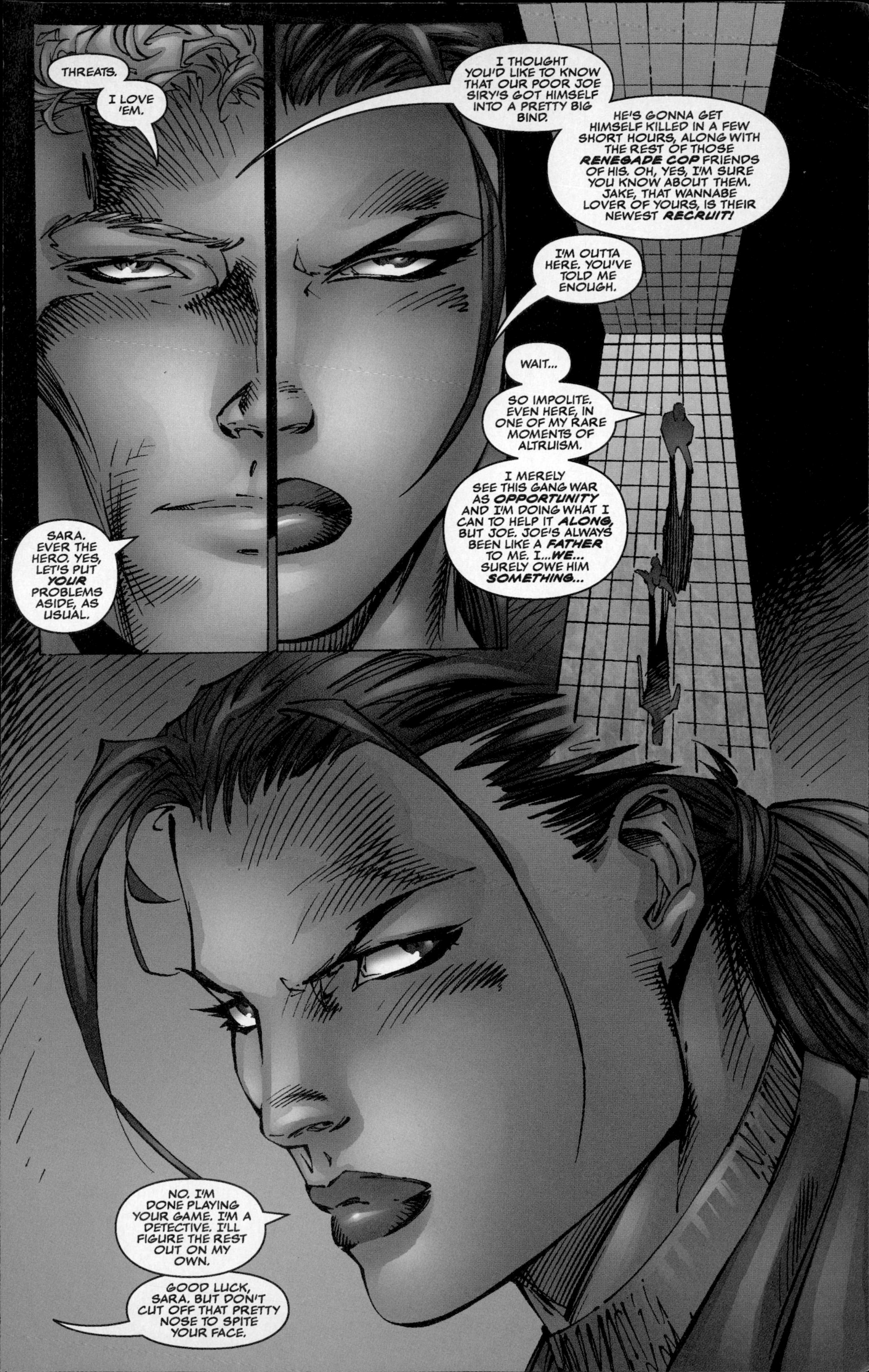
THREATS.
I LOVE 'EM.
I THOUGHT YOU'D LIKE TO KNOW THAT OUR POOR JOE SIRY'S GOT HIMSELF INTO A PRETTY BIG BIND.
HE'S GONNA GET HIMSELF KILLED IN A FEW SHORT HOURS, ALONG WITH THE REST OF THOSE RENEGADE COP FRIENDS OF HIS. OH, YES, I'M SURE YOU KNOW ABOUT THEM. JAKE, THAT WANNABE LOVER OF YOURS, IS THEIR NEWEST RECRUIT!
I'M OUTTA HERE. YOU'VE TOLD ME ENOUGH.
WAIT...
SO IMPOLITE. EVEN HERE, IN ONE OF MY RARE MOMENTS OF ALTRUISM.
I MERELY SEE THIS GANG WAR AS OPPORTUNITY AND I'M DOING WHAT I CAN TO HELP IT ALONG, BUT JOE. JOE'S ALWAYS BEEN LIKE A FATHER TO ME. I...WE... SURELY OWE HIM SOMETHING...
SARA. EVER THE HERO. YES, LET'S PUT YOUR PROBLEMS ASIDE, AS USUAL.
NO. I'M DONE PLAYING YOUR GAME. I'M A DETECTIVE. I'LL FIGURE THE REST OUT ON MY OWN.
GOOD LUCK, SARA. BUT DON'T CUT OFF THAT PRETTY NOSE TO SPITE YOUR FACE.

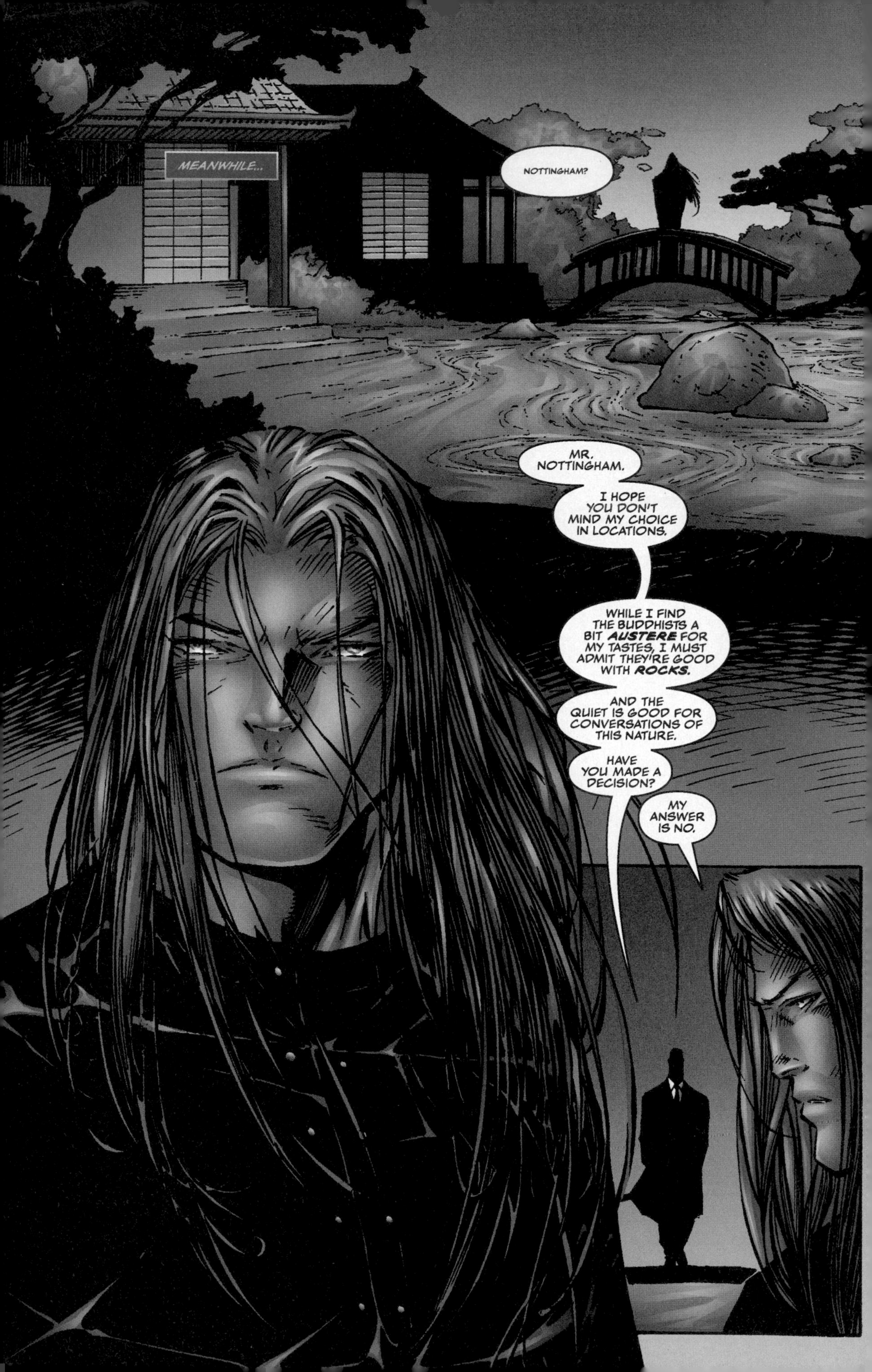
MEANWHILE...
NOTTINGHAM?
MR. NOTTINGHAM.
I HOPE YOU DON'T MIND MY CHOICE IN LOCATIONS.
WHILE I FIND THE BUDDHISTS A BIT AUSTERE FOR MY TASTES, I MUST ADMIT THEY'RE GOOD WITH ROCKS.
AND THE QUIET IS GOOD FOR CONVERSATIONS OF THIS NATURE.
HAVE YOU MADE A DECISION?
MY ANSWER IS NO.

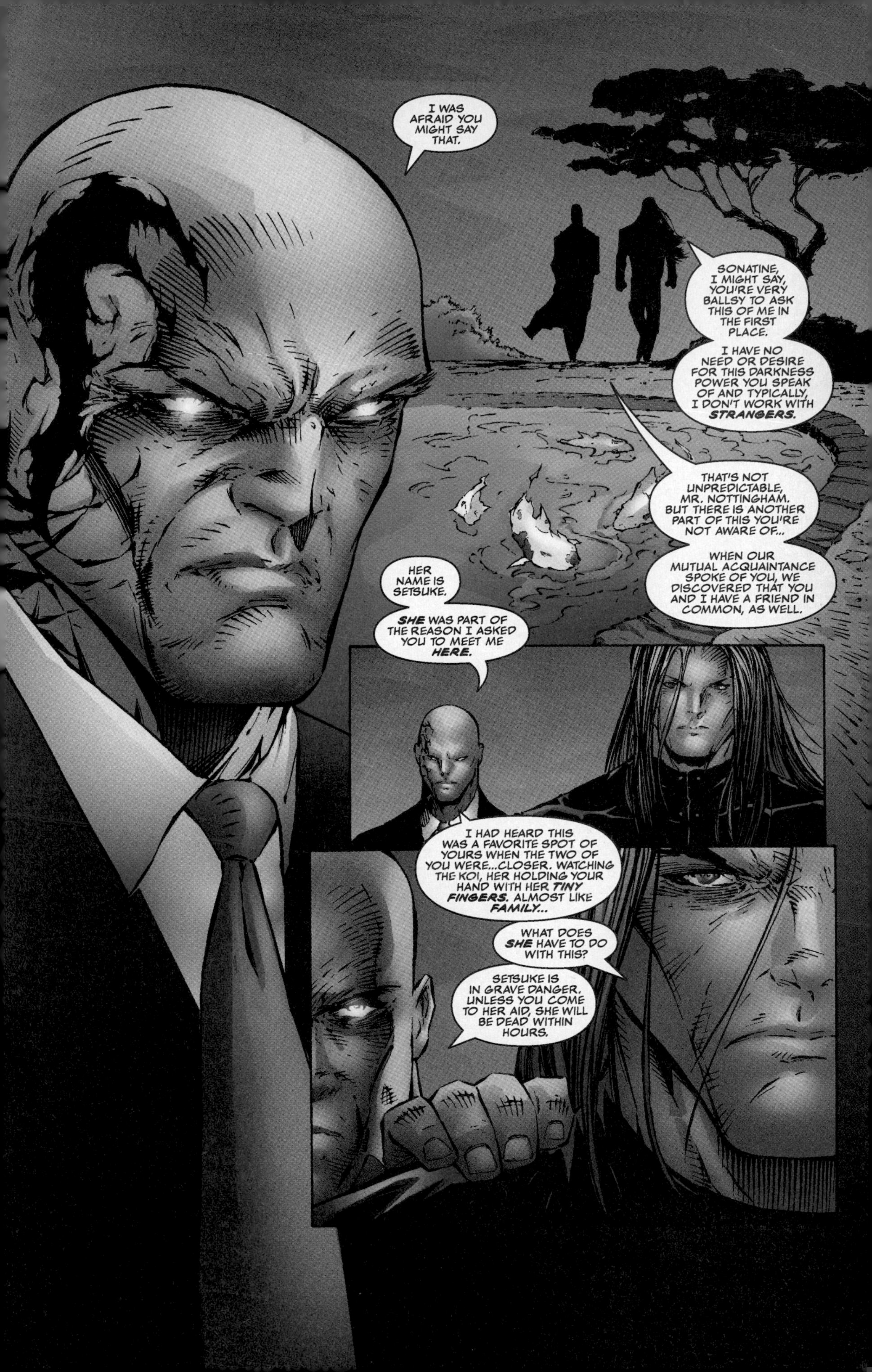

I WAS AFRAID YOU MIGHT SAY THAT.
SONATINE, I MIGHT SAY, YOU'RE VERY BALLSY TO ASK THIS OF ME IN THE FIRST PLACE.
I HAVE NO NEED OR DESIRE FOR THIS DARKNESS POWER YOU SPEAK OF AND TYPICALLY, I DON'T WORK WITH STRANGERS.
THAT'S NOT UNPREDICTABLE, MR. NOTTINGHAM. BUT THERE IS ANOTHER PART OF THIS YOU'RE NOT AWARE OF...
WHEN OUR MUTUAL ACQUAINTANCE SPOKE OF YOU, WE DISCOVERED THAT YOU AND I HAVE A FRIEND IN COMMON, AS WELL.
HER NAME IS SETSUKE.
SHE WAS PART OF THE REASON I ASKED YOU TO MEET ME HERE.
I HAD HEARD THIS WAS A FAVORITE SPOT OF YOURS WHEN THE TWO OF YOU WERE...CLOSER. WATCHING THE KOI, HER HOLDING YOUR HAND WITH HER TINY FINGERS. ALMOST LIKE FAMILY...
WHAT DOES SHE HAVE TO DO WITH THIS?
SETSUKE IS IN GRAVE DANGER. UNLESS YOU COME TO HER AID, SHE WILL BE DEAD WITHIN HOURS.

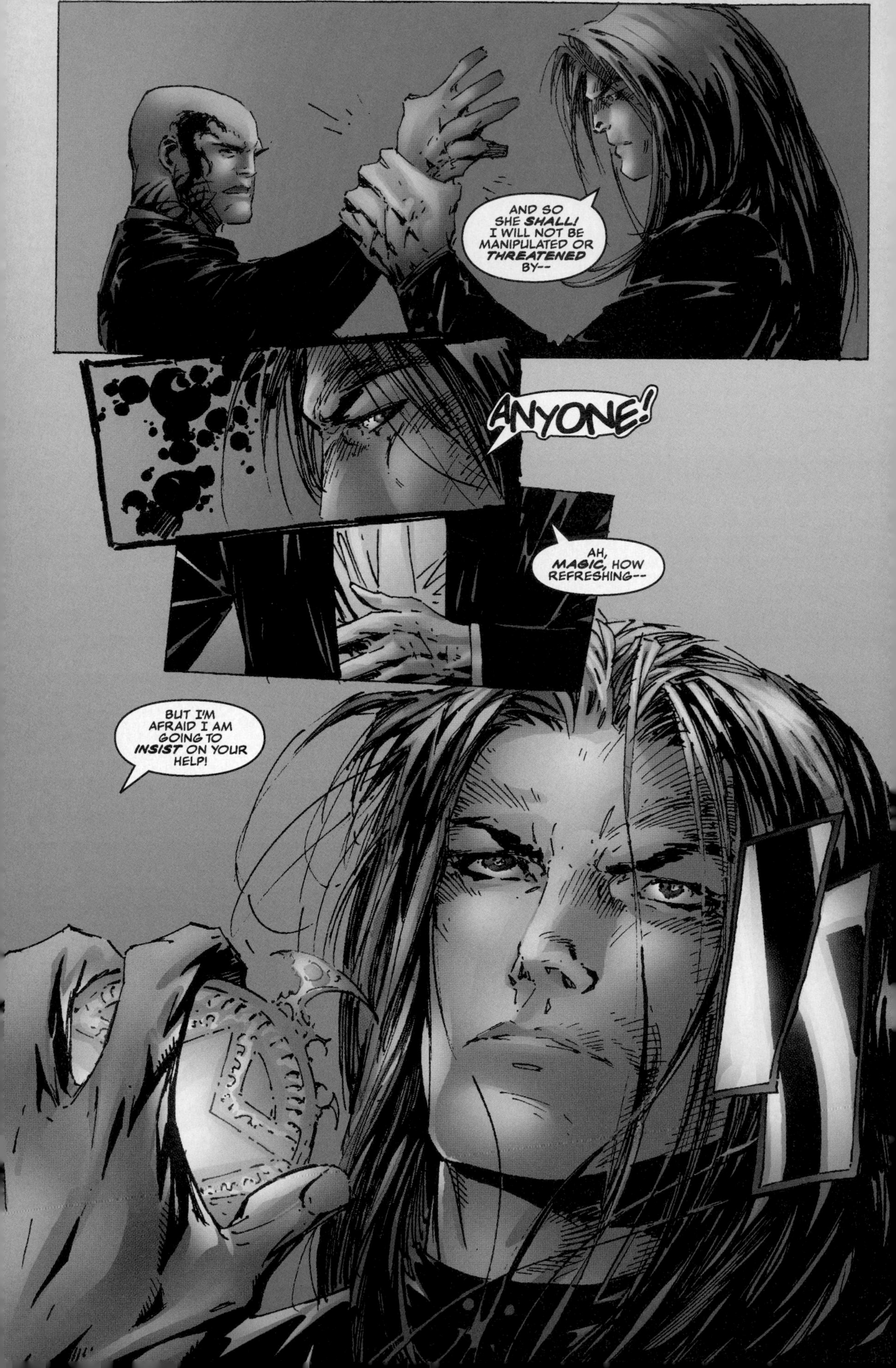
AND SO SHE SHALL! I WILL NOT BE MANIPULATED OR THREATENED BY--
ANYONE!
AH, MAGIC, HOW REFRESHING--
BUT I'M AFRAID I AM GOING TO INSIST ON YOUR HELP!

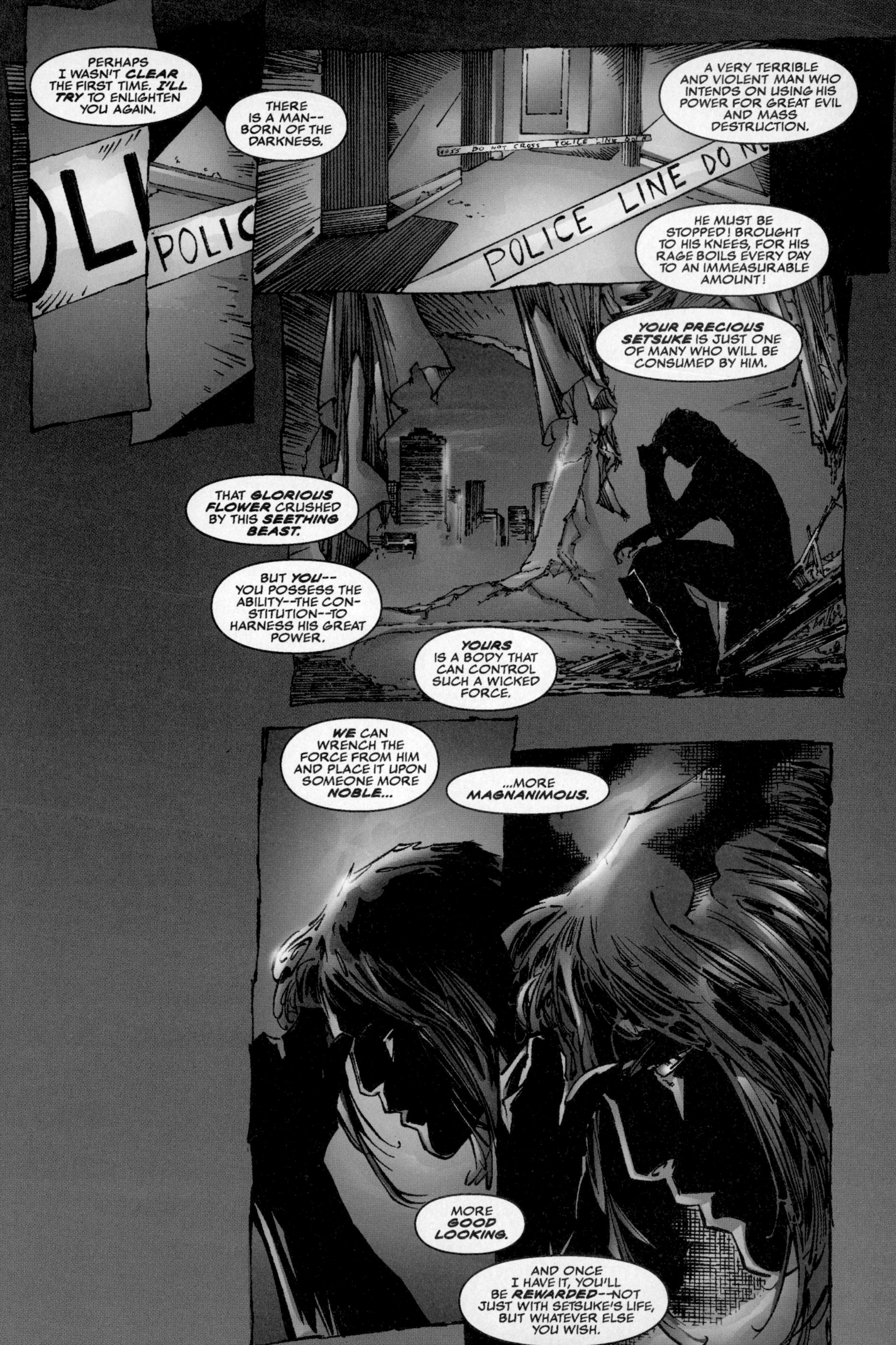
PERHAPS I WASN'T CLEAR THE FIRST TIME. I'LL TRY TO ENLIGHTEN YOU AGAIN.
THERE IS A MAN--BORN OF THE DARKNESS.
A VERY TERRIBLE AND VIOLENT MAN WHO INTENDS ON USING HIS POWER FOR GREAT EVIL AND MASS DESTRUCTION.
POLICE LINE DO NOT CROSS
POLICE LINE DO N
HE MUST BE STOPPED! BROUGHT TO HIS KNEES, FOR HIS RAGE BOILS EVERY DAY TO AN IMMEASURABLE AMOUNT!
YOUR PRECIOUS SETSUKE IS JUST ONE OF MANY WHO WILL BE CONSUMED BY HIM.
THAT GLORIOUS FLOWER CRUSHED BY THIS SEETHING BEAST.
BUT YOU--YOU POSSESS THE ABILITY--THE CONSTITUTION--TO HARNESS HIS GREAT POWER.
YOURS IS A BODY THAT CAN CONTROL SUCH A WICKED FORCE.
WE CAN WRENCH THE FORCE FROM HIM AND PLACE IT UPON SOMEONE MORE NOBLE...
...MORE MAGNANIMOUS.
MORE GOOD LOOKING.
AND ONCE I HAVE IT, YOU'LL BE REWARDED--NOT JUST WITH SETSUKE'S LIFE, BUT WHATEVER ELSE YOU WISH.

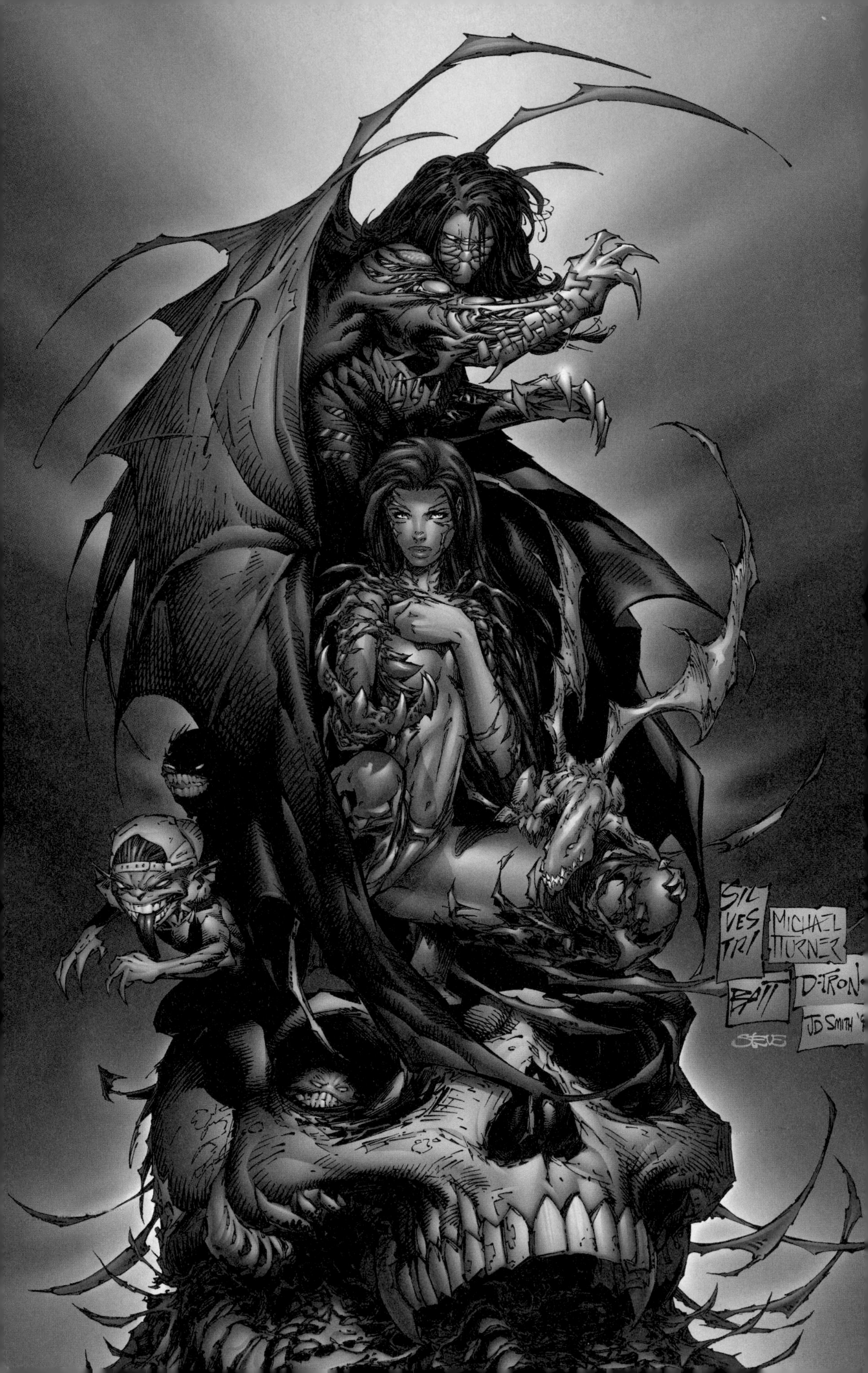
SIL VES TRI
MICHAEL TURNER
BATT
D-TRON
JD SMITH

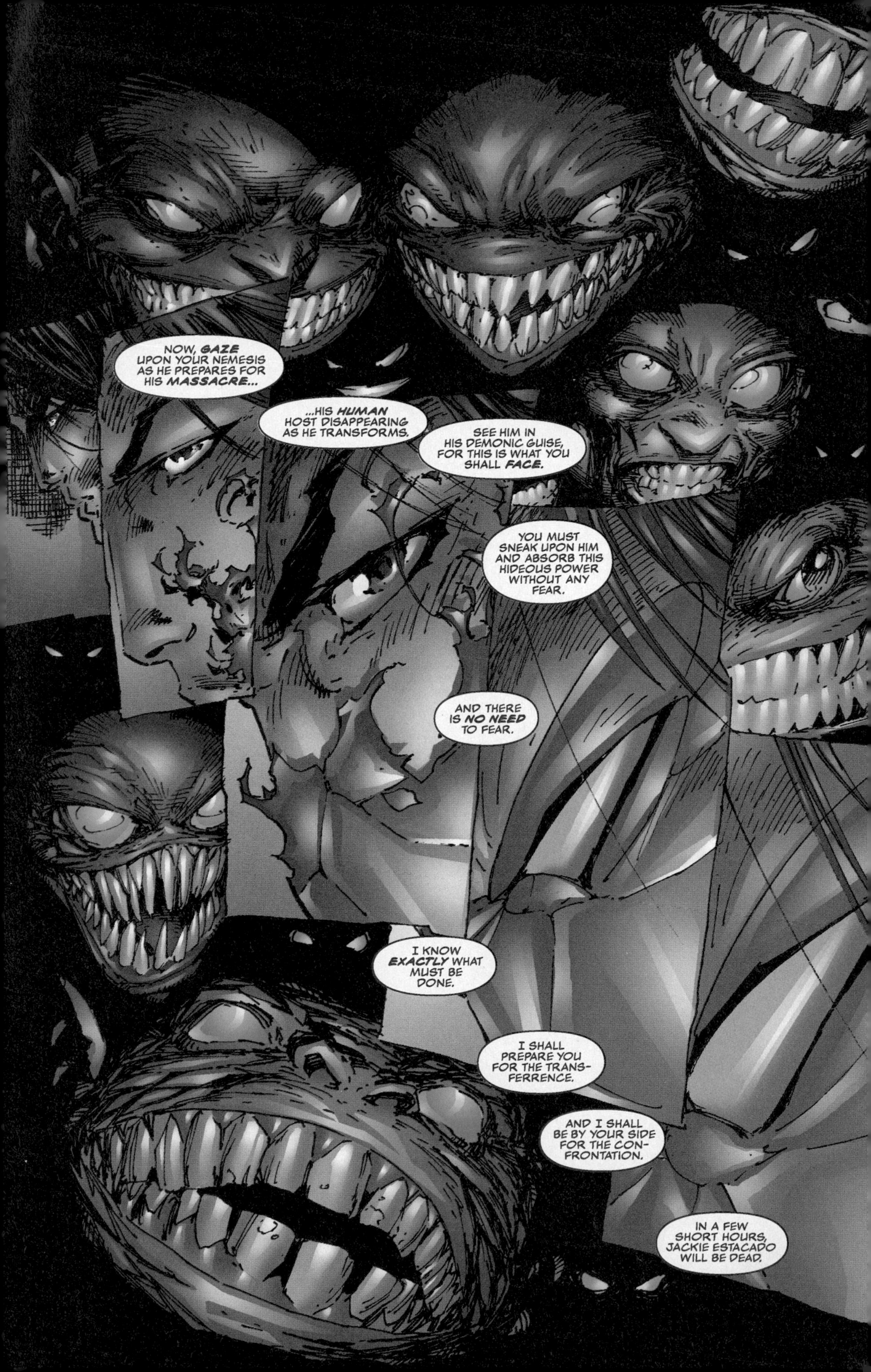
NOW, GAZE UPON YOUR NEMESIS AS HE PREPARES FOR HIS MASSACRE...
...HIS HUMAN HOST DISAPPEARING AS HE TRANSFORMS.
SEE HIM IN HIS DEMONIC GUISE, FOR THIS IS WHAT YOU SHALL FACE.
YOU MUST SNEAK UPON HIM AND ABSORB THIS HIDEOUS POWER WITHOUT ANY FEAR.
AND THERE IS NO NEED TO FEAR.
I KNOW EXACTLY WHAT MUST BE DONE.
I SHALL PREPARE YOU FOR THE TRANS-FERRENCE.
AND I SHALL BE BY YOUR SIDE FOR THE CON-FRONTATION.
IN A FEW SHORT HOURS, JACKIE ESTACADO WILL BE DEAD.

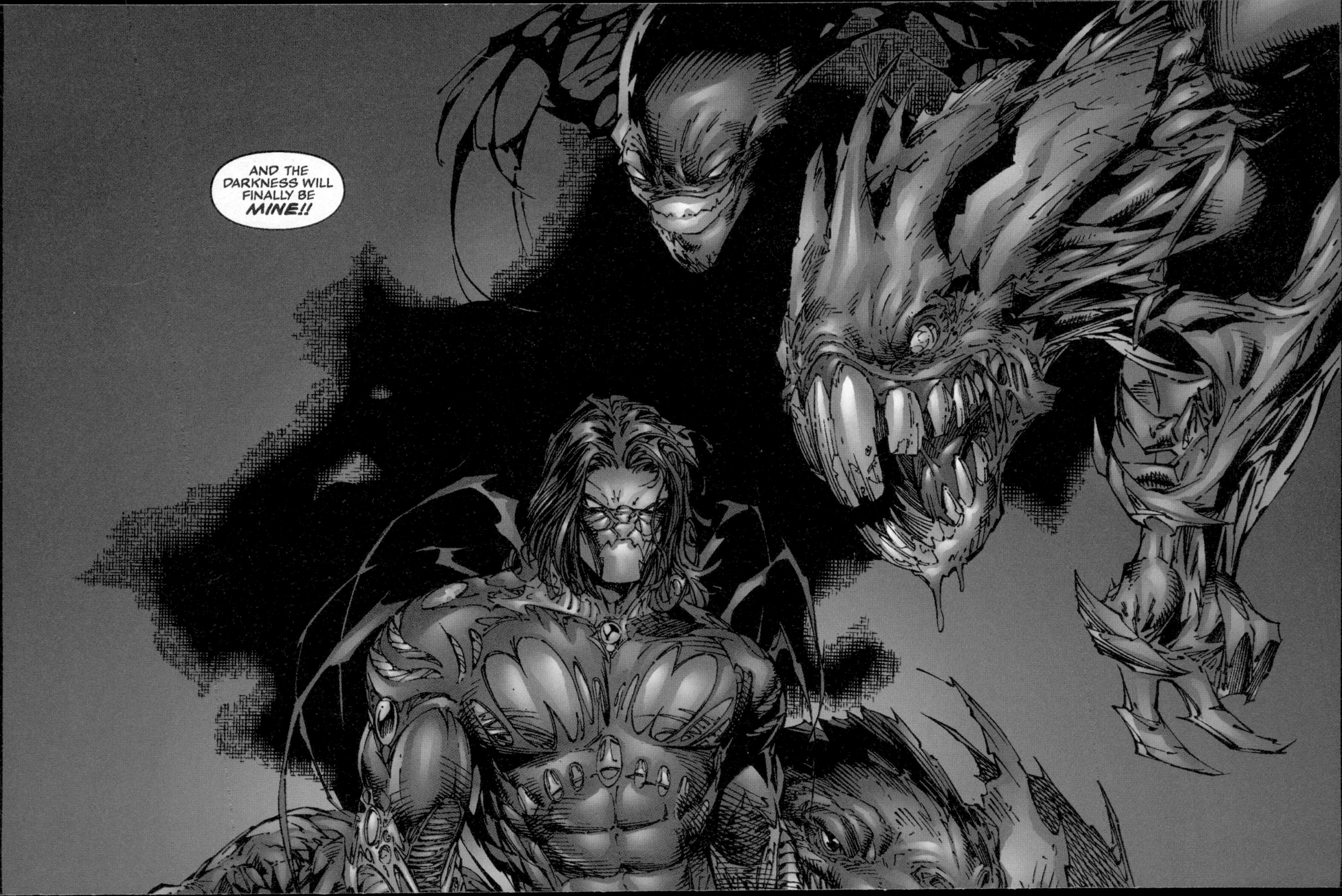
AND THE DARKNESS WILL FINALLY BE MINE!!

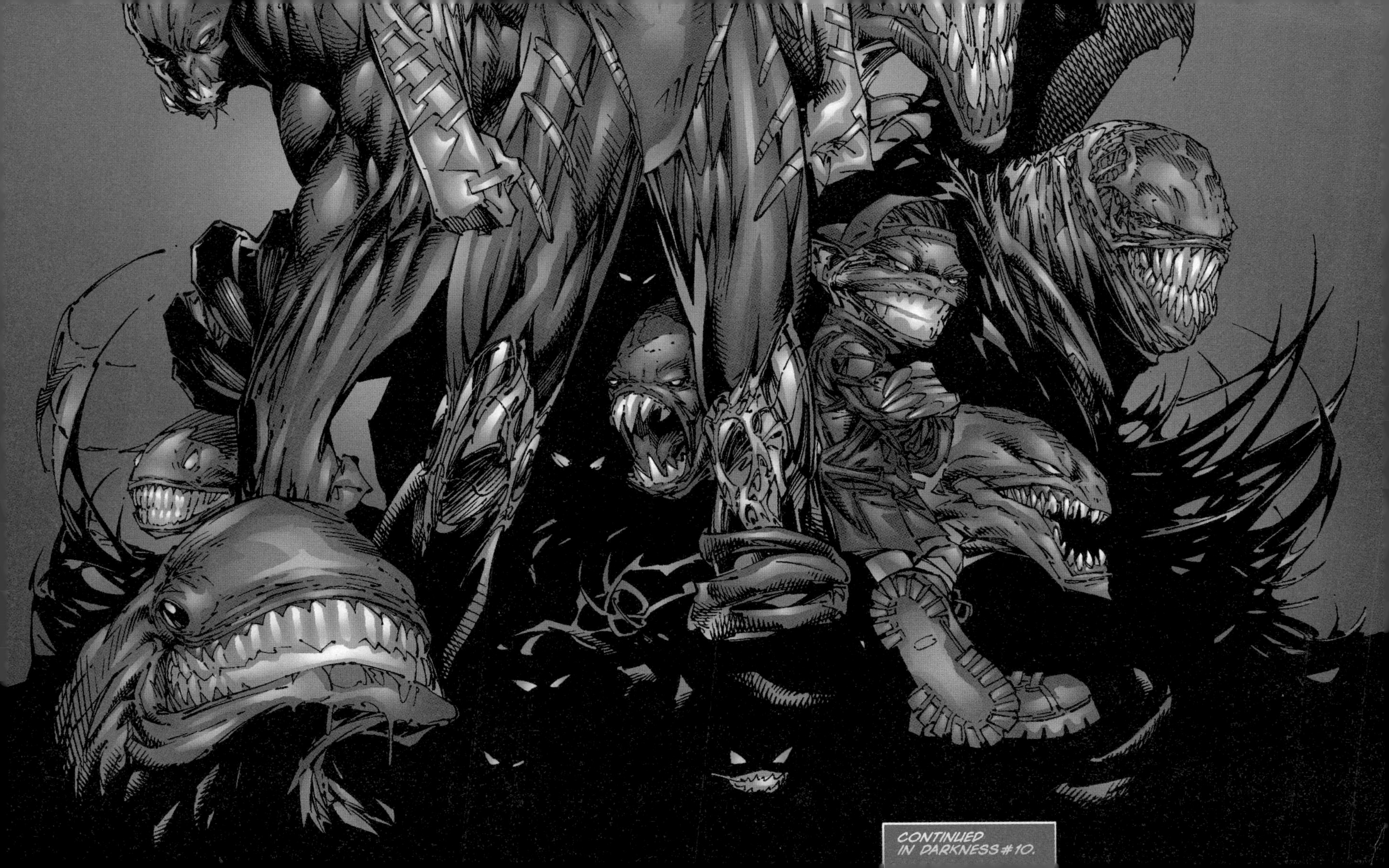
CONTINUED IN DARKNESS #10.

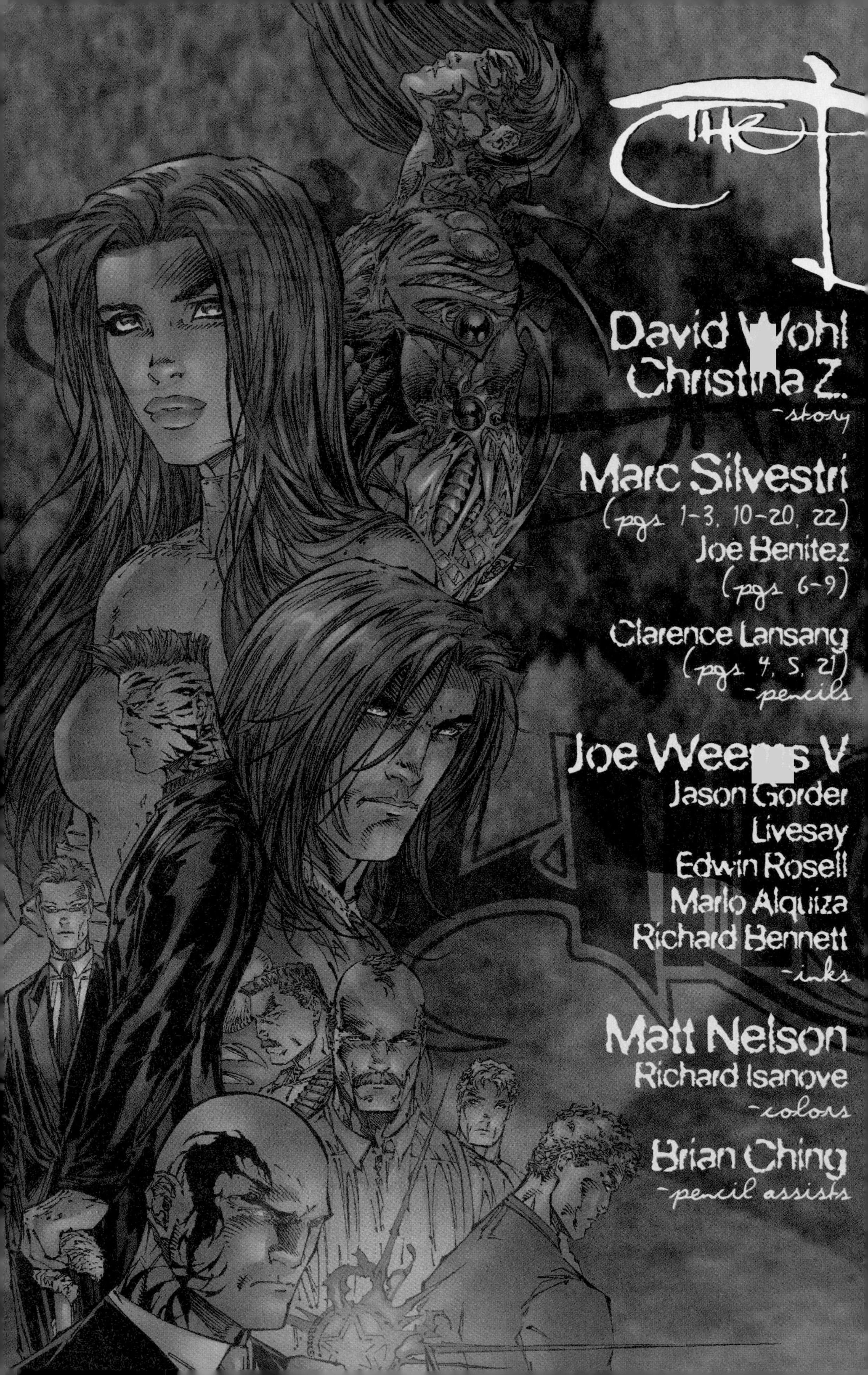

THE
David [redacted]ohl
Christina Z.
-story
Marc Silvestri
(pgs 1-3, 10-20, 22)
Joe Benitez
(pgs 6-9)
Clarence Lansang
(pgs 4, 5, 21)
-pencils
Joe Wee[redacted]s V
Jason Gorder
Livesay
Edwin Rosell
Marlo Alquiza
Richard Bennett
-inks
Matt Nelson
Richard Isanove
-colors
Brian Ching
-pencil assists

DARKNESS 10

Family TIES

PART THREE

Dennis Heisler
Robin Spehar
-letters

Peter Steigerwald
-editor

Sonia Im
-associate editor

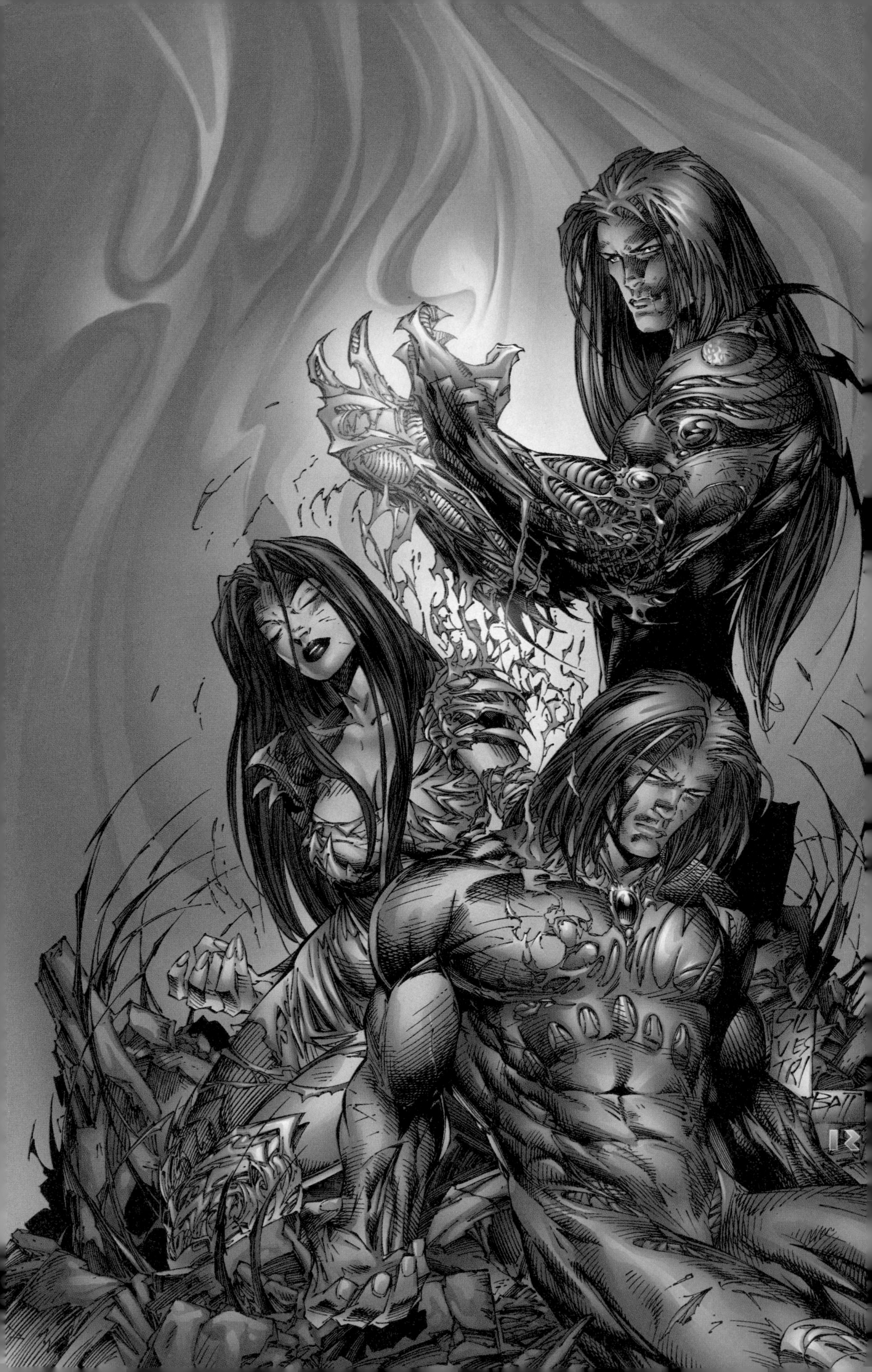

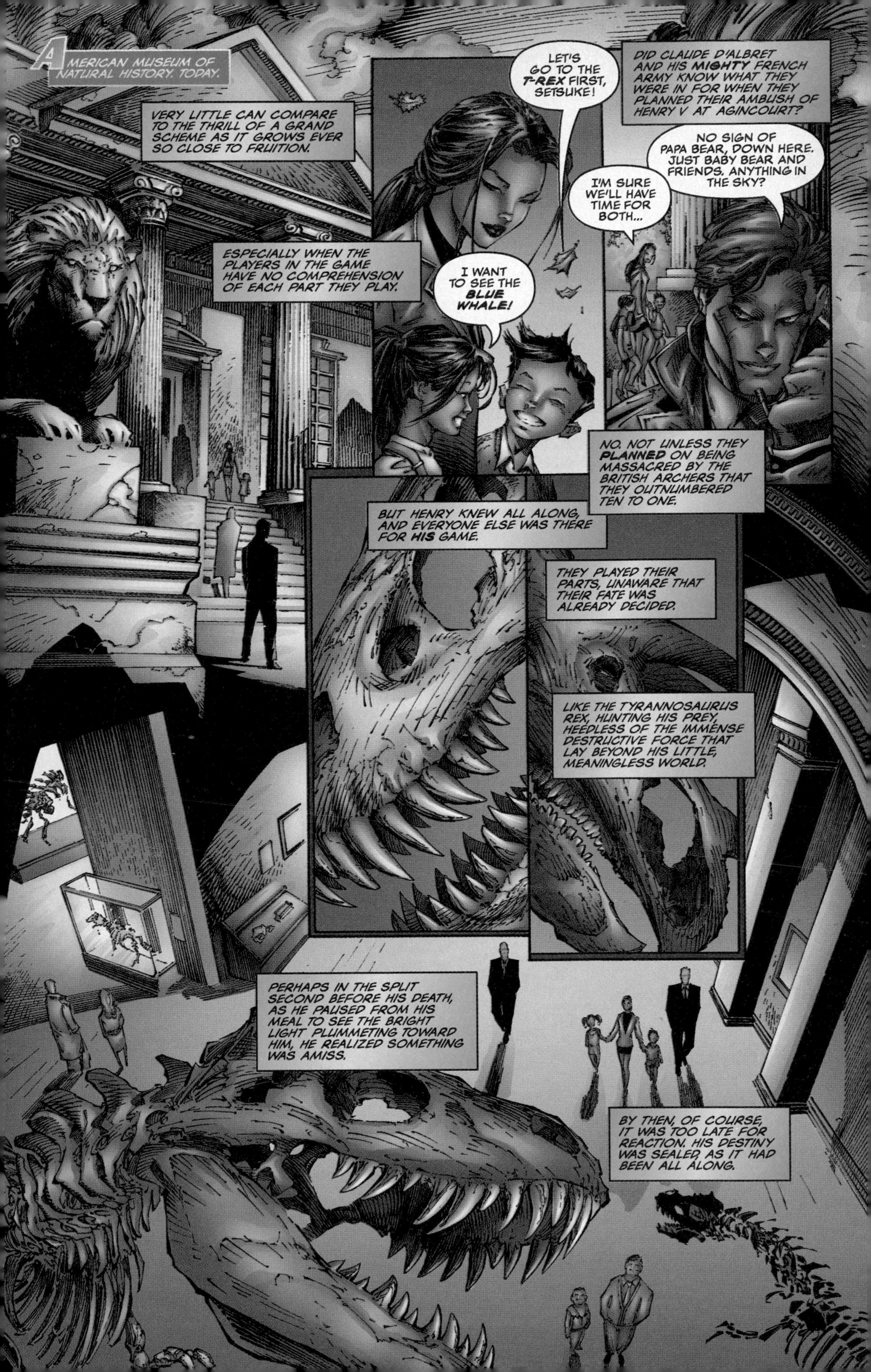
AMERICAN MUSEUM OF NATURAL HISTORY. TODAY.
VERY LITTLE CAN COMPARE TO THE THRILL OF A GRAND SCHEME AS IT GROWS EVER SO CLOSE TO FRUITION.
ESPECIALLY WHEN THE PLAYERS IN THE GAME HAVE NO COMPREHENSION OF EACH PART THEY PLAY.
LET'S GO TO THE T-REX FIRST, SETSUKE!
I'M SURE WE'LL HAVE TIME FOR BOTH...
I WANT TO SEE THE BLUE WHALE!
DID CLAUDE D'ALBRET AND HIS MIGHTY FRENCH ARMY KNOW WHAT THEY WERE IN FOR WHEN THEY PLANNED THEIR AMBUSH OF HENRY V AT AGINCOURT?
NO SIGN OF PAPA BEAR, DOWN HERE. JUST BABY BEAR AND FRIENDS. ANYTHING IN THE SKY?
NO. NOT UNLESS THEY PLANNED ON BEING MASSACRED BY THE BRITISH ARCHERS THAT THEY OUTNUMBERED TEN TO ONE.
BUT HENRY KNEW ALL ALONG, AND EVERYONE ELSE WAS THERE FOR HIS GAME.
THEY PLAYED THEIR PARTS, UNAWARE THAT THEIR FATE WAS ALREADY DECIDED.
LIKE THE TYRANNOSAURUS REX, HUNTING HIS PREY, HEEDLESS OF THE IMMENSE DESTRUCTIVE FORCE THAT LAY BEYOND HIS LITTLE, MEANINGLESS WORLD.
PERHAPS IN THE SPLIT SECOND BEFORE HIS DEATH, AS HE PAUSED FROM HIS MEAL TO SEE THE BRIGHT LIGHT PLUMMETING TOWARD HIM, HE REALIZED SOMETHING WAS AMISS.
BY THEN, OF COURSE, IT WAS TOO LATE FOR REACTION. HIS DESTINY WAS SEALED, AS IT HAD BEEN ALL ALONG.

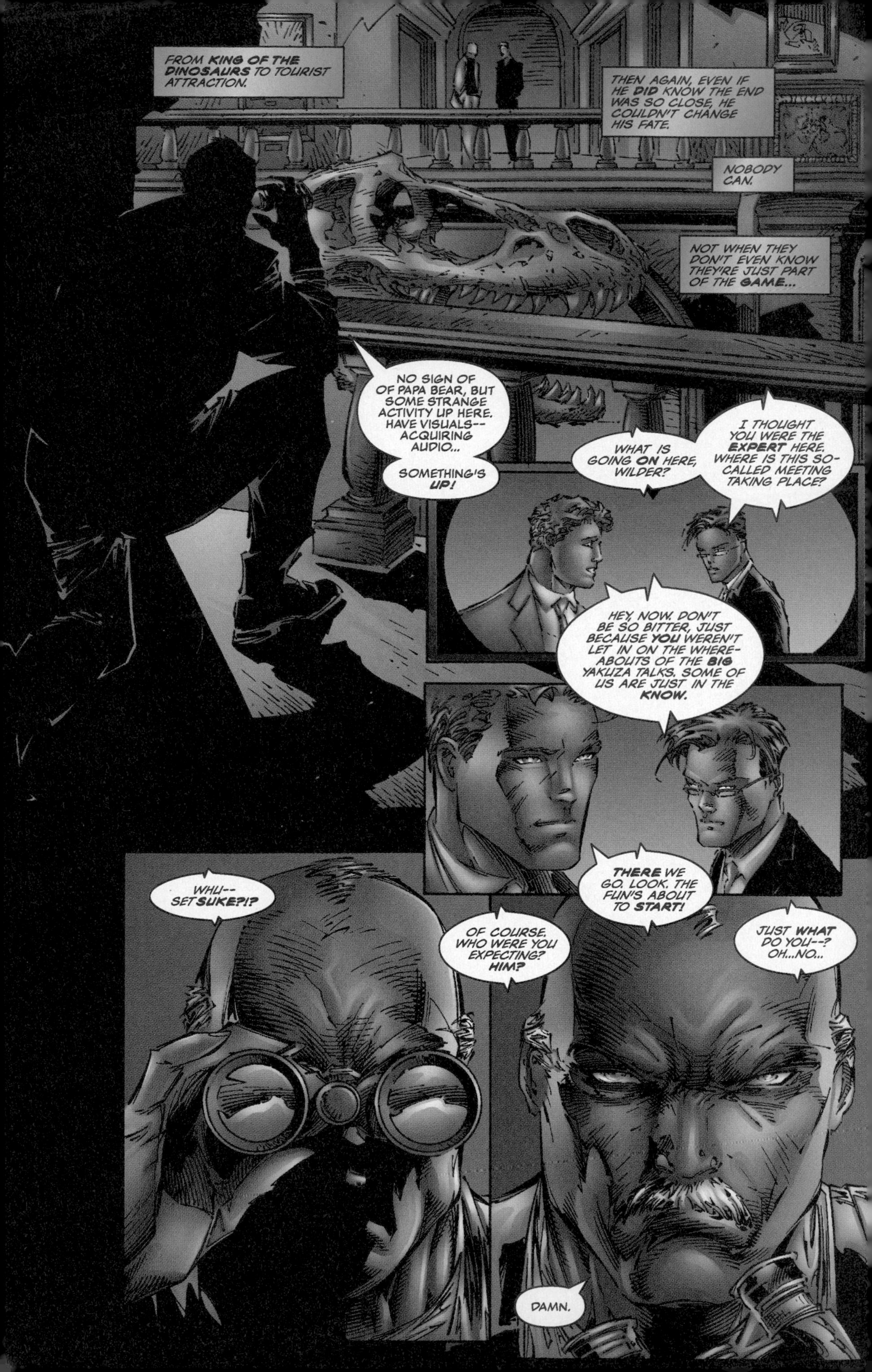
FROM KING OF THE DINOSAURS TO TOURIST ATTRACTION.
THEN AGAIN, EVEN IF HE DID KNOW THE END WAS SO CLOSE, HE COULDN'T CHANGE HIS FATE.
NOBODY CAN.
NOT WHEN THEY DON'T EVEN KNOW THEY'RE JUST PART OF THE GAME...
NO SIGN OF OF PAPA BEAR, BUT SOME STRANGE ACTIVITY UP HERE. HAVE VISUALS-- ACQUIRING AUDIO...
SOMETHING'S UP!
WHAT IS GOING ON HERE, WILDER?
I THOUGHT YOU WERE THE EXPERT HERE. WHERE IS THIS SO-CALLED MEETING TAKING PLACE?
HEY, NOW. DON'T BE SO BITTER, JUST BECAUSE YOU WEREN'T LET IN ON THE WHERE-ABOUTS OF THE BIG YAKUZA TALKS. SOME OF US ARE JUST IN THE KNOW.
THERE WE GO. LOOK. THE FUN'S ABOUT TO START!
WHU-- SET SUKE?!?
OF COURSE. WHO WERE YOU EXPECTING? HIM?
JUST WHAT DO YOU--? OH...NO...
DAMN.

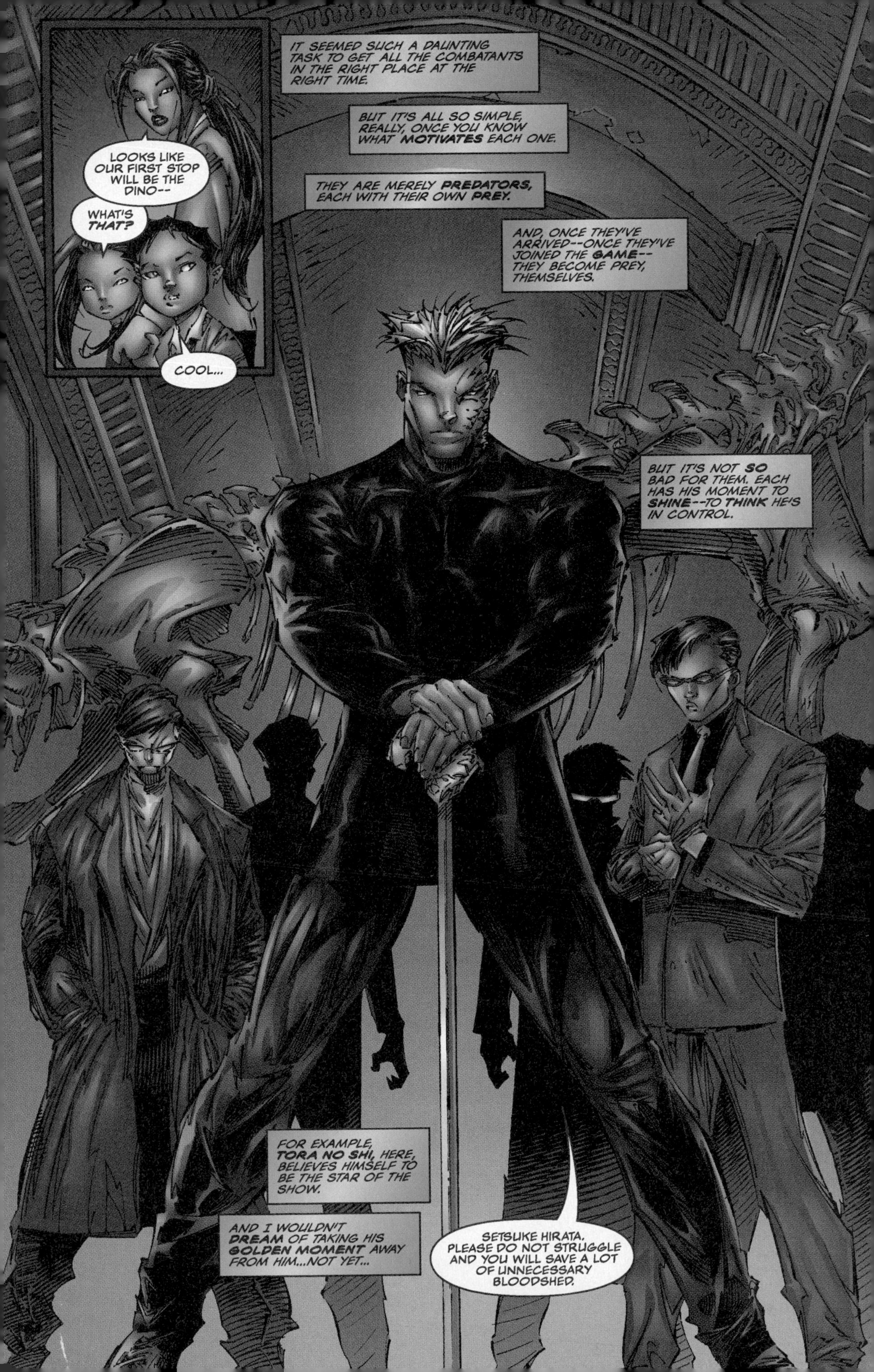
LOOKS LIKE OUR FIRST STOP WILL BE THE DINO--
WHAT'S THAT?
COOL...
IT SEEMED SUCH A DAUNTING TASK TO GET ALL THE COMBATANTS IN THE RIGHT PLACE AT THE RIGHT TIME.
BUT IT'S ALL SO SIMPLE, REALLY, ONCE YOU KNOW WHAT MOTIVATES EACH ONE.
THEY ARE MERELY PREDATORS, EACH WITH THEIR OWN PREY.
AND, ONCE THEY'VE ARRIVED--ONCE THEY'VE JOINED THE GAME--THEY BECOME PREY, THEMSELVES.
BUT IT'S NOT SO BAD FOR THEM. EACH HAS HIS MOMENT TO SHINE--TO THINK HE'S IN CONTROL.
FOR EXAMPLE, TORA NO SHI, HERE, BELIEVES HIMSELF TO BE THE STAR OF THE SHOW.
AND I WOULDN'T DREAM OF TAKING HIS GOLDEN MOMENT AWAY FROM HIM...NOT YET...
SETSUKE HIRATA, PLEASE DO NOT STRUGGLE AND YOU WILL SAVE A LOT OF UNNECESSARY BLOODSHED.

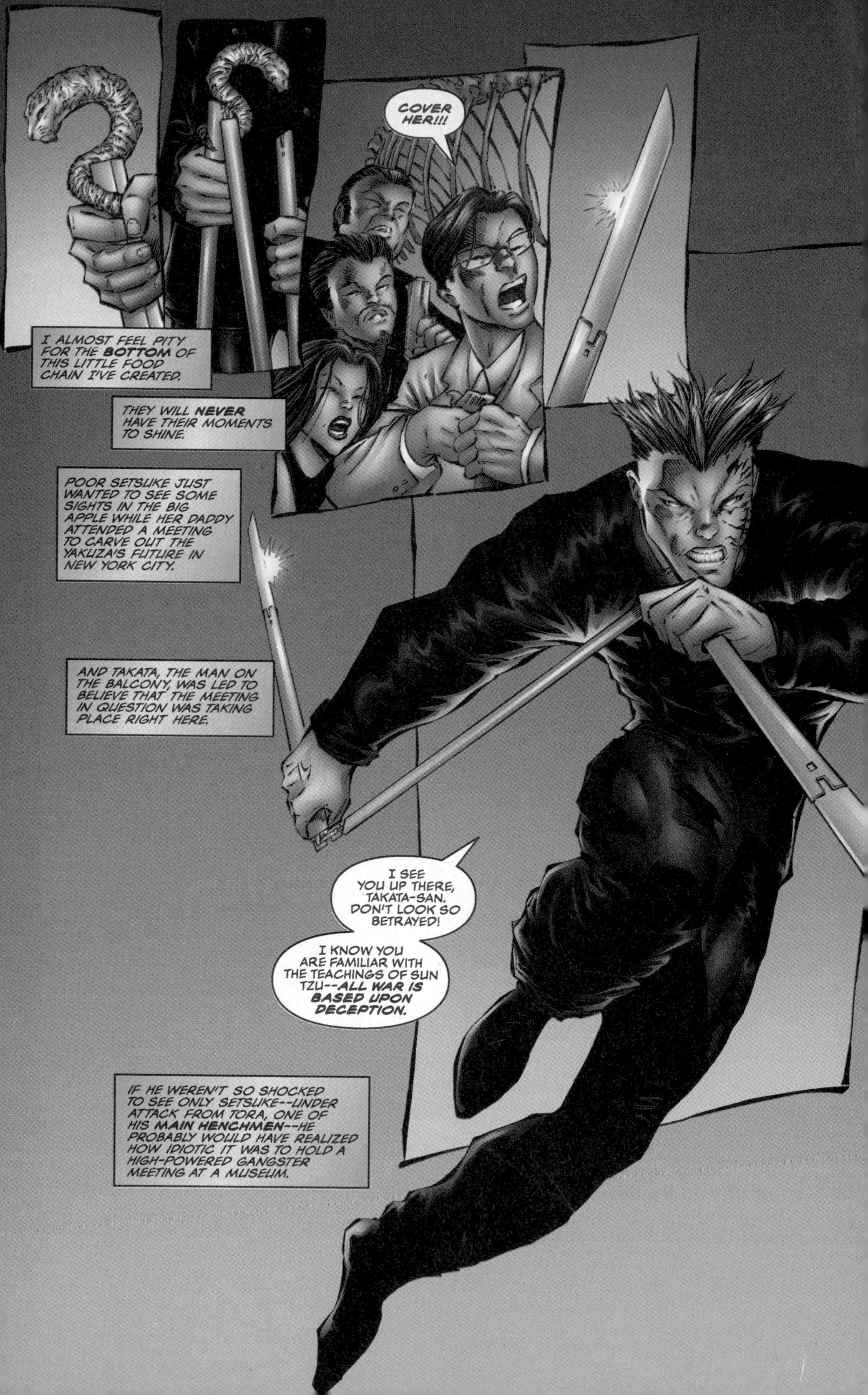

COVER HER!!!
I ALMOST FEEL PITY FOR THE **BOTTOM** OF THIS LITTLE FOOD CHAIN I'VE CREATED.
THEY WILL **NEVER** HAVE THEIR MOMENTS TO SHINE.
POOR SETSUKE JUST WANTED TO SEE SOME SIGHTS IN THE BIG APPLE WHILE HER DADDY ATTENDED A MEETING TO CARVE OUT THE YAKUZA'S FUTURE IN NEW YORK CITY.
AND TAKATA, THE MAN ON THE BALCONY, WAS LED TO BELIEVE THAT THE MEETING IN QUESTION WAS TAKING PLACE RIGHT HERE.
I SEE YOU UP THERE, TAKATA-SAN. DON'T LOOK SO BETRAYED!
I KNOW YOU ARE FAMILIAR WITH THE TEACHINGS OF SUN TZU--**ALL WAR IS BASED UPON DECEPTION.**
IF HE WEREN'T SO SHOCKED TO SEE ONLY SETSUKE--UNDER ATTACK FROM TORA, ONE OF HIS **MAIN HENCHMEN**--HE PROBABLY WOULD HAVE REALIZED HOW IDIOTIC IT WAS TO HOLD A HIGH-POWERED GANGSTER MEETING AT A MUSEUM.

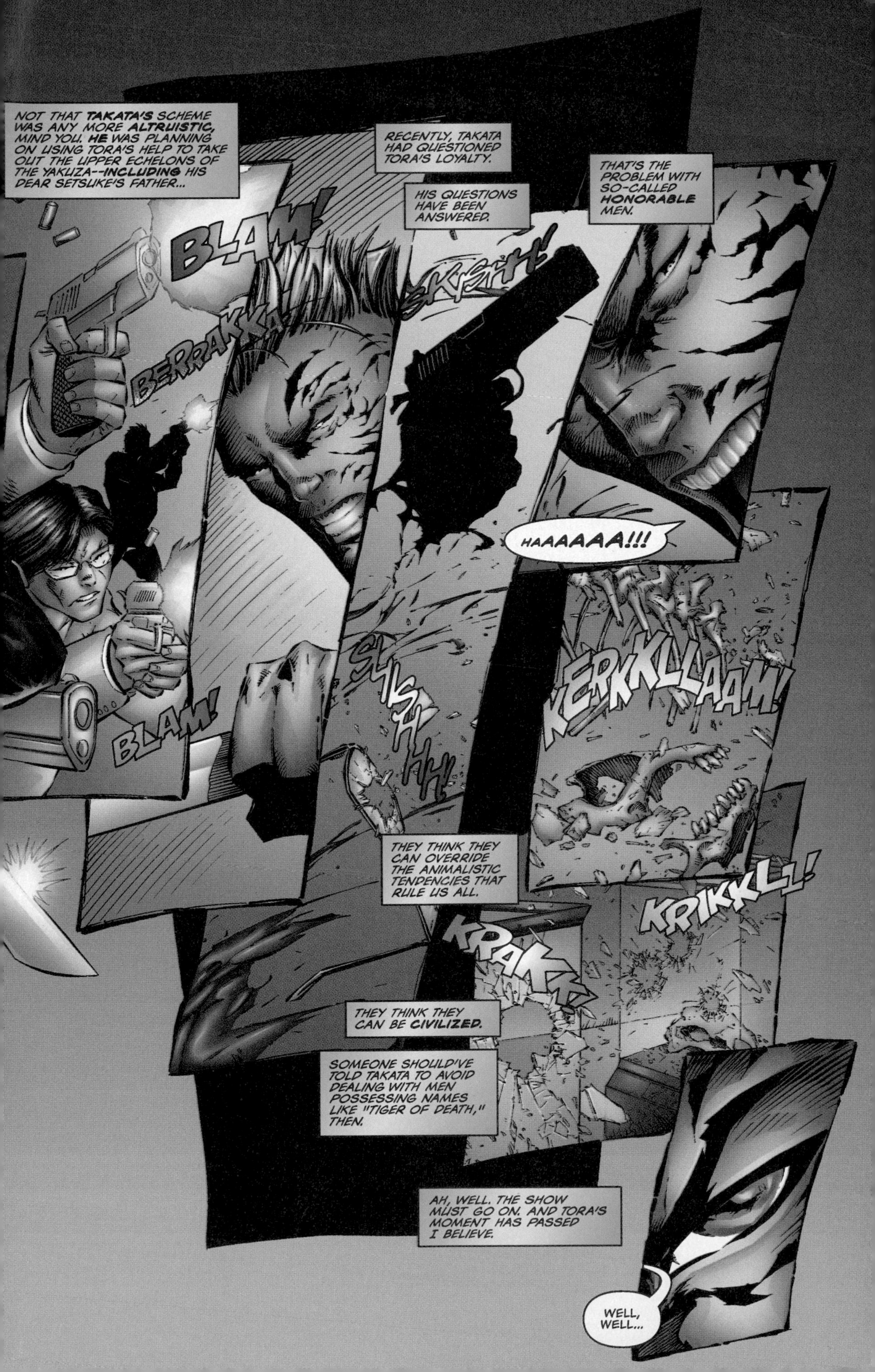

NOT THAT TAKATA'S SCHEME WAS ANY MORE ALTRUISTIC, MIND YOU. HE WAS PLANNING ON USING TORA'S HELP TO TAKE OUT THE UPPER ECHELONS OF THE YAKUZA--INCLUDING HIS DEAR SETSUKE'S FATHER...
BLAM!
BERRAKKA!
BLAM!
RECENTLY, TAKATA HAD QUESTIONED TORA'S LOYALTY.
HIS QUESTIONS HAVE BEEN ANSWERED.
SKSSH!
SLISHHH!
THAT'S THE PROBLEM WITH SO-CALLED HONORABLE MEN.
HAAAAAA!!!
KERKKLLAAM!
THEY THINK THEY CAN OVERRIDE THE ANIMALISTIC TENDENCIES THAT RULE US ALL.
KRIKKLL!
KRAKK
THEY THINK THEY CAN BE CIVILIZED.
SOMEONE SHOULD'VE TOLD TAKATA TO AVOID DEALING WITH MEN POSSESSING NAMES LIKE "TIGER OF DEATH," THEN.
AH, WELL. THE SHOW MUST GO ON. AND TORA'S MOMENT HAS PASSED I BELIEVE.
WELL, WELL...

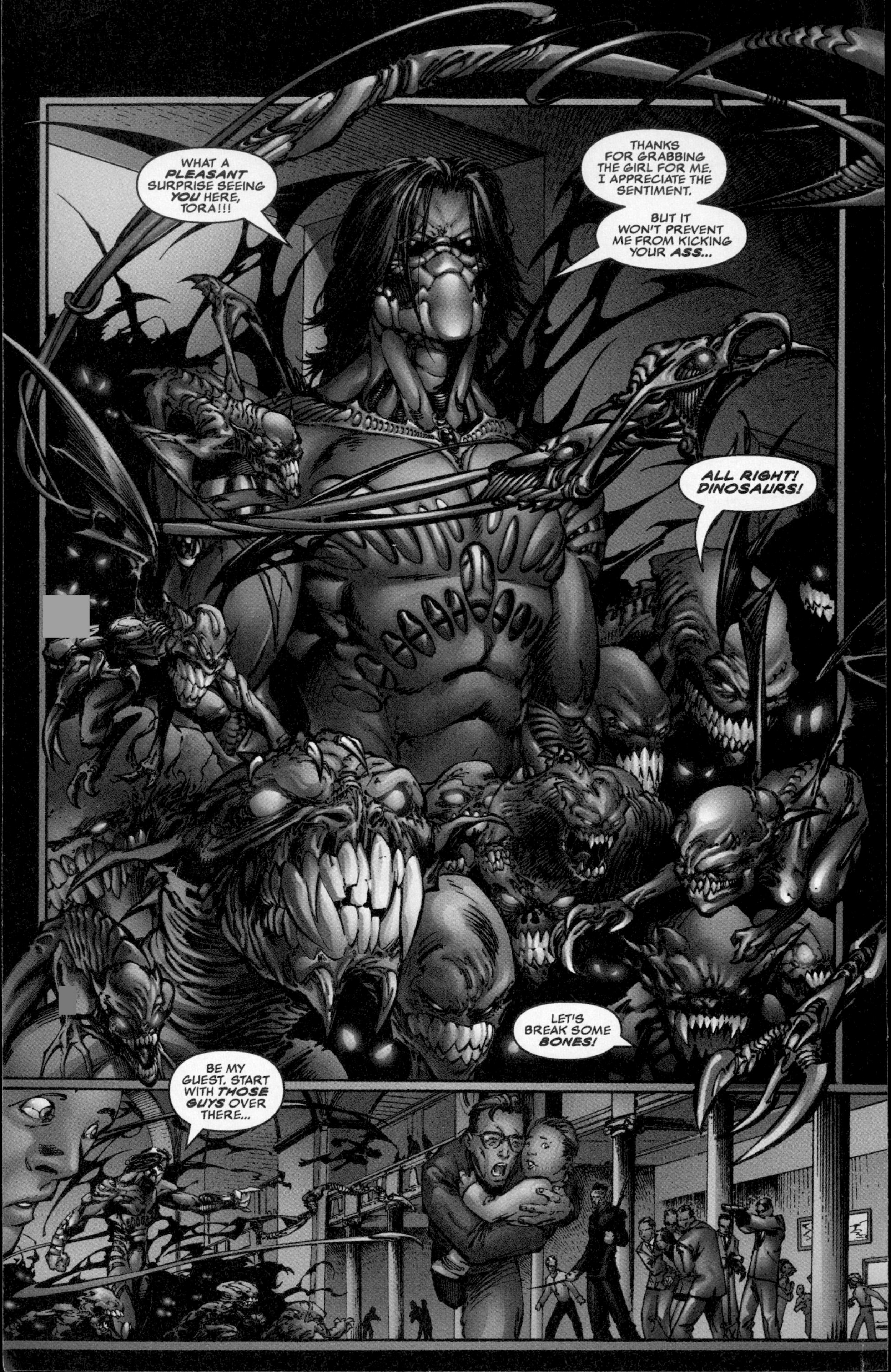
WHAT A PLEASANT SURPRISE SEEING YOU HERE, TORA!!!
THANKS FOR GRABBING THE GIRL FOR ME. I APPRECIATE THE SENTIMENT.
BUT IT WON'T PREVENT ME FROM KICKING YOUR ASS...
ALL RIGHT! DINOSAURS!
LET'S BREAK SOME BONES!
BE MY GUEST. START WITH THOSE GUYS OVER THERE...

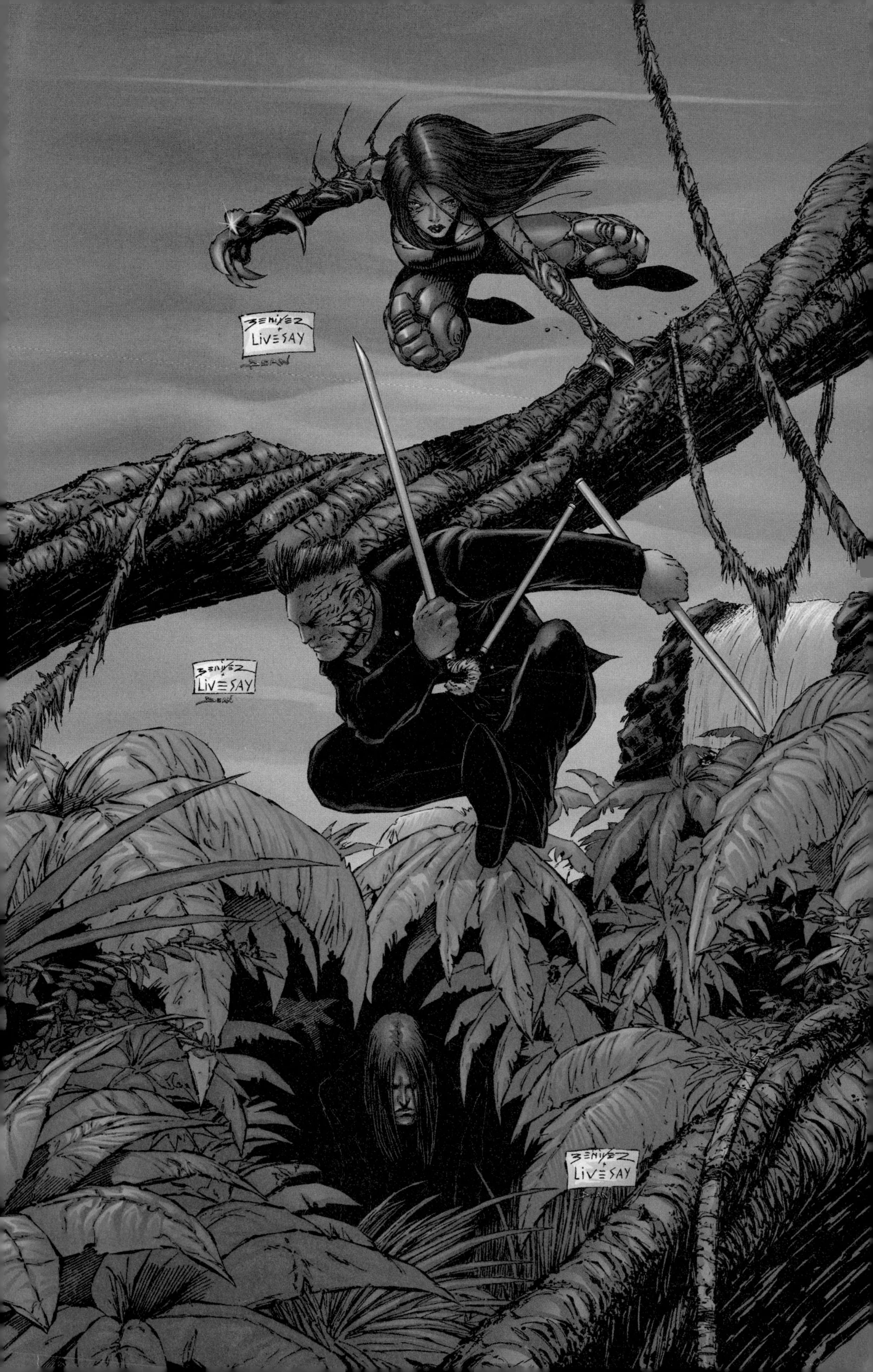
BENITEZ + LIVESAY
BENITEZ + LIVESAY
BENITEZ + LIVESAY

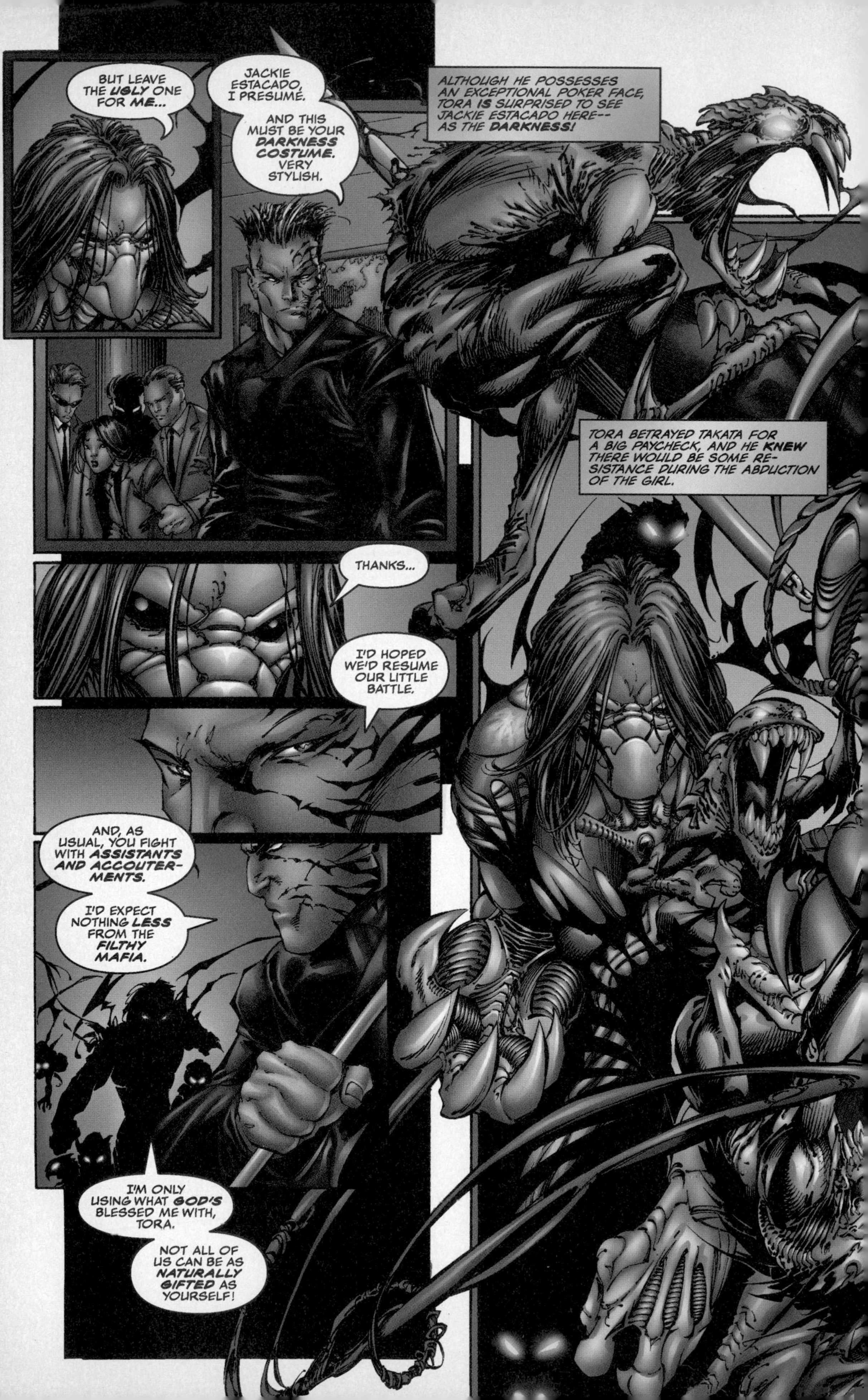
BUT LEAVE THE UGLY ONE FOR ME...
JACKIE ESTACADO, I PRESUME.
AND THIS MUST BE YOUR DARKNESS COSTUME. VERY STYLISH.
ALTHOUGH HE POSSESSES AN EXCEPTIONAL POKER FACE, TORA IS SURPRISED TO SEE JACKIE ESTACADO HERE-- AS THE DARKNESS!
TORA BETRAYED TAKATA FOR A BIG PAYCHECK, AND HE KNEW THERE WOULD BE SOME RESISTANCE DURING THE ABDUCTION OF THE GIRL.
THANKS...
I'D HOPED WE'D RESUME OUR LITTLE BATTLE.
AND, AS USUAL, YOU FIGHT WITH ASSISTANTS AND ACCOUTERMENTS.
I'D EXPECT NOTHING LESS FROM THE FILTHY MAFIA.
I'M ONLY USING WHAT GOD'S BLESSED ME WITH, TORA.
NOT ALL OF US CAN BE AS NATURALLY GIFTED AS YOURSELF!

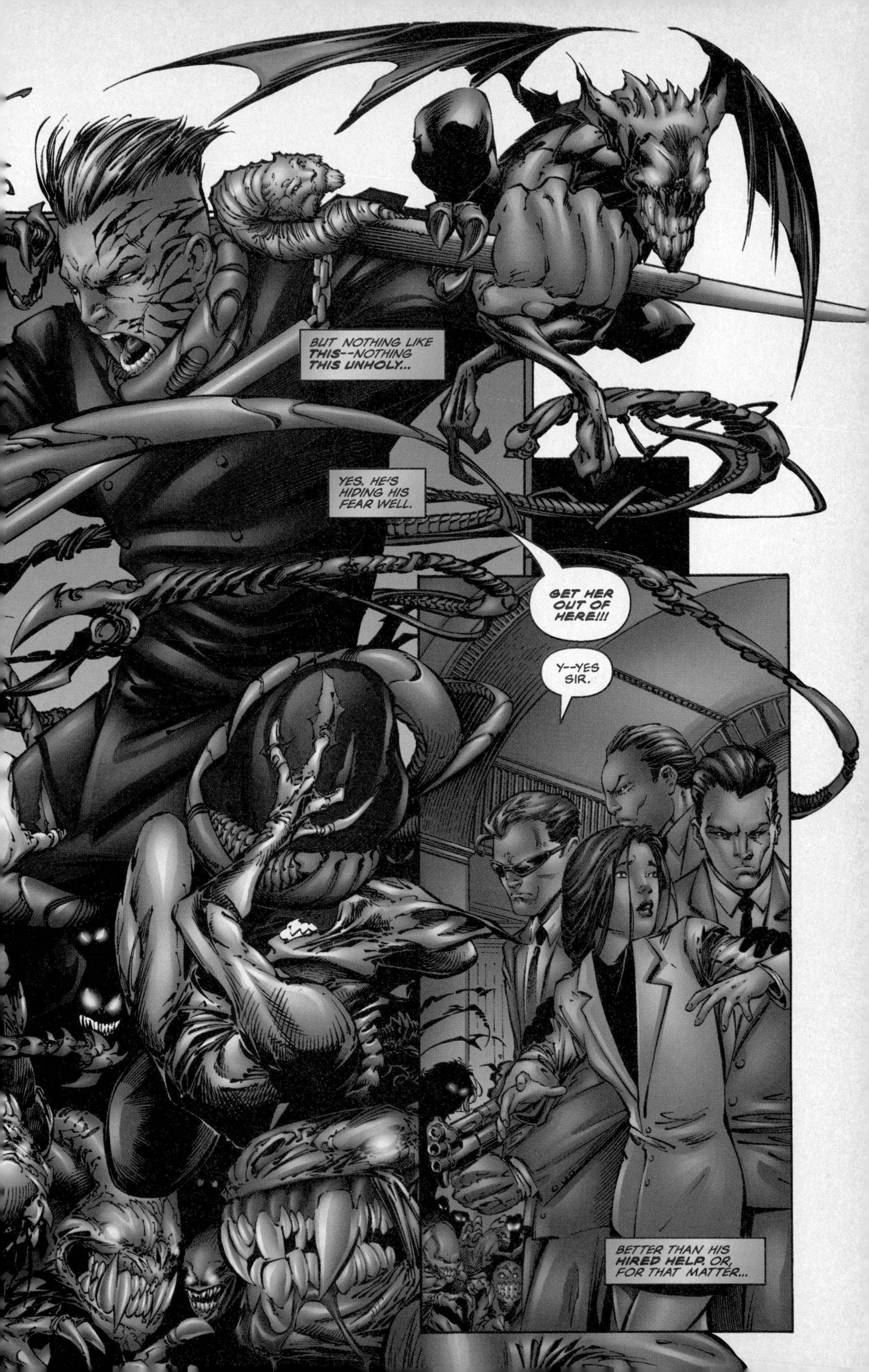
BUT NOTHING LIKE THIS--NOTHING THIS UNHOLY...
YES. HE'S HIDING HIS FEAR WELL.
GET HER OUT OF HERE!!!
Y--YES SIR.
BETTER THAN HIS HIRED HELP. OR, FOR THAT MATTER...

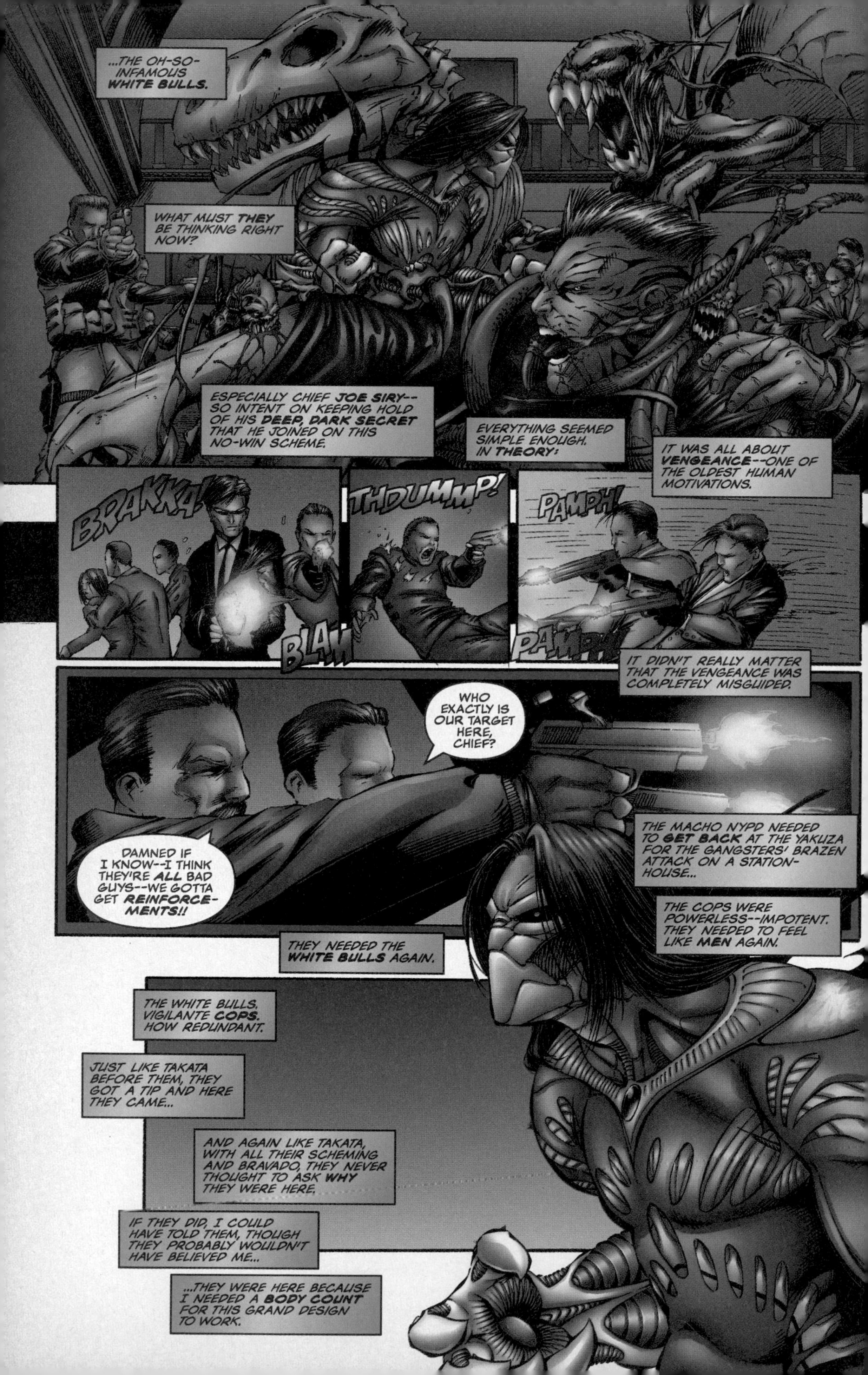
...THE OH-SO-INFAMOUS WHITE BULLS.
WHAT MUST THEY BE THINKING RIGHT NOW?
ESPECIALLY CHIEF JOE SIRY--SO INTENT ON KEEPING HOLD OF HIS DEEP, DARK SECRET THAT HE JOINED ON THIS NO-WIN SCHEME.
EVERYTHING SEEMED SIMPLE ENOUGH. IN THEORY:
IT WAS ALL ABOUT VENGEANCE--ONE OF THE OLDEST HUMAN MOTIVATIONS.
BRAKKA!
BLAM
THDUMMP!
PAMPH!
PAMPH!
IT DIDN'T REALLY MATTER THAT THE VENGEANCE WAS COMPLETELY MISGUIDED.
WHO EXACTLY IS OUR TARGET HERE, CHIEF?
DAMNED IF I KNOW--I THINK THEY'RE ALL BAD GUYS--WE GOTTA GET REINFORCE-MENTS!!
THE MACHO NYPD NEEDED TO GET BACK AT THE YAKUZA FOR THE GANGSTERS' BRAZEN ATTACK ON A STATION-HOUSE...
THE COPS WERE POWERLESS--IMPOTENT. THEY NEEDED TO FEEL LIKE MEN AGAIN.
THEY NEEDED THE WHITE BULLS AGAIN.
THE WHITE BULLS. VIGILANTE COPS. HOW REDUNDANT.
JUST LIKE TAKATA BEFORE THEM, THEY GOT A TIP AND HERE THEY CAME...
AND AGAIN LIKE TAKATA, WITH ALL THEIR SCHEMING AND BRAVADO, THEY NEVER THOUGHT TO ASK WHY THEY WERE HERE.
IF THEY DID, I COULD HAVE TOLD THEM, THOUGH THEY PROBABLY WOULDN'T HAVE BELIEVED ME...
...THEY WERE HERE BECAUSE I NEEDED A BODY COUNT FOR THIS GRAND DESIGN TO WORK.

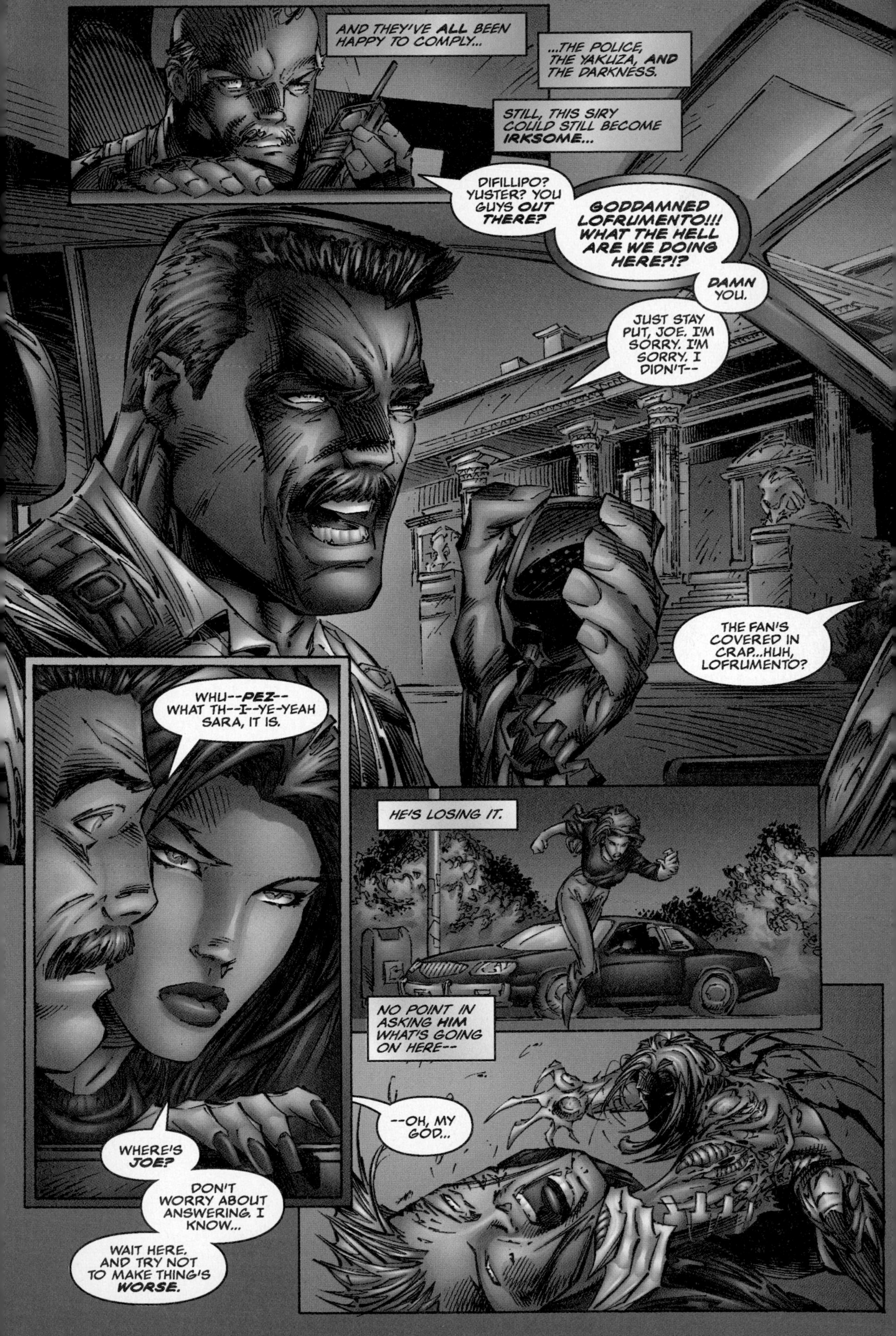

AND THEY'VE ALL BEEN HAPPY TO COMPLY...
...THE POLICE, THE YAKUZA, AND THE DARKNESS.
STILL, THIS SIRY COULD STILL BECOME IRKSOME...
DIFILLIPO? YUSTER? YOU GUYS OUT THERE?
GODDAMNED LOFRUMENTO!!! WHAT THE HELL ARE WE DOING HERE?!?
DAMN YOU.
JUST STAY PUT, JOE. I'M SORRY. I'M SORRY. I DIDN'T--
THE FAN'S COVERED IN CRAP...HUH, LOFRUMENTO?
WHU--PEZ--WHAT TH--I--YE-YEAH SARA, IT IS.
WHERE'S JOE?
DON'T WORRY ABOUT ANSWERING. I KNOW...
WAIT HERE. AND TRY NOT TO MAKE THING'S WORSE.
HE'S LOSING IT.
NO POINT IN ASKING HIM WHAT'S GOING ON HERE--
--OH, MY GOD...

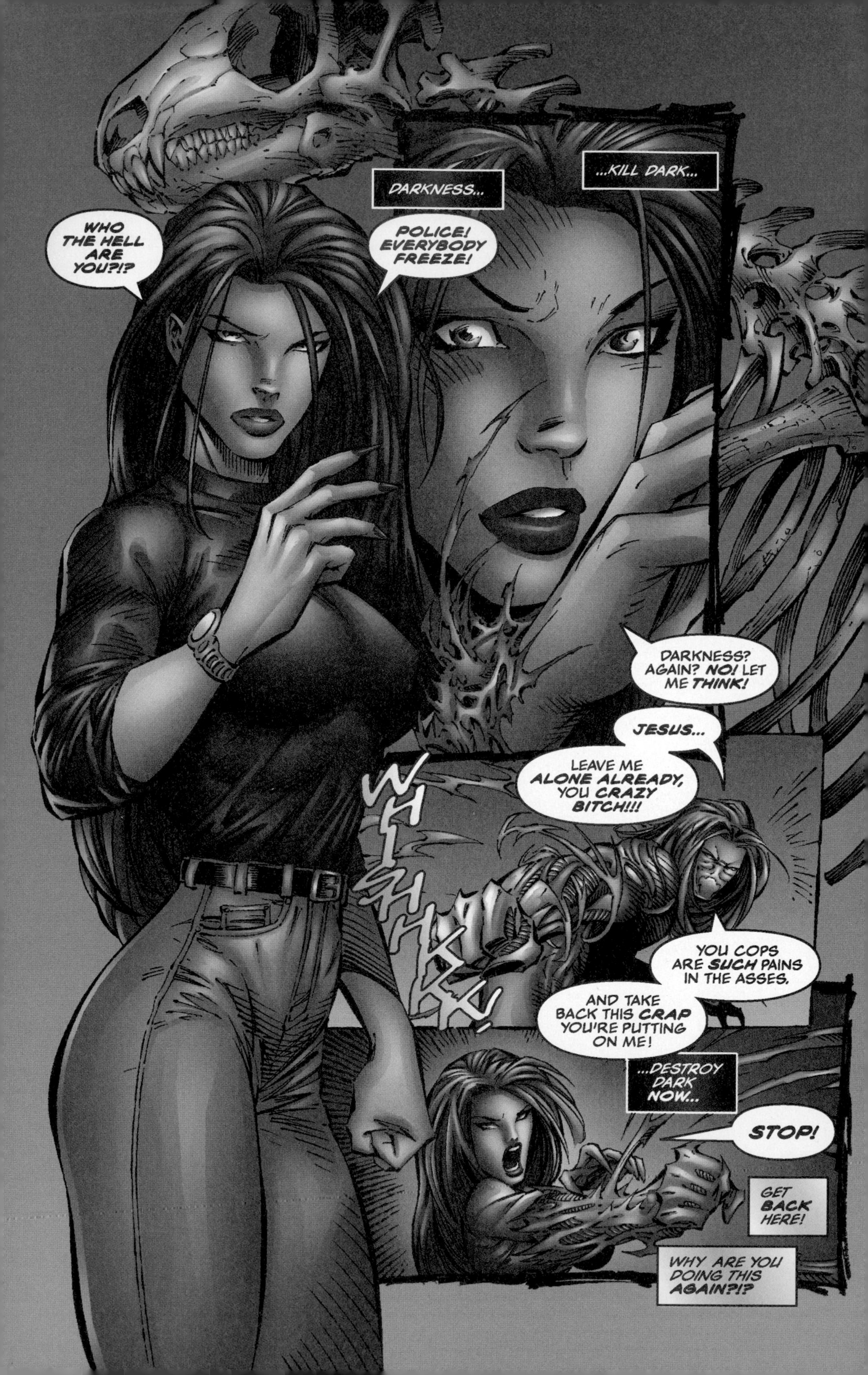
DARKNESS...
...KILL DARK...
WHO THE HELL ARE YOU?!?
POLICE! EVERYBODY FREEZE!
DARKNESS? AGAIN? NO! LET ME THINK!
JESUS...
LEAVE ME ALONE ALREADY, YOU CRAZY BITCH!!!
WHISHKK!
YOU COPS ARE SUCH PAINS IN THE ASSES.
AND TAKE BACK THIS CRAP YOU'RE PUTTING ON ME!
...DESTROY DARK NOW...
STOP!
GET BACK HERE!
WHY ARE YOU DOING THIS AGAIN?!?

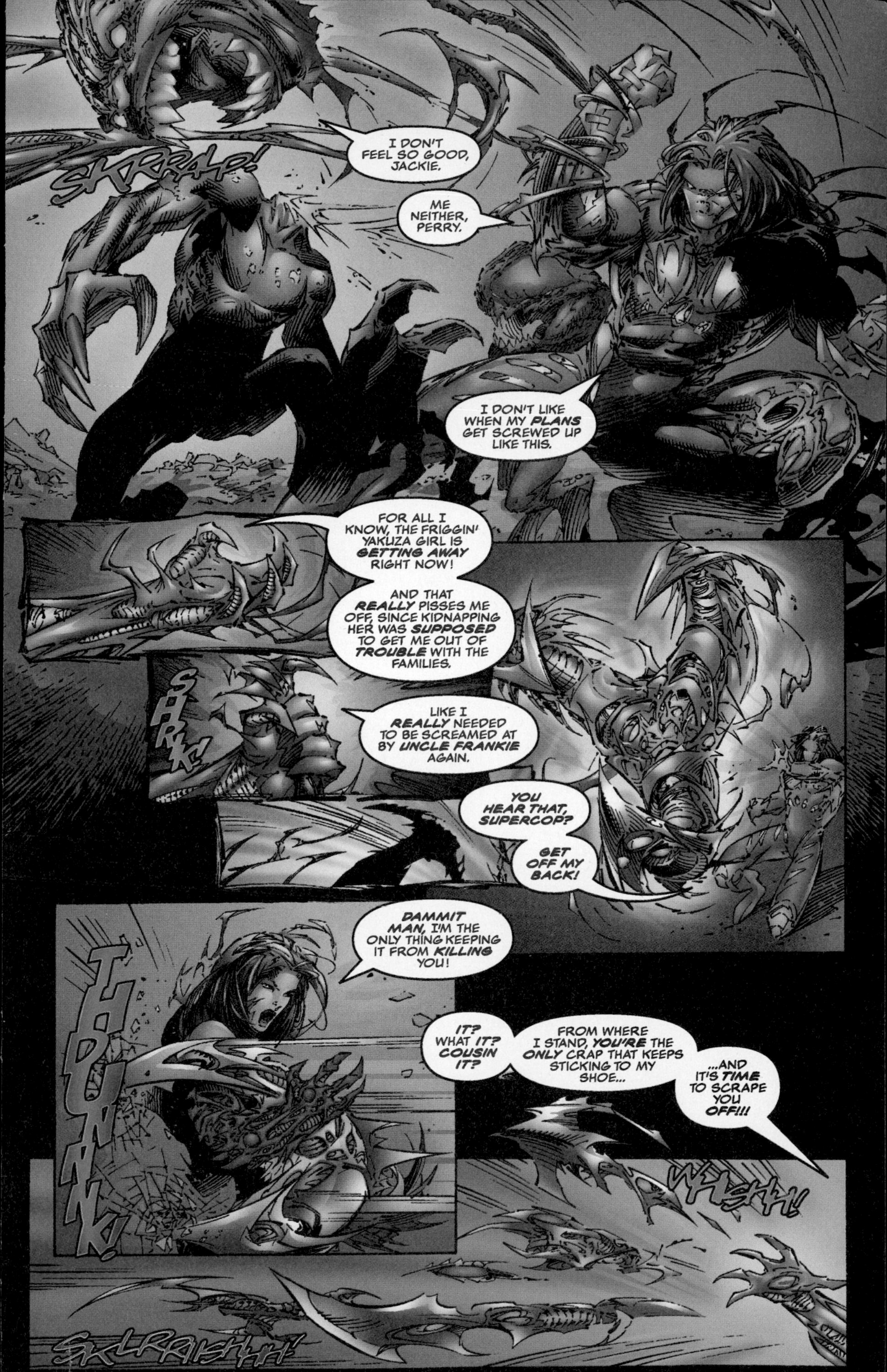
SKRRAAP!
I DON'T FEEL SO GOOD, JACKIE.
ME NEITHER, PERRY.
I DON'T LIKE WHEN MY PLANS GET SCREWED UP LIKE THIS.
FOR ALL I KNOW, THE FRIGGIN' YAKUZA GIRL IS GETTING AWAY RIGHT NOW!
AND THAT REALLY PISSES ME OFF, SINCE KIDNAPPING HER WAS SUPPOSED TO GET ME OUT OF TROUBLE WITH THE FAMILIES.
SHRAK!
LIKE I REALLY NEEDED TO BE SCREAMED AT BY UNCLE FRANKIE AGAIN.
YOU HEAR THAT, SUPERCOP?
GET OFF MY BACK!
DAMMIT MAN, I'M THE ONLY THING KEEPING IT FROM KILLING YOU!
THUNNK!
IT? WHAT IT? COUSIN IT?
FROM WHERE I STAND, YOU'RE THE ONLY CRAP THAT KEEPS STICKING TO MY SHOE...
...AND IT'S TIME TO SCRAPE YOU OFF!!!
WSSHH!
SKLRAASHHH!

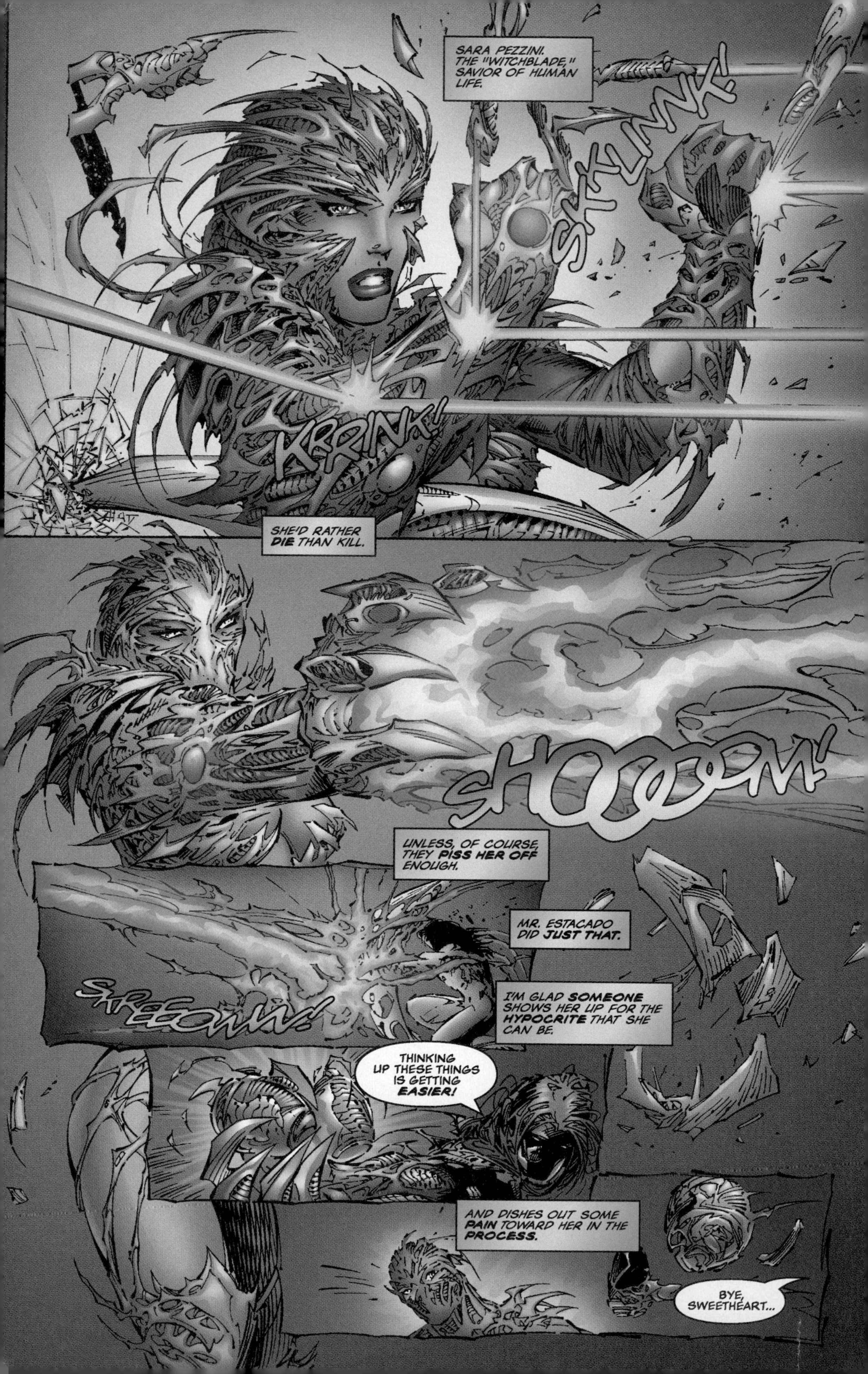
SARA PEZZINI. THE "WITCHBLADE," SAVIOR OF HUMAN LIFE.
SKLUNK!
KRRINK!
SHE'D RATHER DIE THAN KILL.
SHOOOOM!
UNLESS, OF COURSE, THEY PISS HER OFF ENOUGH.
MR. ESTACADO DID JUST THAT.
SKREEOWW!
I'M GLAD SOMEONE SHOWS HER UP FOR THE HYPOCRITE THAT SHE CAN BE.
THINKING UP THESE THINGS IS GETTING EASIER!
AND DISHES OUT SOME PAIN TOWARD HER IN THE PROCESS.
BYE, SWEETHEART...

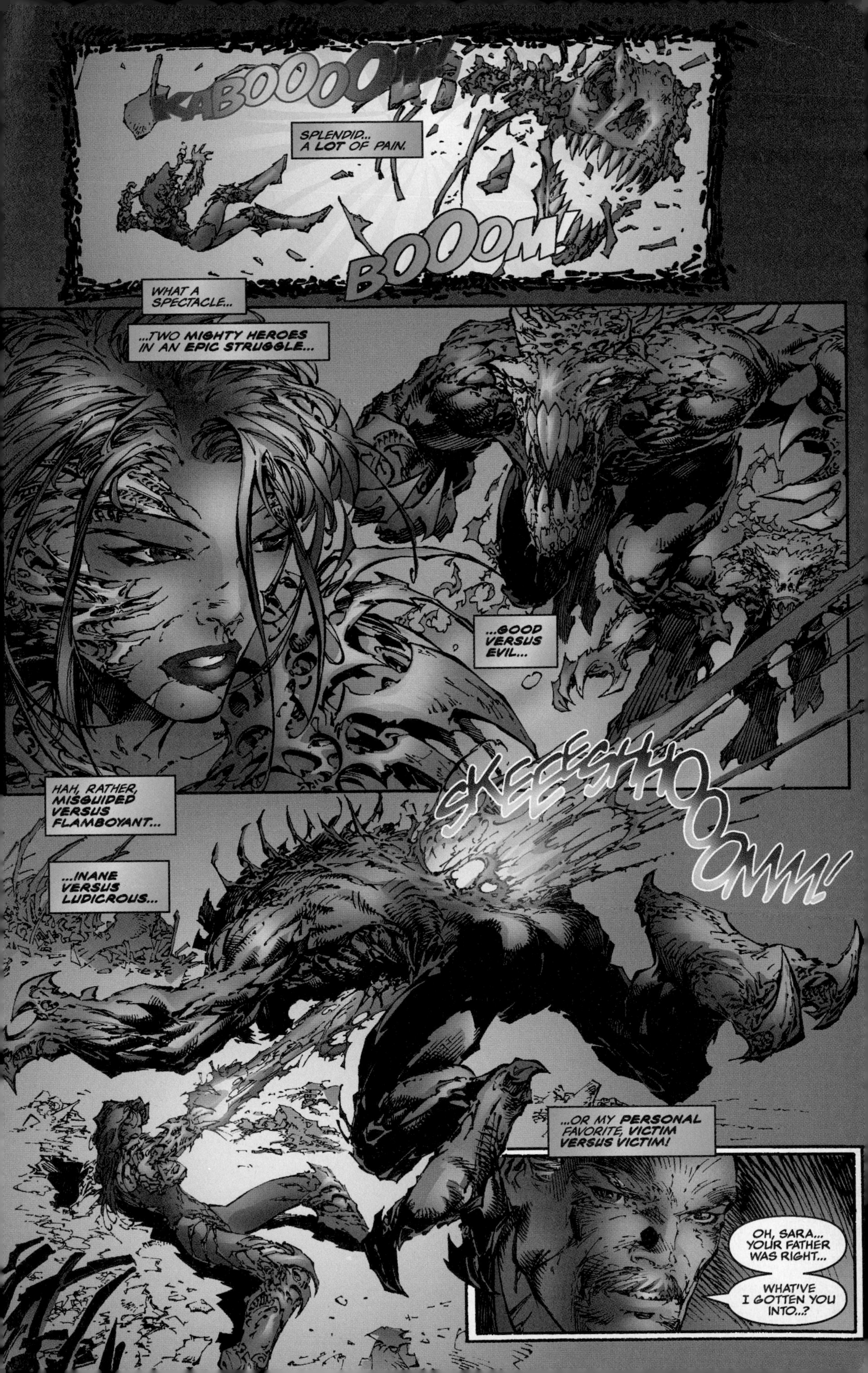
KABOOOOM!
SPLENDID... A LOT OF PAIN.
BOOOM!
WHAT A SPECTACLE...
...TWO MIGHTY HEROES IN AN EPIC STRUGGLE...
...GOOD VERSUS EVIL...
HAH, RATHER, MISGUIDED VERSUS FLAMBOYANT...
...INANE VERSUS LUDICROUS...
SKEEESHOOOMM!
...OR MY PERSONAL FAVORITE, VICTIM VERSUS VICTIM!
OH, SARA... YOUR FATHER WAS RIGHT...
WHAT'VE I GOTTEN YOU INTO..?

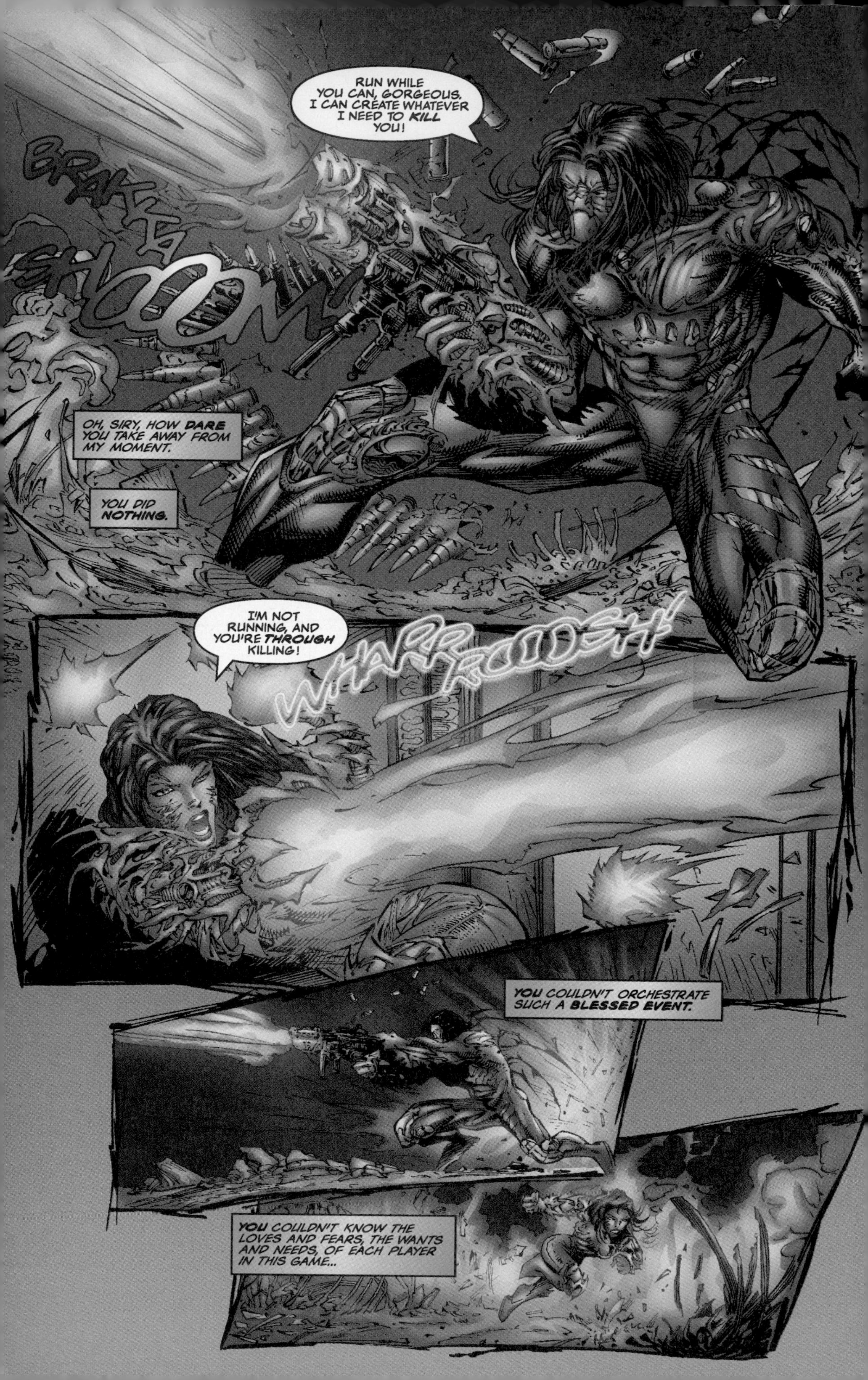
BRAKKA SHOOOM!
RUN WHILE YOU CAN, GORGEOUS. I CAN CREATE WHATEVER I NEED TO KILL YOU!
OH, SIRY, HOW DARE YOU TAKE AWAY FROM MY MOMENT.
YOU DID NOTHING.
I'M NOT RUNNING, AND YOU'RE THROUGH KILLING!
WHARRROOOSH!
YOU COULDN'T ORCHESTRATE SUCH A BLESSED EVENT.
YOU COULDN'T KNOW THE LOVES AND FEARS, THE WANTS AND NEEDS, OF EACH PLAYER IN THIS GAME...

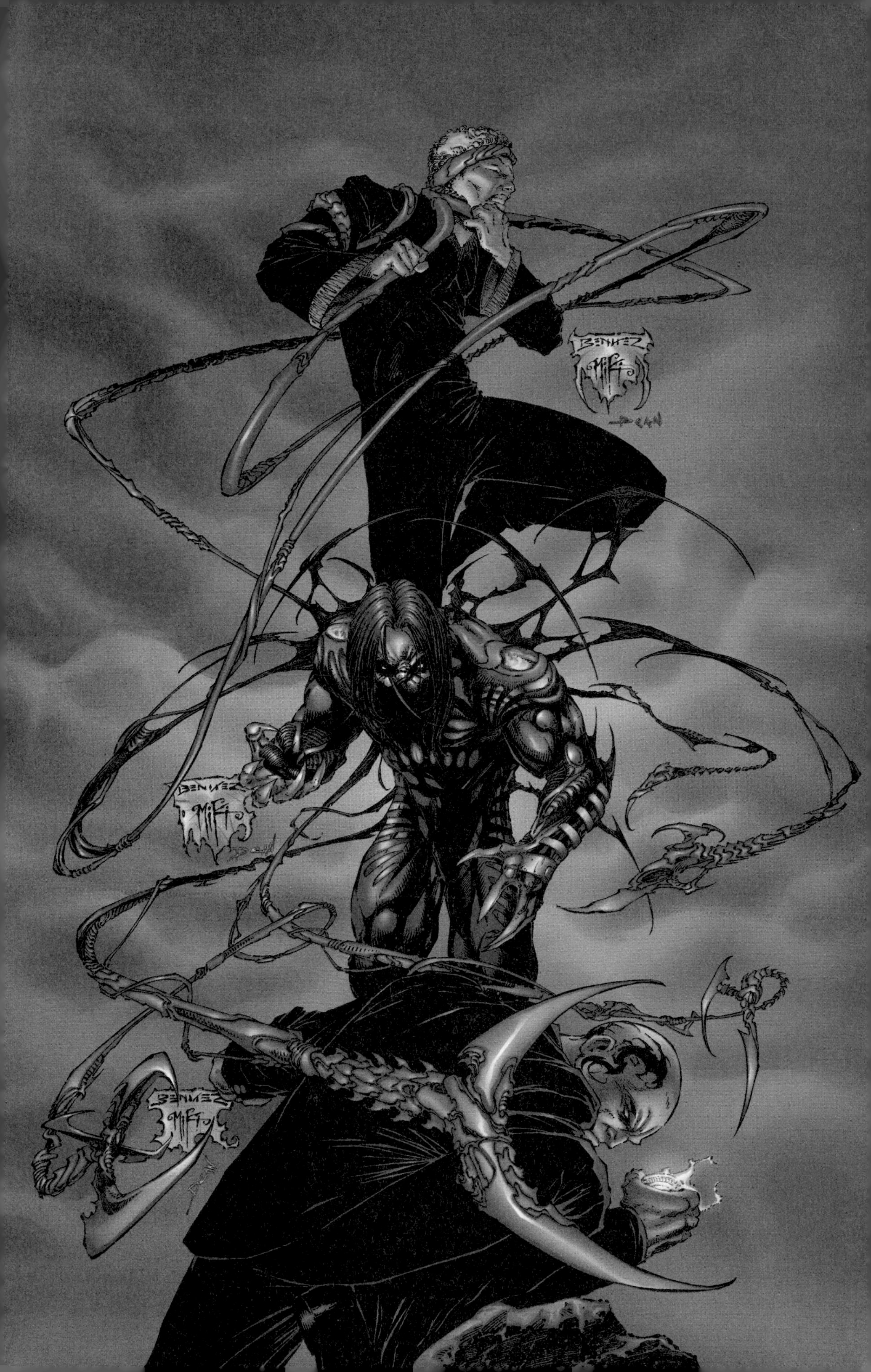

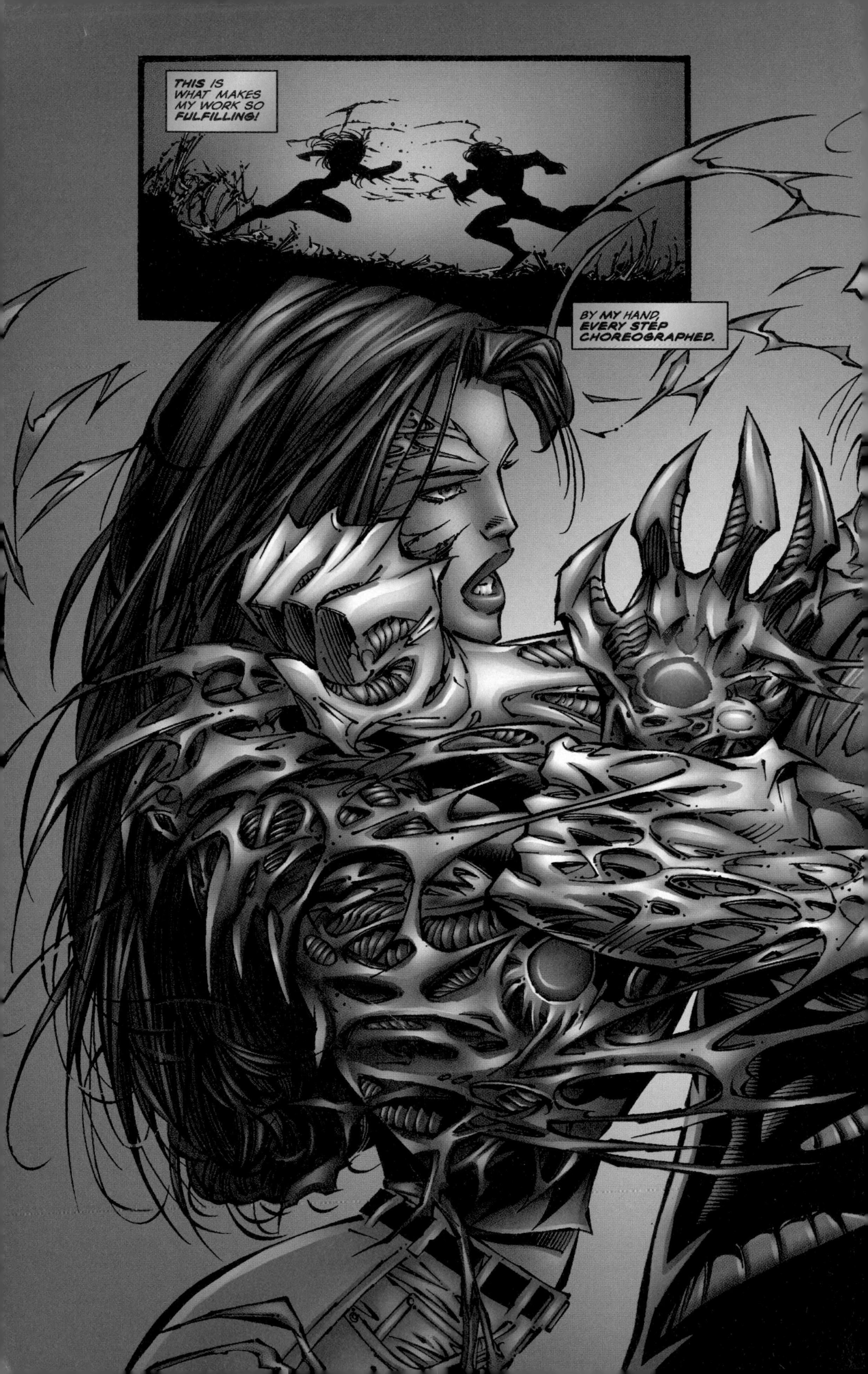
THIS IS WHAT MAKES MY WORK SO FULFILLING!
BY MY HAND, EVERY STEP CHOREOGRAPHED.

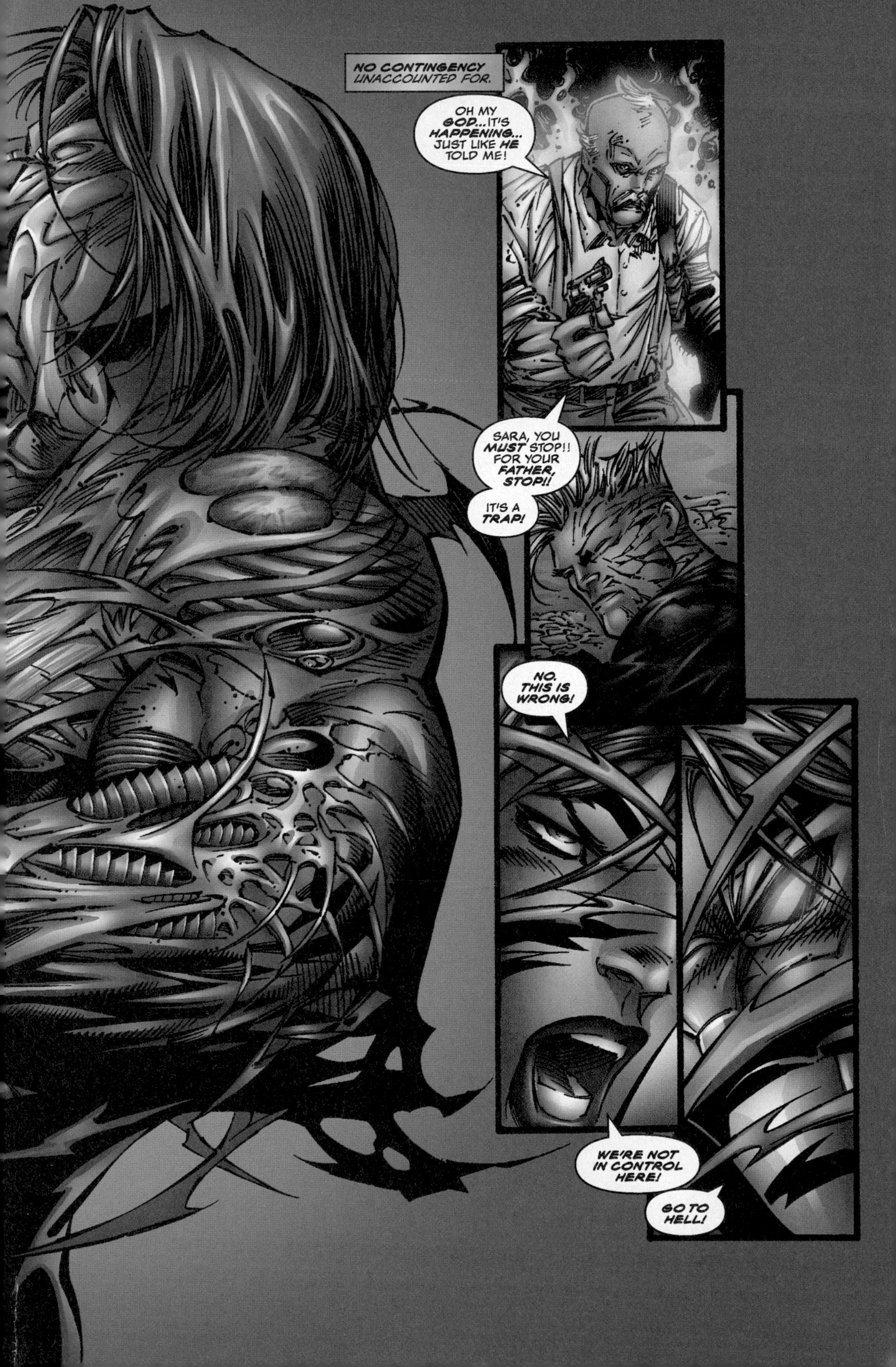
NO CONTINGENCY UNACCOUNTED FOR.
OH MY GOD...IT'S HAPPENING... JUST LIKE HE TOLD ME!
SARA, YOU MUST STOP!! FOR YOUR FATHER, STOP!!
IT'S A TRAP!
NO. THIS IS WRONG!
WE'RE NOT IN CONTROL HERE!
GO TO HELL!

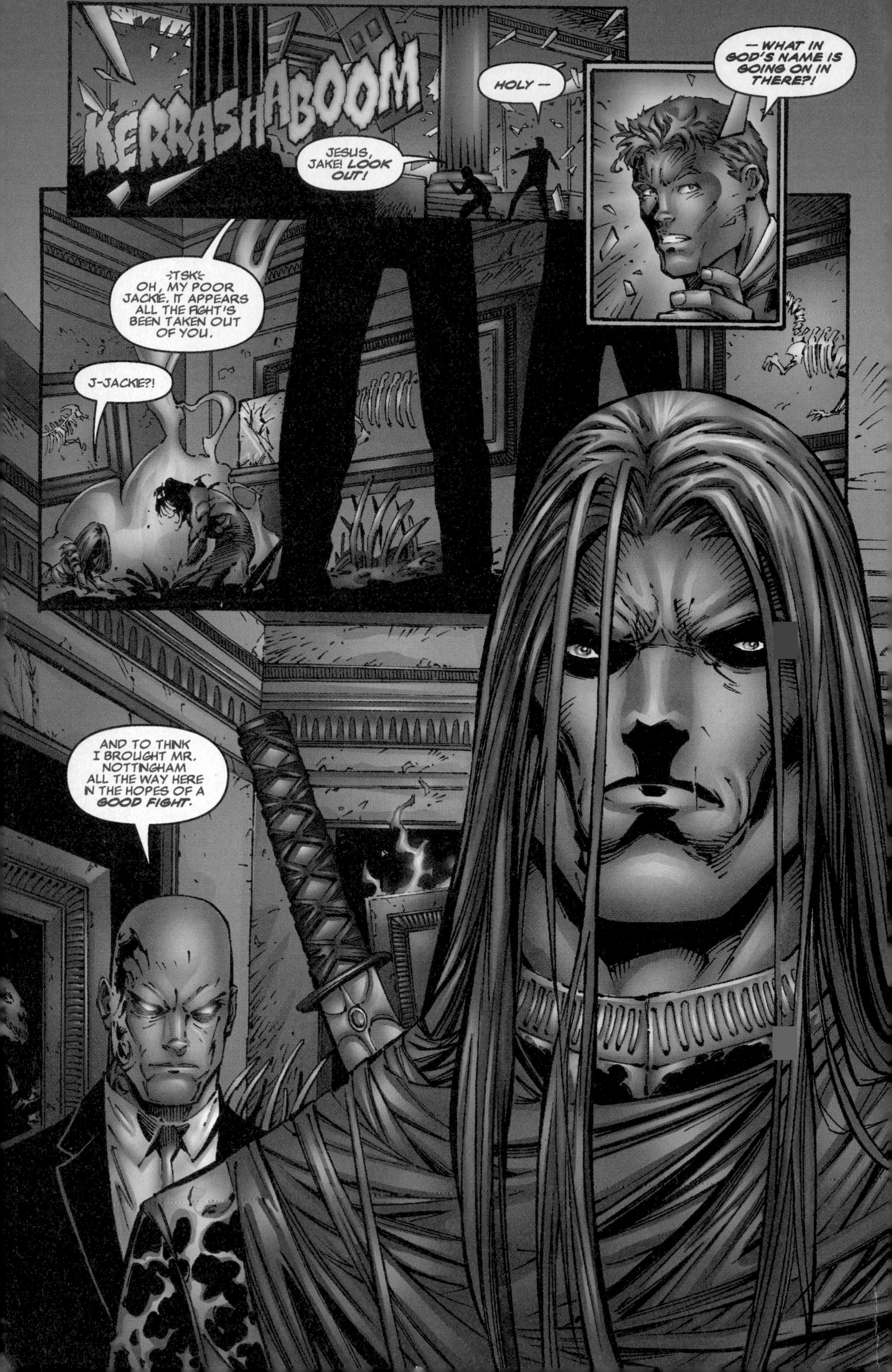
KERRASHABOOM
HOLY —
— WHAT IN GOD'S NAME IS GOING ON IN THERE?!
JESUS, JAKE! LOOK OUT!
-TSK- OH, MY POOR JACKIE. IT APPEARS ALL THE FIGHT'S BEEN TAKEN OUT OF YOU.
J-JACKIE?!
AND TO THINK I BROUGHT MR. NOTTINGHAM ALL THE WAY HERE IN THE HOPES OF A GOOD FIGHT.

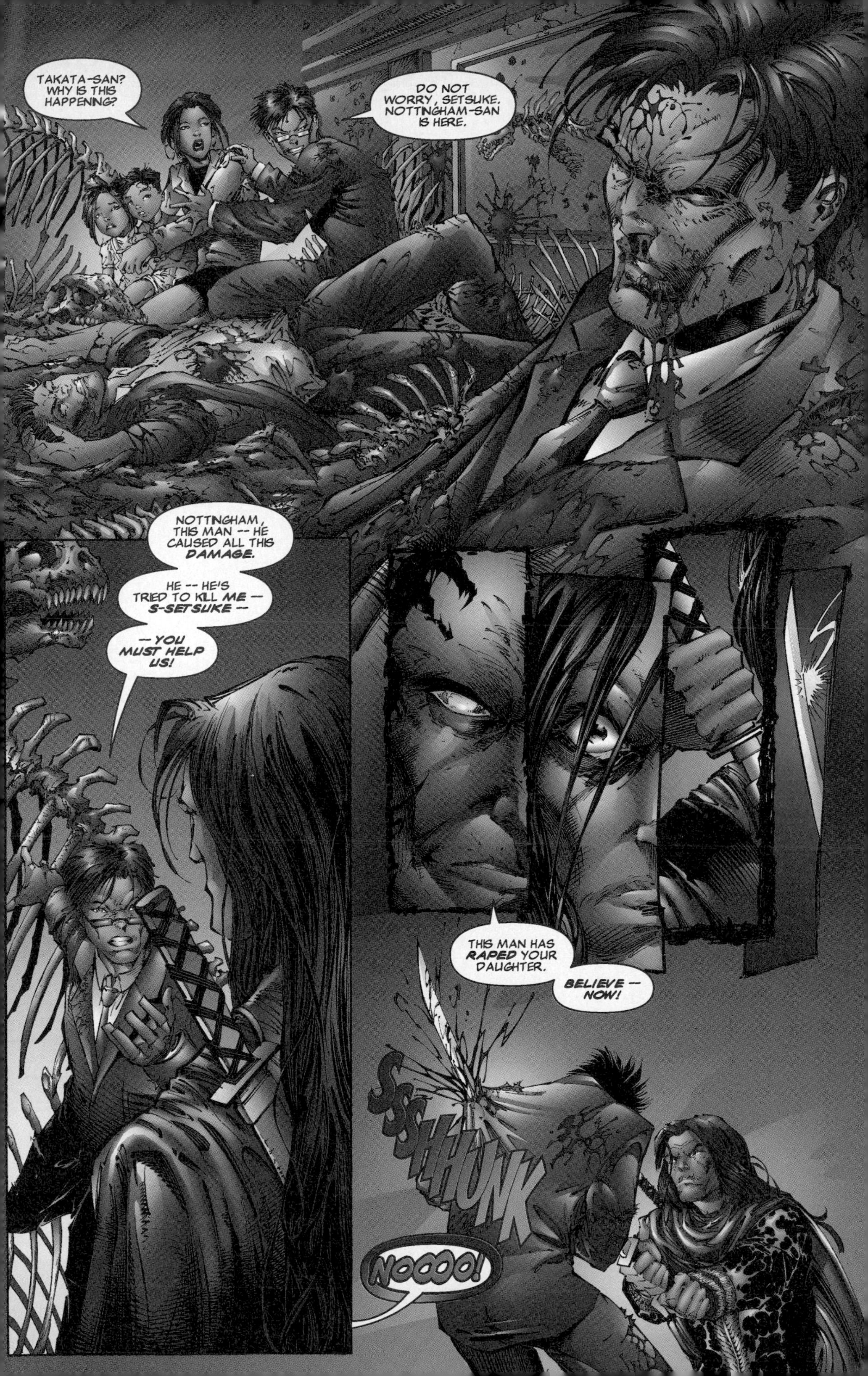
TAKATA-SAN? WHY IS THIS HAPPENING?
DO NOT WORRY, SETSUKE. NOTTINGHAM-SAN IS HERE.
NOTTINGHAM, THIS MAN -- HE CAUSED ALL THIS DAMAGE.
HE -- HE'S TRIED TO KILL ME -- S-SETSUKE --
-- YOU MUST HELP US!
THIS MAN HAS RAPED YOUR DAUGHTER.
BELIEVE -- NOW!
SSSHHUNK
NOOOO!

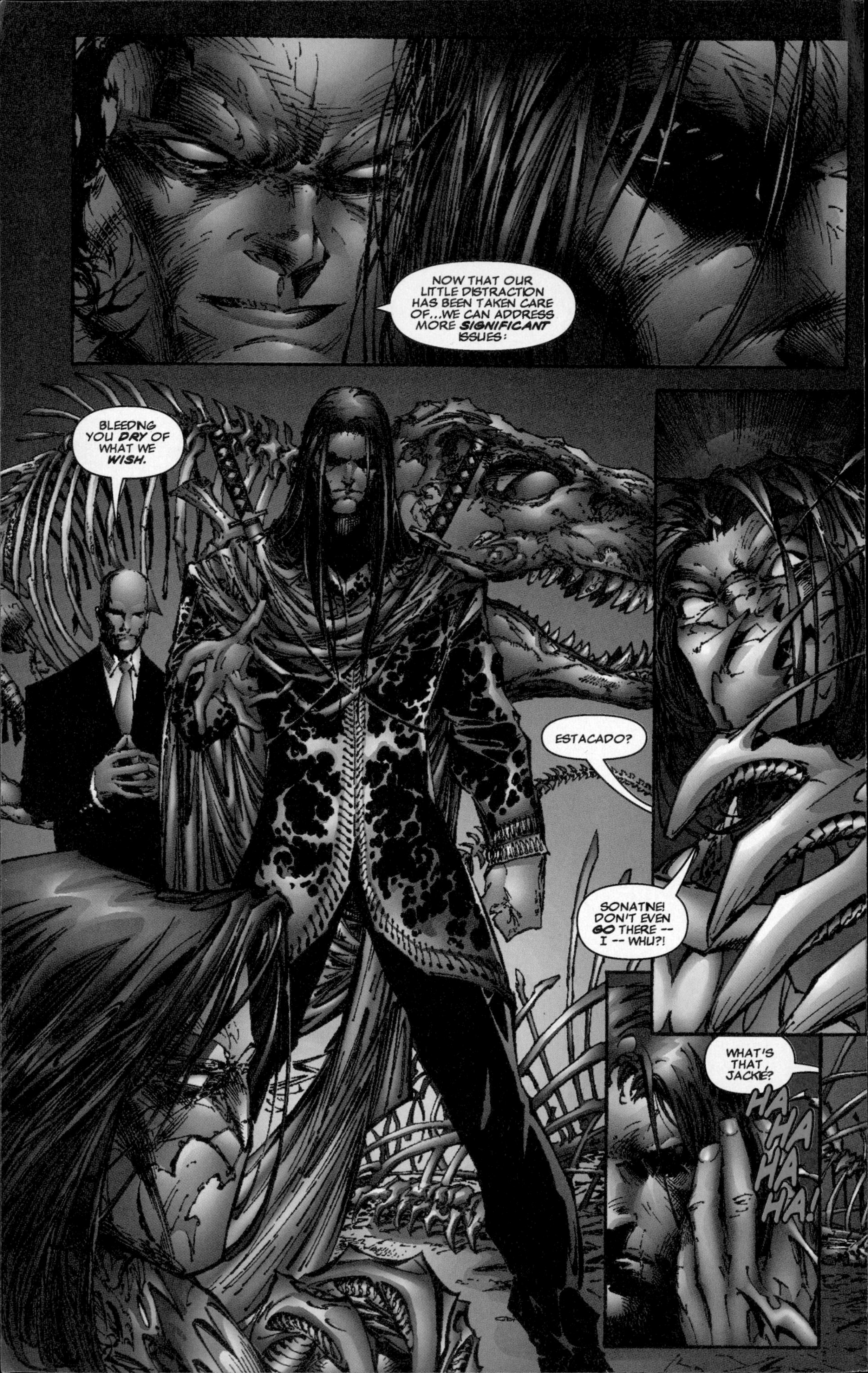
NOW THAT OUR LITTLE DISTRACTION HAS BEEN TAKEN CARE OF...WE CAN ADDRESS MORE SIGNIFICANT ISSUES:
BLEEDING YOU DRY OF WHAT WE WISH.
ESTACADO?
SONATINE! DON'T EVEN GO THERE -- I -- WHU?!
WHAT'S THAT, JACKIE?
HA HA HA HA HA!

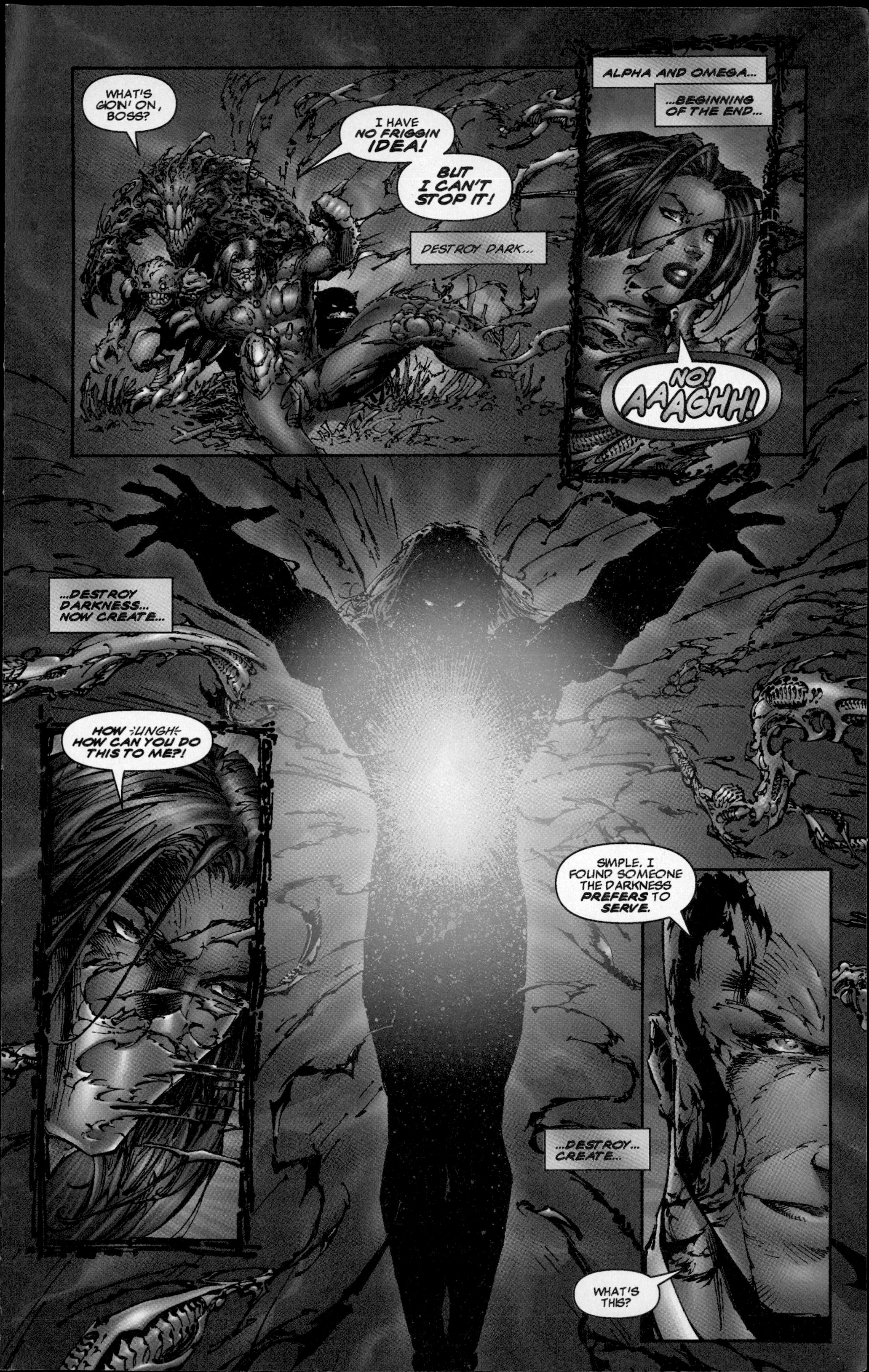
WHAT'S GION' ON, BOSS?
I HAVE NO FRIGGIN IDEA!
BUT I CAN'T STOP IT!
DESTROY DARK...
ALPHA AND OMEGA...
...BEGINNING OF THE END...
NO! AAAGHH!
...DESTROY DARKNESS... NOW CREATE...
HOW -UNGH- HOW CAN YOU DO THIS TO ME?!
SIMPLE. I FOUND SOMEONE THE DARKNESS PREFERS TO SERVE.
...DESTROY... CREATE...
WHAT'S THIS?

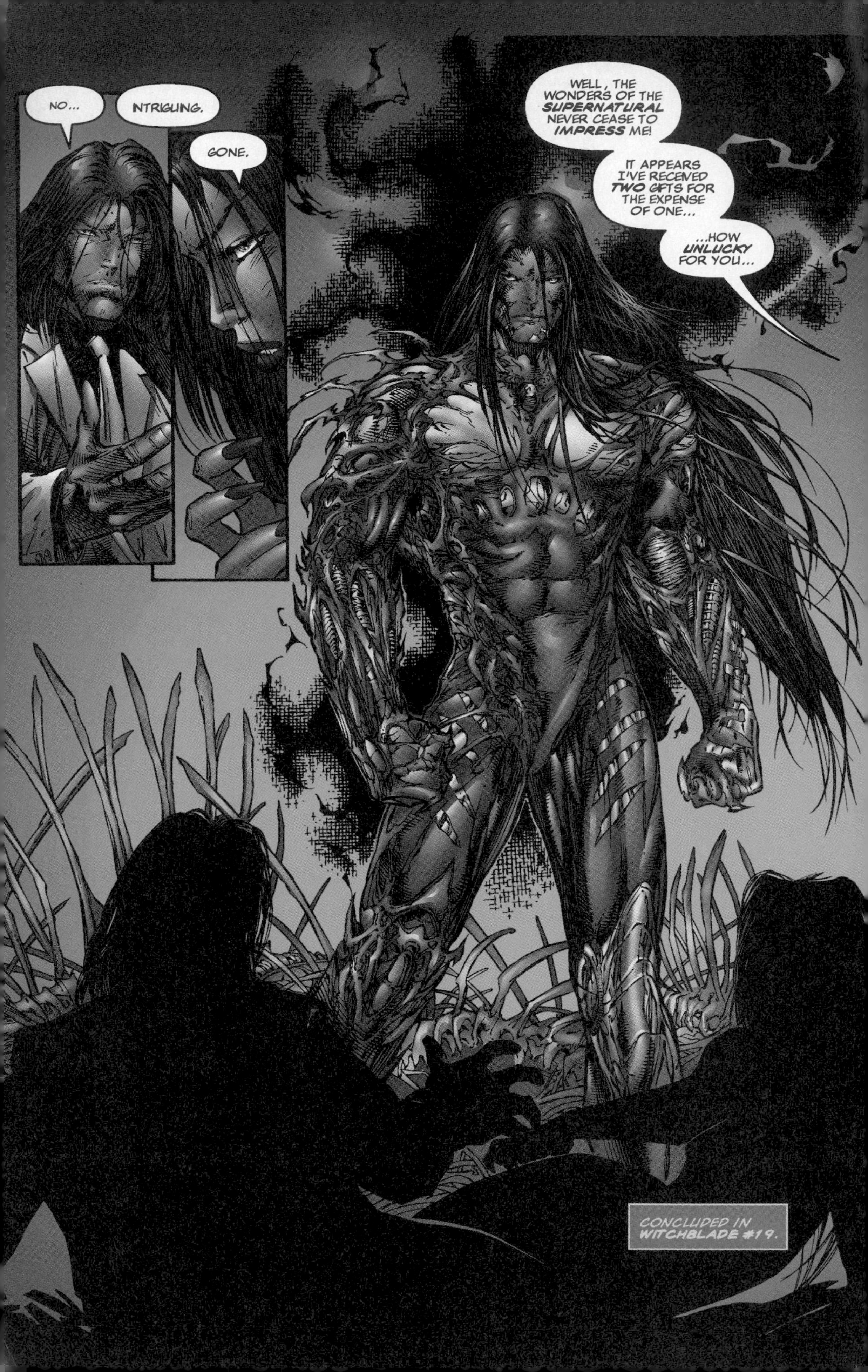

NO...
INTRIGUING.
GONE.
WELL, THE WONDERS OF THE SUPERNATURAL NEVER CEASE TO IMPRESS ME!
IT APPEARS I'VE RECEIVED TWO GIFTS FOR THE EXPENSE OF ONE...
...HOW UNLUCKY FOR YOU...
CONCLUDED IN WITCHBLADE #19.

WITCHBLADE 19

Christina Z
David Wohl
-story

Michael Turner
-pencils/ co-plot

D-Tron·
-inks

Jonathan D. Smith
-colors

Family TIES

PART FOUR

Dennis Heisler
-letters

Brad Foxhoven
-editor

Sonia Im
Aaron Michiel
-associate editors

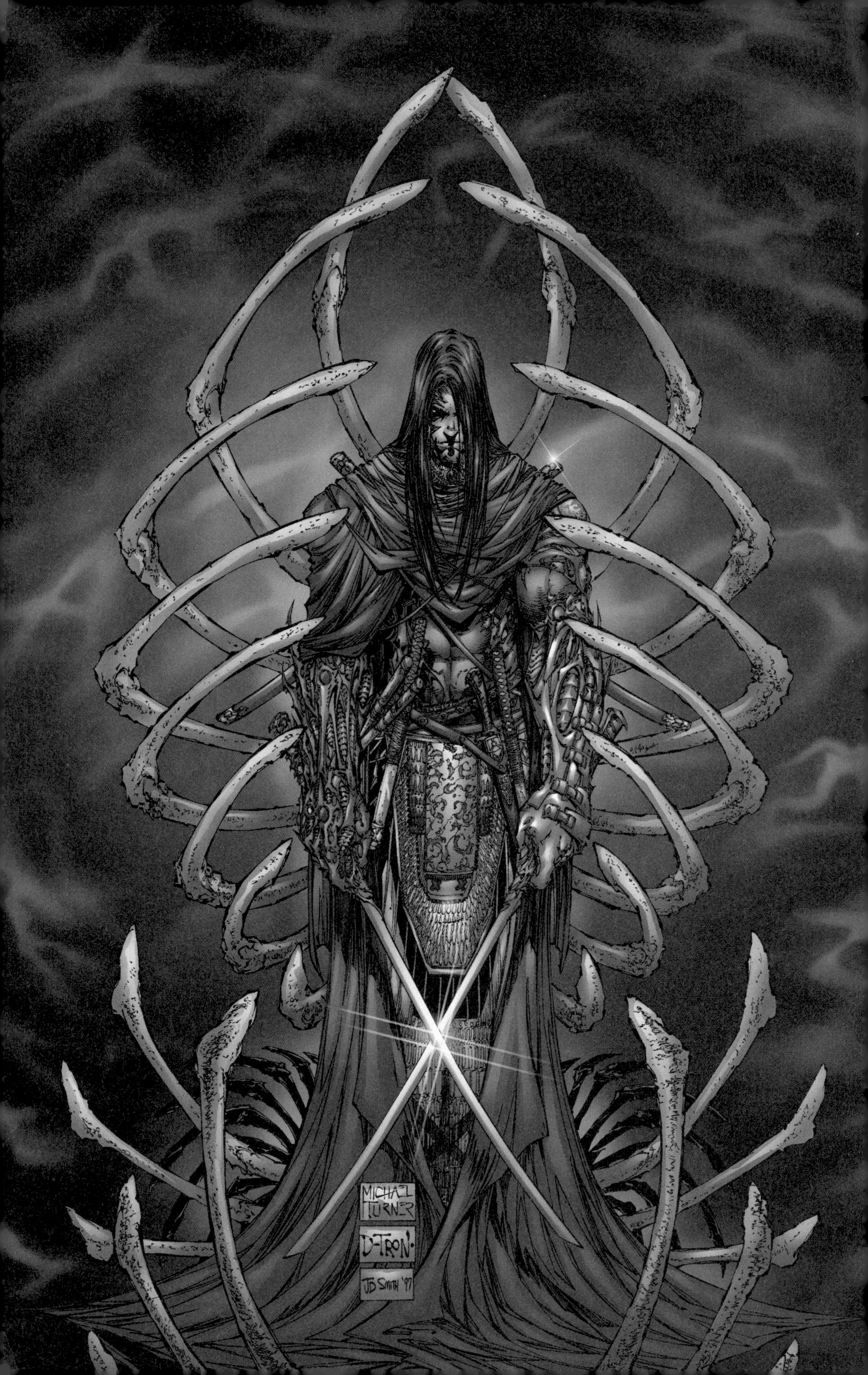
MICHAEL TURNER
D-TRON
JD SMITH '97

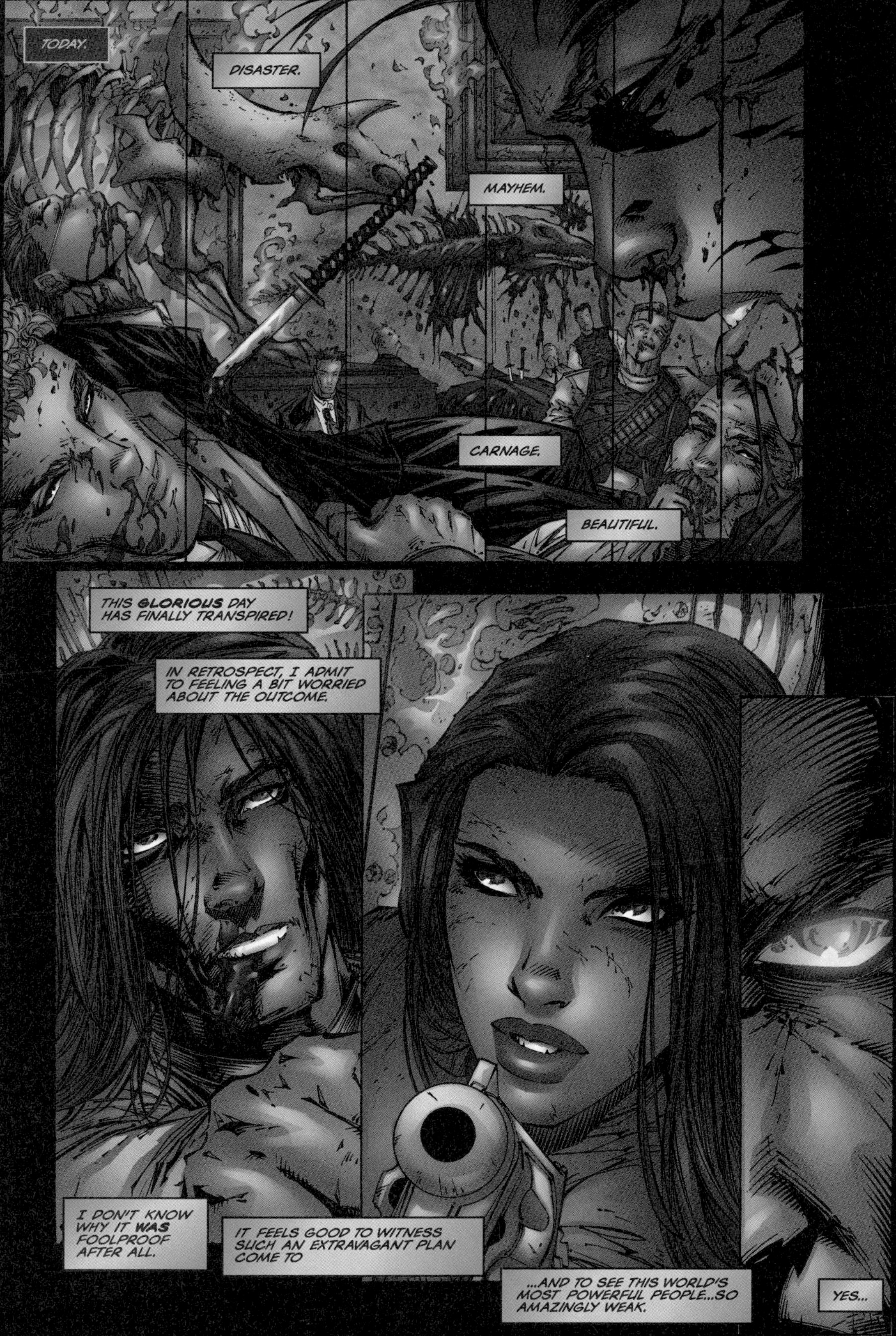
TODAY.
DISASTER.
MAYHEM.
CARNAGE.
BEAUTIFUL.
THIS GLORIOUS DAY HAS FINALLY TRANSPIRED!
IN RETROSPECT, I ADMIT TO FEELING A BIT WORRIED ABOUT THE OUTCOME.
I DON'T KNOW WHY IT WAS FOOLPROOF AFTER ALL.
IT FEELS GOOD TO WITNESS SUCH AN EXTRAVAGANT PLAN COME TO
...AND TO SEE THIS WORLD'S MOST POWERFUL PEOPLE...SO AMAZINGLY WEAK.
YES...

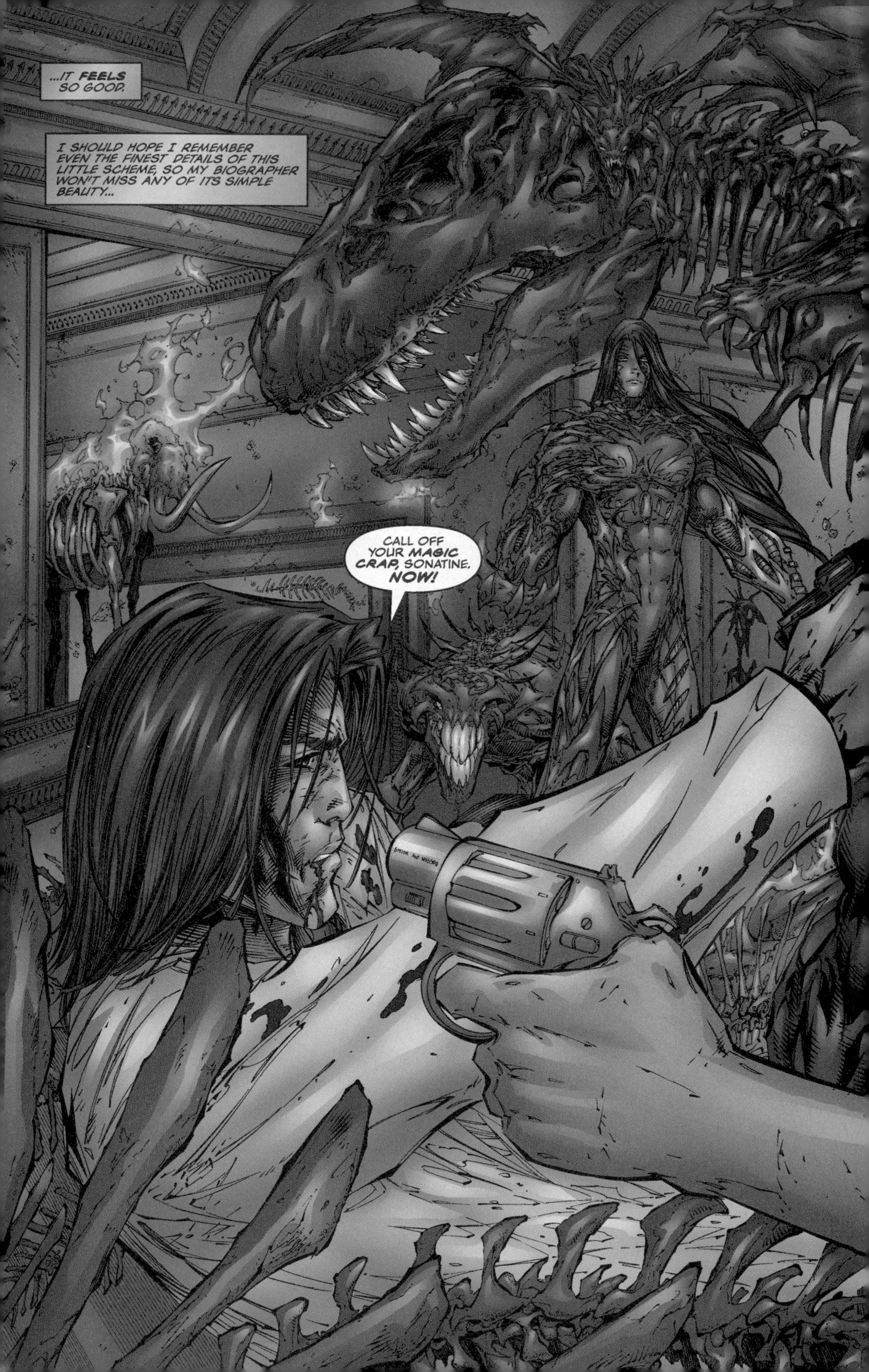
...IT FEELS SO GOOD.
I SHOULD HOPE I REMEMBER EVEN THE FINEST DETAILS OF THIS LITTLE SCHEME, SO MY BIOGRAPHER WON'T MISS ANY OF ITS SIMPLE BEAUTY...
CALL OFF YOUR MAGIC CRAP, SONATINE. NOW!

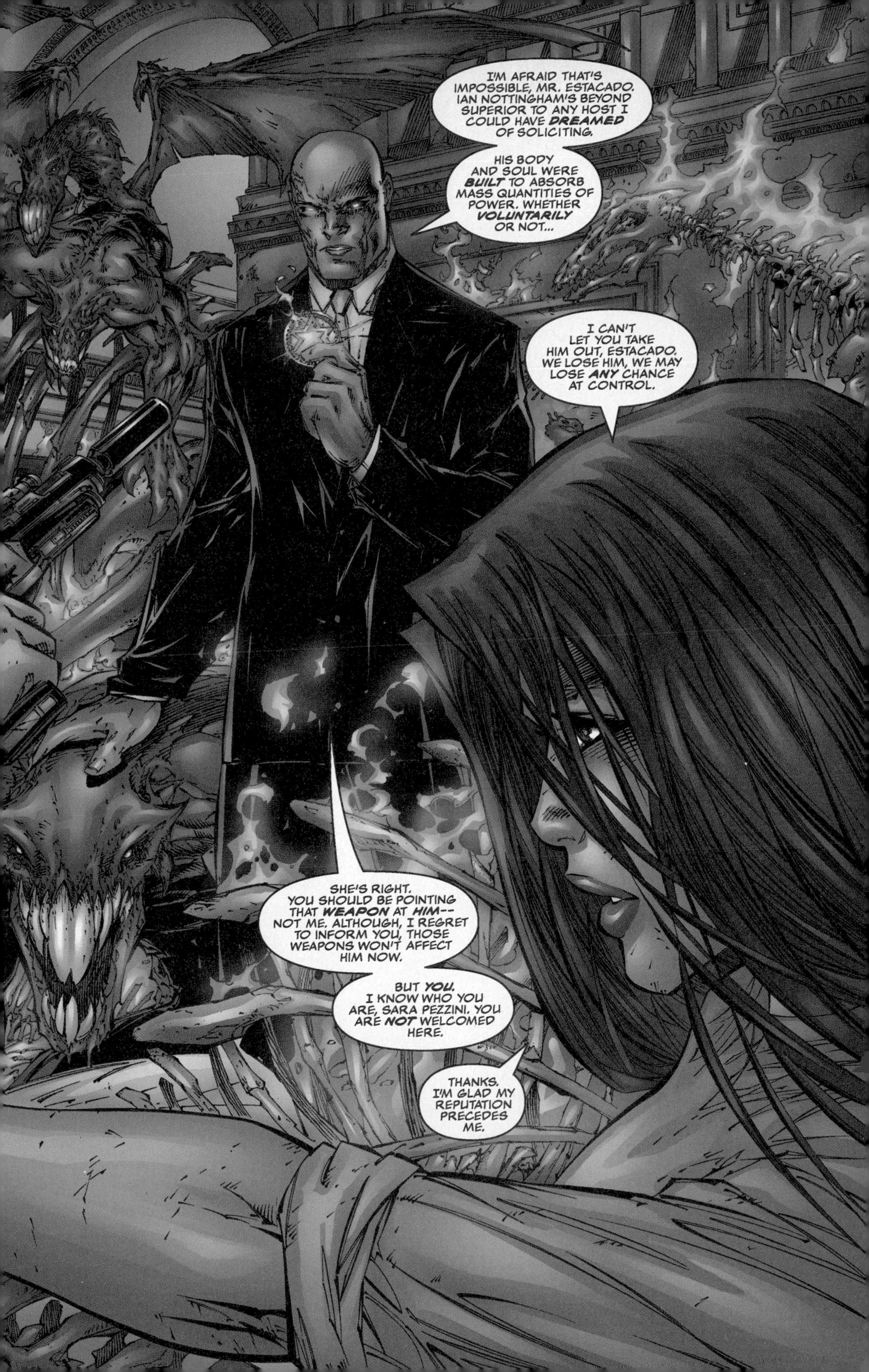
I'M AFRAID THAT'S IMPOSSIBLE, MR. ESTACADO. IAN NOTTINGHAM'S BEYOND SUPERIOR TO ANY HOST I COULD HAVE DREAMED OF SOLICITING.
HIS BODY AND SOUL WERE BUILT TO ABSORB MASS QUANTITIES OF POWER. WHETHER VOLUNTARILY OR NOT...
I CAN'T LET YOU TAKE HIM OUT, ESTACADO. WE LOSE HIM, WE MAY LOSE ANY CHANCE AT CONTROL.
SHE'S RIGHT. YOU SHOULD BE POINTING THAT WEAPON AT HIM-- NOT ME. ALTHOUGH, I REGRET TO INFORM YOU, THOSE WEAPONS WON'T AFFECT HIM NOW.
BUT YOU. I KNOW WHO YOU ARE, SARA PEZZINI. YOU ARE NOT WELCOMED HERE.
THANKS. I'M GLAD MY REPUTATION PRECEDES ME.

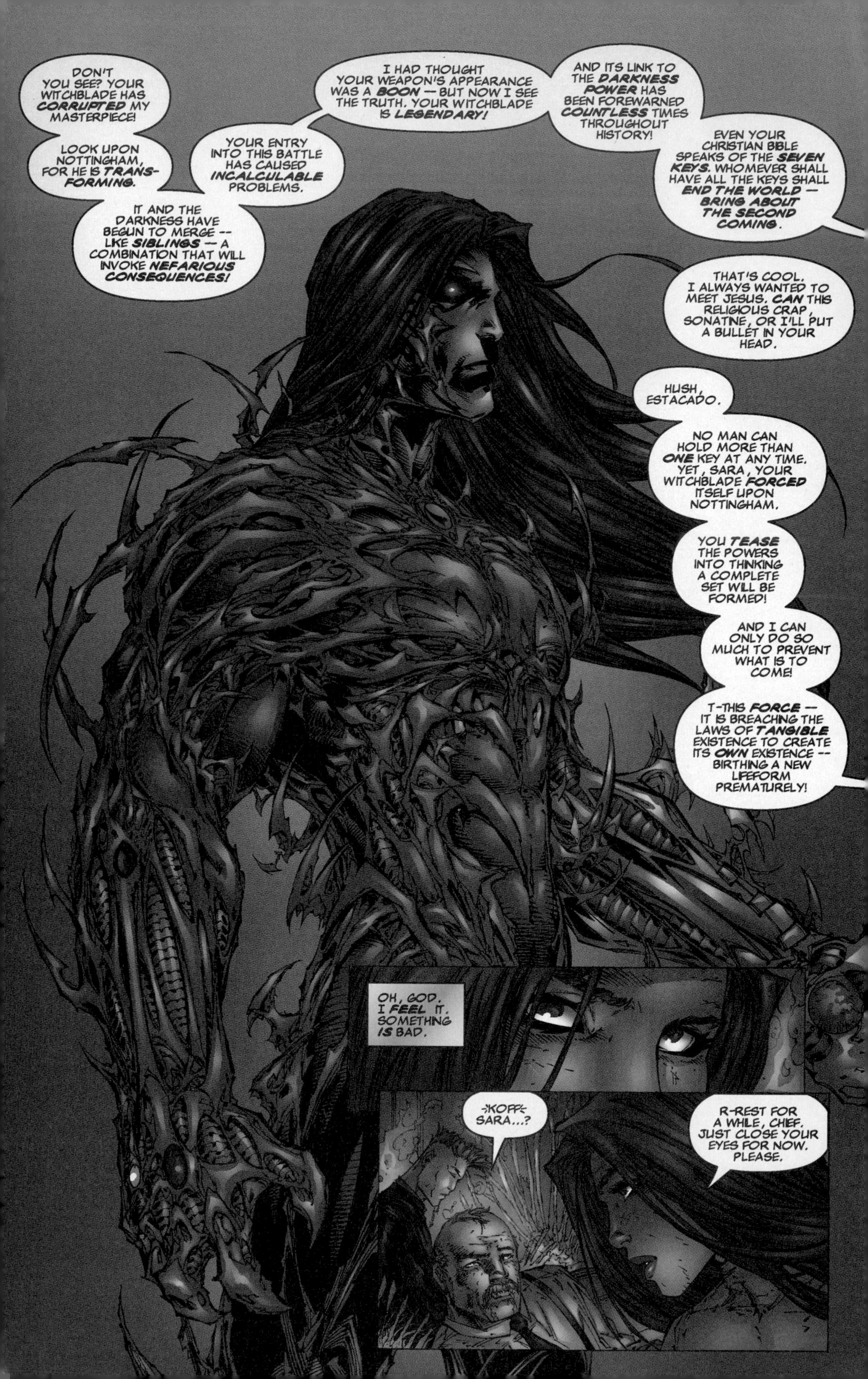
DON'T YOU SEE? YOUR WITCHBLADE HAS CORRUPTED MY MASTERPIECE!
LOOK UPON NOTTINGHAM, FOR HE IS TRANS-FORMING.
IT AND THE DARKNESS HAVE BEGUN TO MERGE -- LIKE SIBLINGS -- A COMBINATION THAT WILL INVOKE NEFARIOUS CONSEQUENCES!
YOUR ENTRY INTO THIS BATTLE HAS CAUSED INCALCULABLE PROBLEMS.
I HAD THOUGHT YOUR WEAPON'S APPEARANCE WAS A BOON -- BUT NOW I SEE THE TRUTH. YOUR WITCHBLADE IS LEGENDARY!
AND ITS LINK TO THE DARKNESS POWER HAS BEEN FOREWARNED COUNTLESS TIMES THROUGHOUT HISTORY!
EVEN YOUR CHRISTIAN BIBLE SPEAKS OF THE SEVEN KEYS. WHOMEVER SHALL HAVE ALL THE KEYS SHALL END THE WORLD -- BRING ABOUT THE SECOND COMING.
THAT'S COOL. I ALWAYS WANTED TO MEET JESUS. CAN THIS RELIGIOUS CRAP, SONATINE, OR I'LL PUT A BULLET IN YOUR HEAD.
HUSH, ESTACADO.
NO MAN CAN HOLD MORE THAN ONE KEY AT ANY TIME. YET, SARA, YOUR WITCHBLADE FORCED ITSELF UPON NOTTINGHAM.
YOU TEASE THE POWERS INTO THINKING A COMPLETE SET WILL BE FORMED!
AND I CAN ONLY DO SO MUCH TO PREVENT WHAT IS TO COME!
T-THIS FORCE -- IT IS BREACHING THE LAWS OF TANGIBLE EXISTENCE TO CREATE ITS OWN EXISTENCE -- BIRTHING A NEW LIFEFORM PREMATURELY!
OH, GOD. I FEEL IT. SOMETHING IS BAD.
KOFF SARA...?
R-REST FOR A WHILE, CHIEF. JUST CLOSE YOUR EYES FOR NOW. PLEASE.

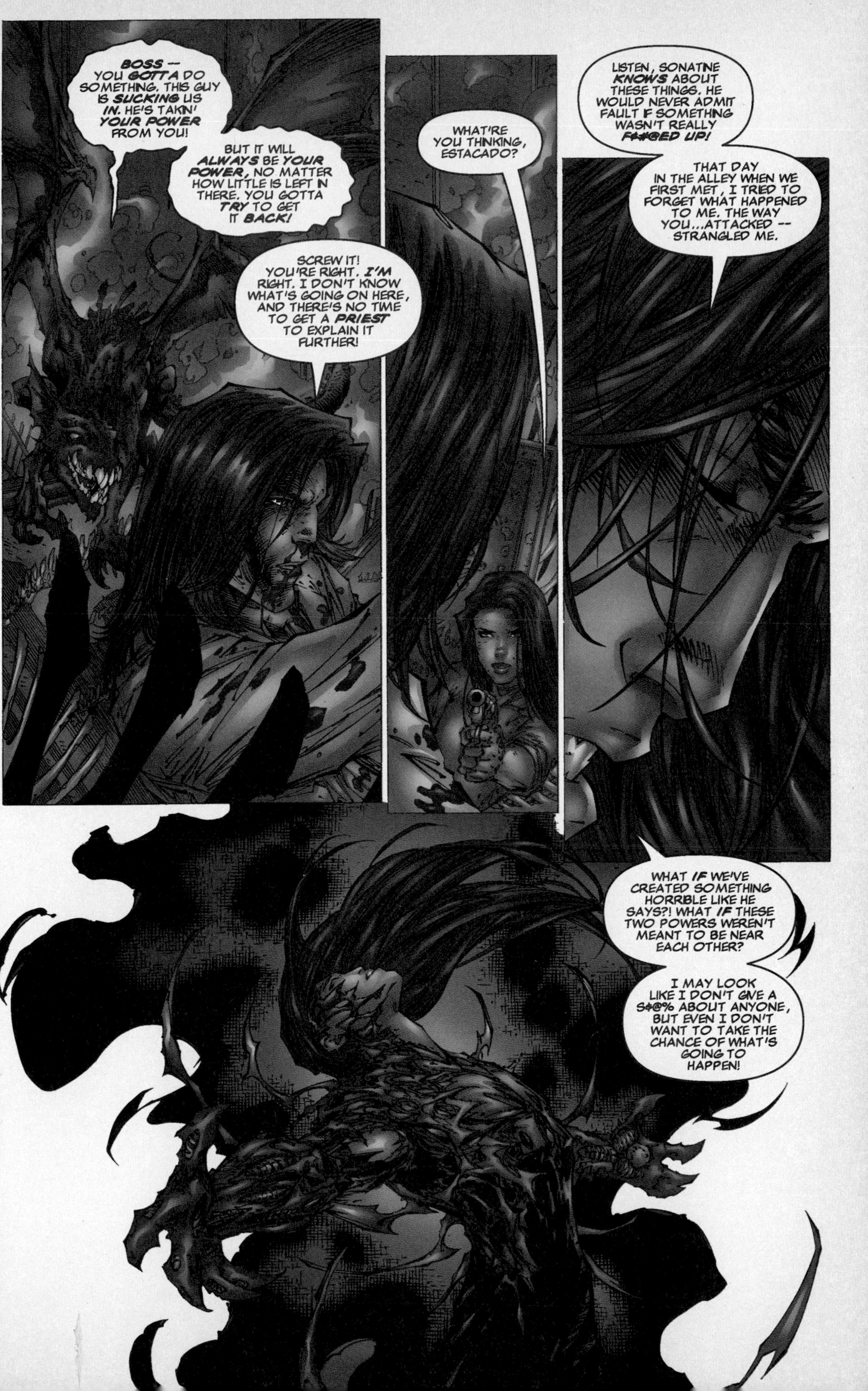
BOSS -- YOU GOTTA DO SOMETHING. THIS GUY IS SUCKING US IN. HE'S TAKIN' YOUR POWER FROM YOU!
BUT IT WILL ALWAYS BE YOUR POWER, NO MATTER HOW LITTLE IS LEFT IN THERE. YOU GOTTA TRY TO GET IT BACK!
SCREW IT! YOU'RE RIGHT. I'M RIGHT. I DON'T KNOW WHAT'S GOING ON HERE, AND THERE'S NO TIME TO GET A PRIEST TO EXPLAIN IT FURTHER!
WHAT'RE YOU THINKING, ESTACADO?
LISTEN, SONATINE KNOWS ABOUT THESE THINGS. HE WOULD NEVER ADMIT FAULT IF SOMETHING WASN'T REALLY F#*@ED UP!
THAT DAY IN THE ALLEY WHEN WE FIRST MET, I TRIED TO FORGET WHAT HAPPENED TO ME. THE WAY YOU...ATTACKED -- STRANGLED ME.
WHAT IF WE'VE CREATED SOMETHING HORRIBLE LIKE HE SAYS?! WHAT IF THESE TWO POWERS WEREN'T MEANT TO BE NEAR EACH OTHER?
I MAY LOOK LIKE I DON'T GIVE A S#@% ABOUT ANYONE, BUT EVEN I DON'T WANT TO TAKE THE CHANCE OF WHAT'S GOING TO HAPPEN!

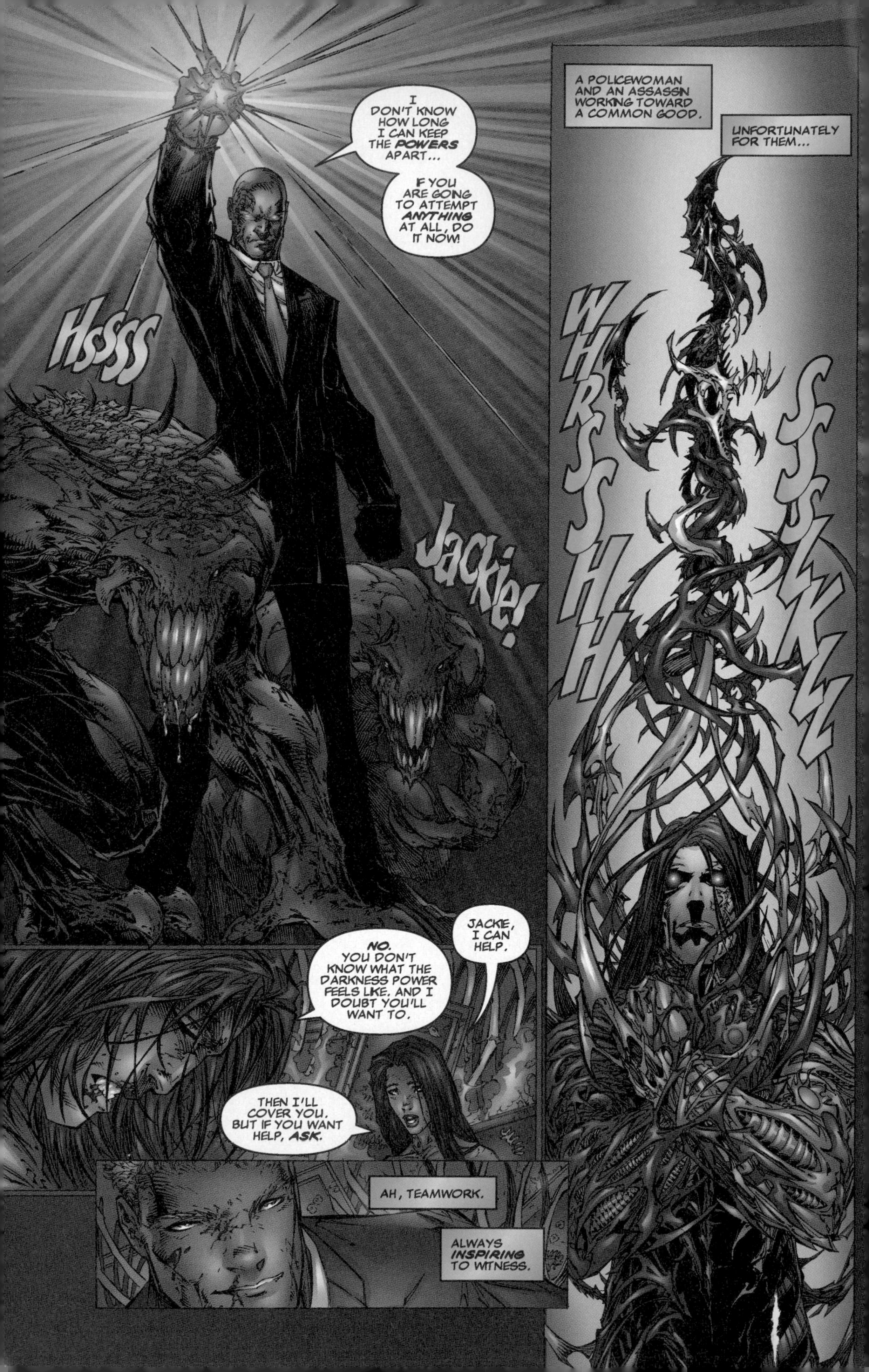

I DON'T KNOW HOW LONG I CAN KEEP THE POWERS APART...
IF YOU ARE GOING TO ATTEMPT ANYTHING AT ALL, DO IT NOW!
HSSSS
JACKIE!
A POLICEWOMAN AND AN ASSASSIN WORKING TOWARD A COMMON GOOD.
UNFORTUNATELY FOR THEM...
WHRSSHHH
SSSKKKK
JACKE, I CAN HELP.
NO. YOU DON'T KNOW WHAT THE DARKNESS POWER FEELS LIKE, AND I DOUBT YOU'LL WANT TO.
THEN I'LL COVER YOU. BUT IF YOU WANT HELP, ASK.
AH, TEAMWORK.
ALWAYS INSPIRING TO WITNESS.

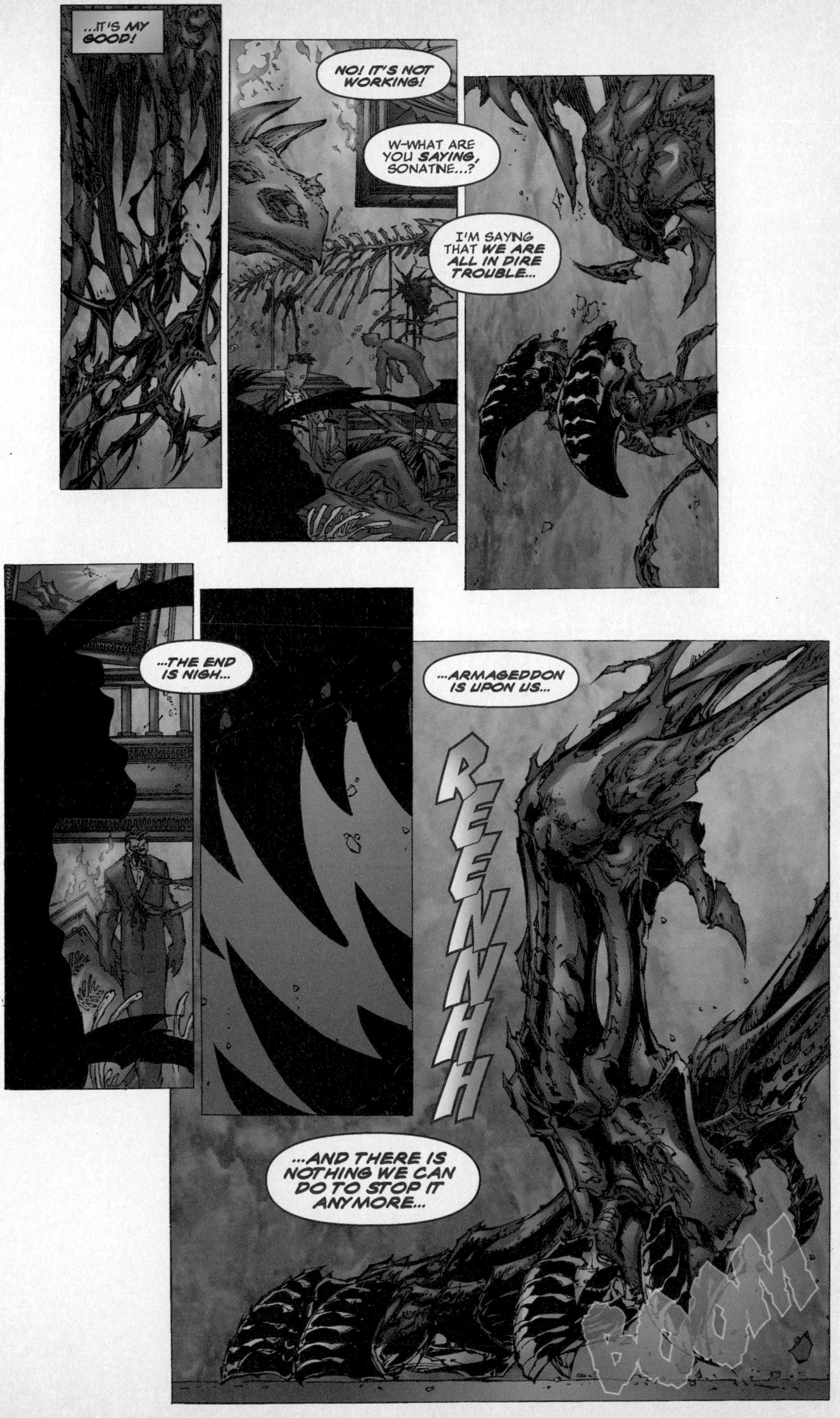

...IT'S MY GOOD!
NO! IT'S NOT WORKING!
W-WHAT ARE YOU SAYING, SONATINE...?
I'M SAYING THAT WE ARE ALL IN DIRE TROUBLE...
...THE END IS NIGH...
...ARMAGEDDON IS UPON US...
REENNHH
...AND THERE IS NOTHING WE CAN DO TO STOP IT ANYMORE...
BOOM

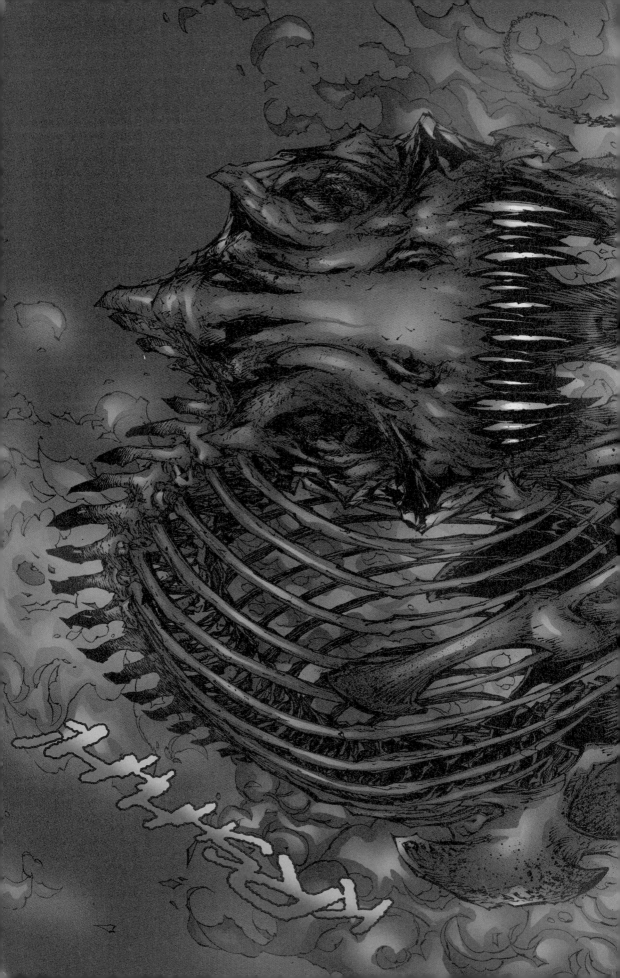

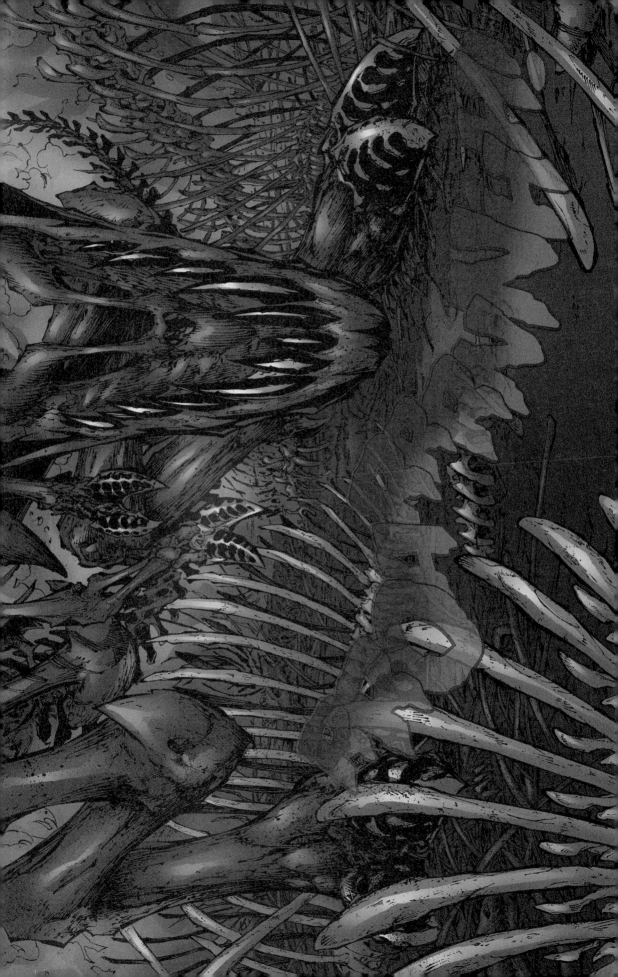

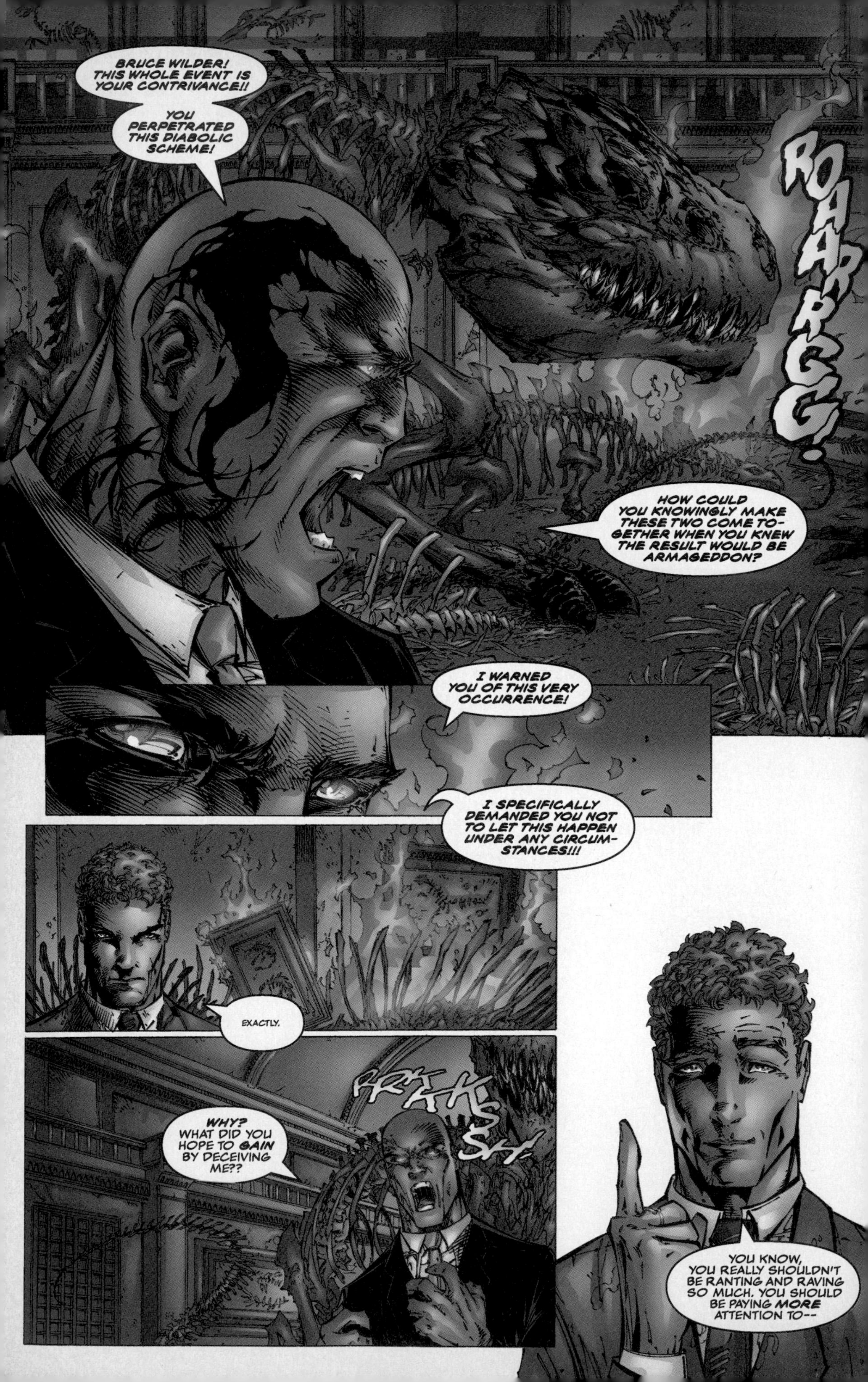
BRUCE WILDER! THIS WHOLE EVENT IS YOUR CONTRIVANCE!!
YOU PERPETRATED THIS DIABOLIC SCHEME!
ROAARRGG!
HOW COULD YOU KNOWINGLY MAKE THESE TWO COME TO-GETHER WHEN YOU KNEW THE RESULT WOULD BE ARMAGEDDON?
I WARNED YOU OF THIS VERY OCCURRENCE!
I SPECIFICALLY DEMANDED YOU NOT TO LET THIS HAPPEN UNDER ANY CIRCUM-STANCES!!!
EXACTLY.
WHY? WHAT DID YOU HOPE TO GAIN BY DECEIVING ME??
YOU KNOW, YOU REALLY SHOULDN'T BE RANTING AND RAVING SO MUCH. YOU SHOULD BE PAYING MORE ATTENTION TO--

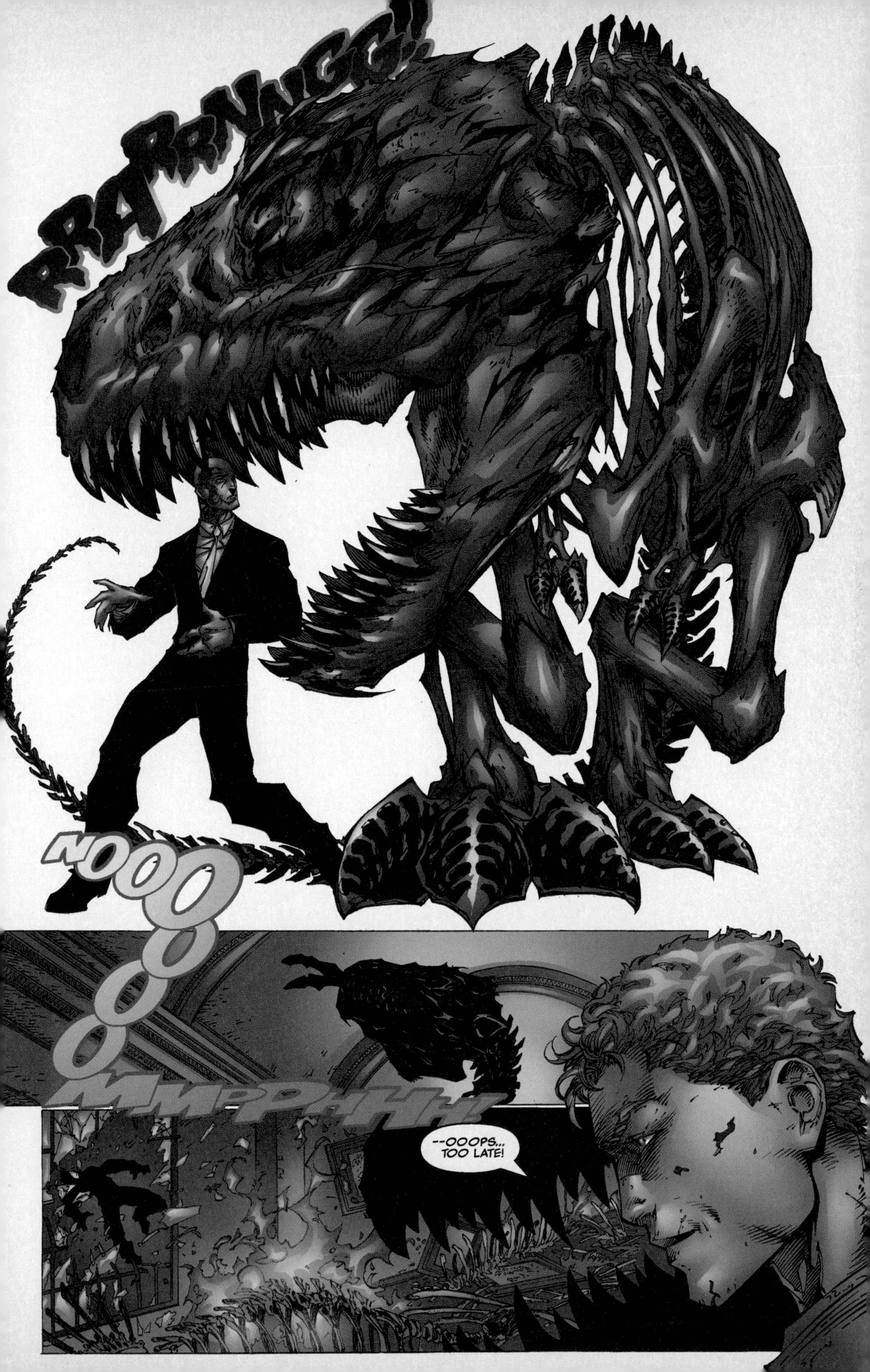
RRARRNNGG!!
NOOOOOOO
MMPHHH!
--OOOPS... TOO LATE!

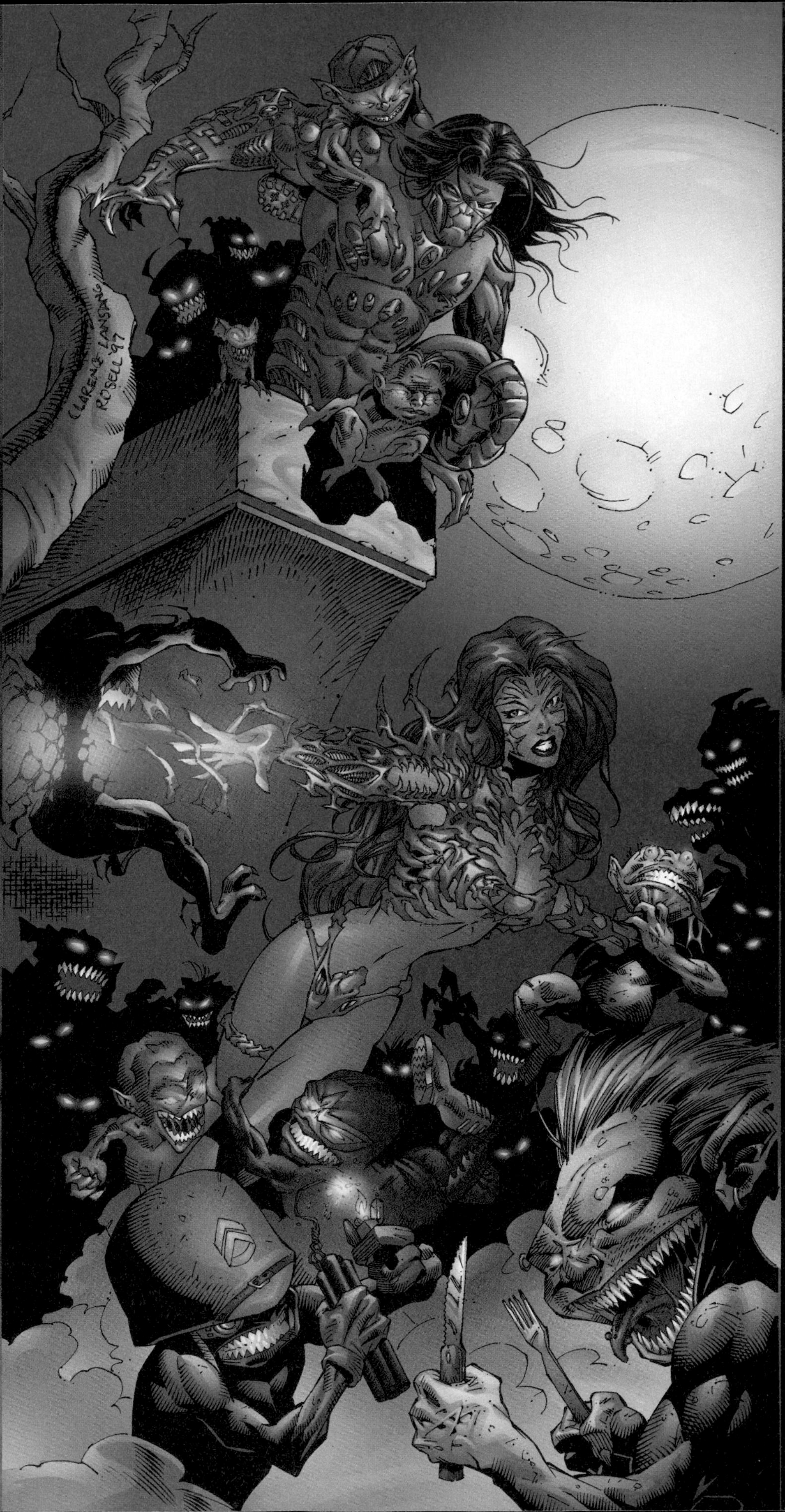

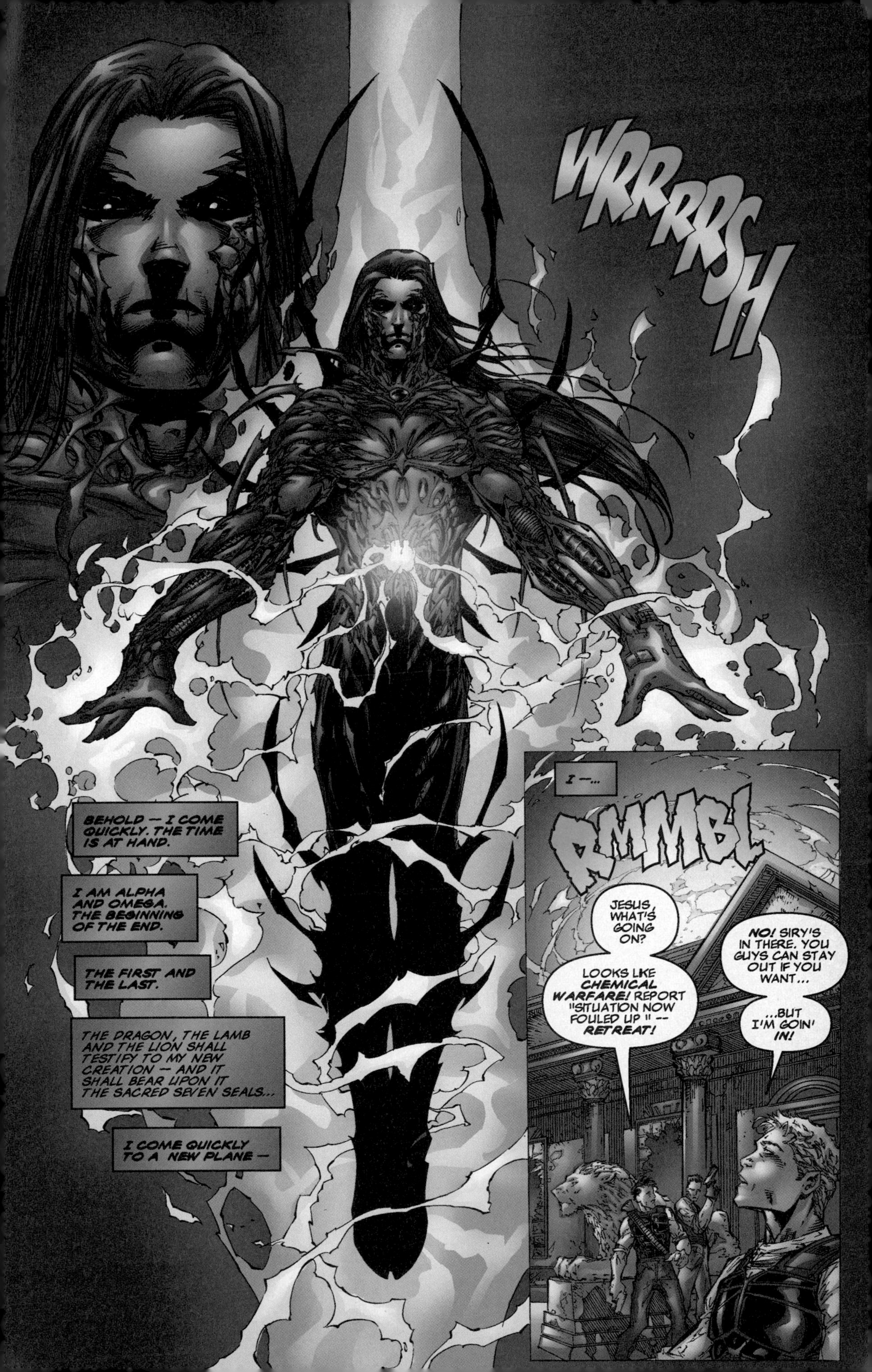
WRRRRSH
BEHOLD — I COME QUICKLY. THE TIME IS AT HAND.
I AM ALPHA AND OMEGA. THE BEGINNING OF THE END.
THE FIRST AND THE LAST.
THE DRAGON, THE LAMB AND THE LION SHALL TESTIFY TO MY NEW CREATION — AND IT SHALL BEAR UPON IT THE SACRED SEVEN SEALS...
I COME QUICKLY TO A NEW PLANE —
I —...
RMMBL
JESUS, WHAT'S GOING ON?
LOOKS LIKE CHEMICAL WARFARE! REPORT "SITUATION NOW FOULED UP" -- RETREAT!
NO! SIRY'S IN THERE. YOU GUYS CAN STAY OUT IF YOU WANT...
...BUT I'M GOIN' IN!

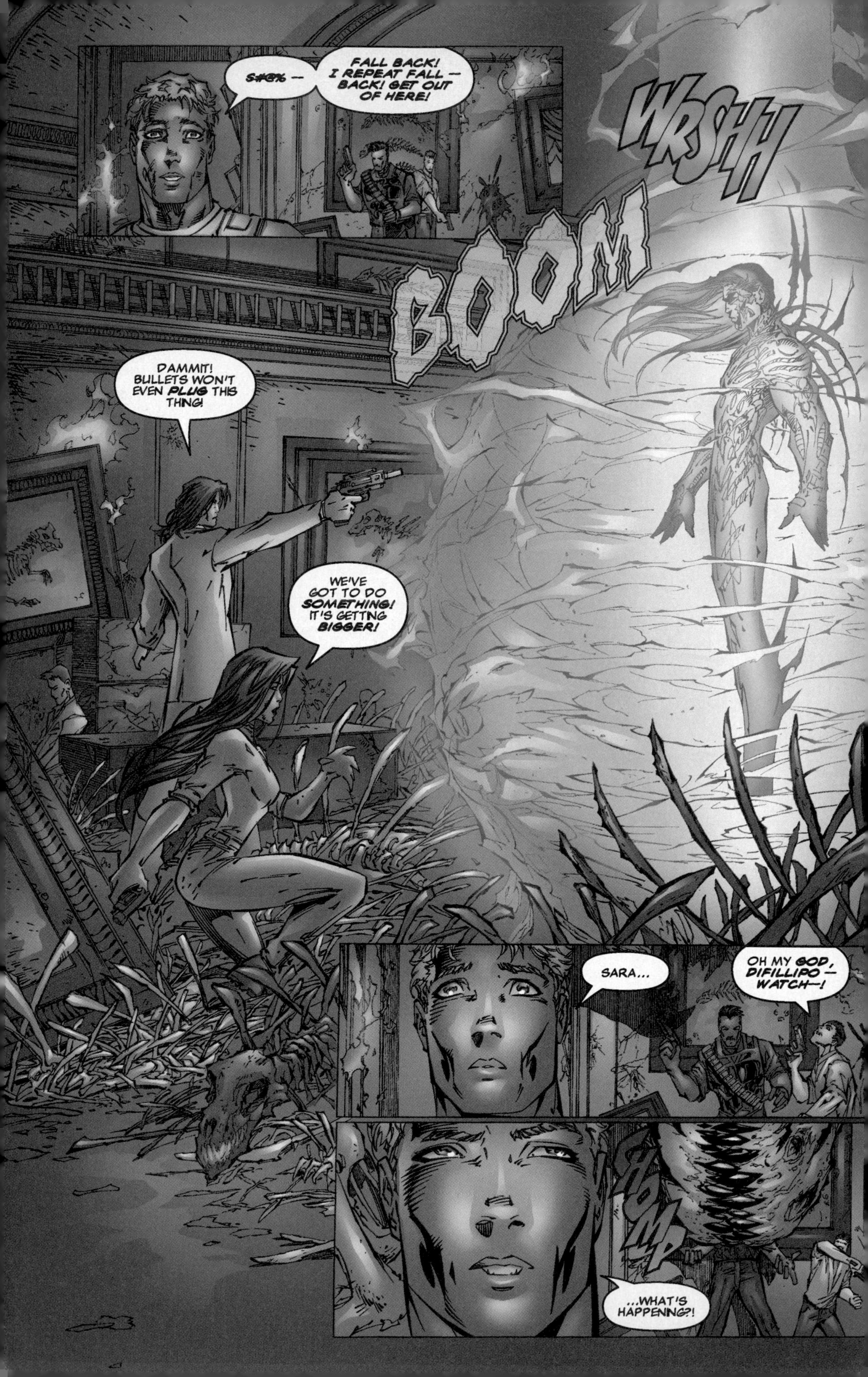
S#@% --
FALL BACK! I REPEAT FALL -- BACK! GET OUT OF HERE!
WRSHH
BOOM
DAMMIT! BULLETS WON'T EVEN PLUG THIS THING!
WE'VE GOT TO DO SOMETHING! IT'S GETTING BIGGER!
SARA...
OH MY GOD, DIFILLIPO -- WATCH--!
...WHAT'S HAPPENING?!

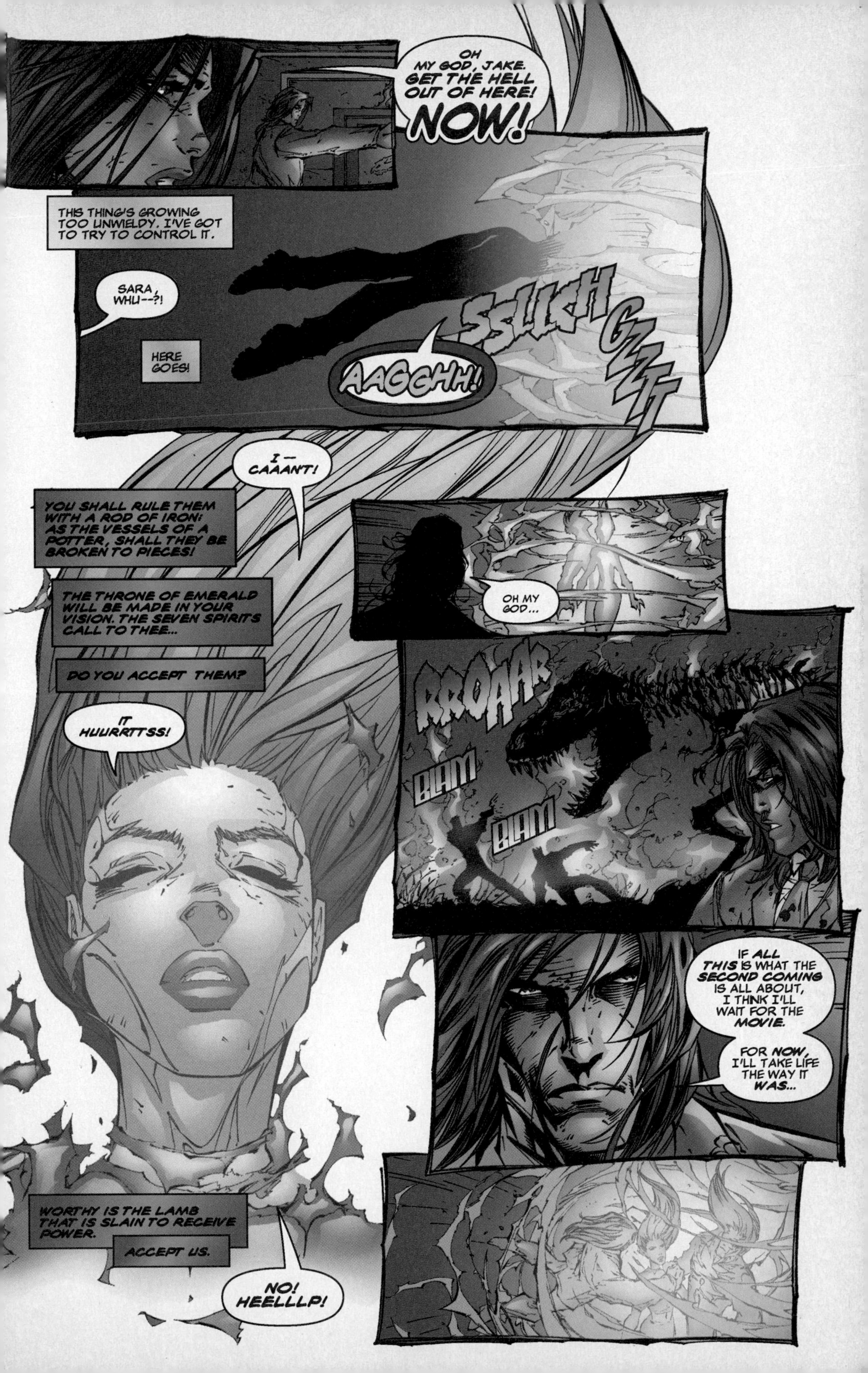
OH MY GOD, JAKE. GET THE HELL OUT OF HERE! NOW!
THIS THING'S GROWING TOO UNWIELDY. I'VE GOT TO TRY TO CONTROL IT.
SARA, WHU--?!
HERE GOES!
SSLICH
GZZZT
AAGGHH!
I — CAAAN'T!
YOU SHALL RULE THEM WITH A ROD OF IRON; AS THE VESSELS OF A POTTER, SHALL THEY BE BROKEN TO PIECES!
THE THRONE OF EMERALD WILL BE MADE IN YOUR VISION. THE SEVEN SPIRITS CALL TO THEE...
DO YOU ACCEPT THEM?
IT HUURRTTSS!
OH MY GOD...
RROAAR
BLAM
BLAM
IF ALL THIS IS WHAT THE SECOND COMING IS ALL ABOUT, I THINK I'LL WAIT FOR THE MOVIE.
FOR NOW, I'LL TAKE LIFE THE WAY IT WAS...
WORTHY IS THE LAMB THAT IS SLAIN TO RECEIVE POWER.
ACCEPT US.
NO! HEELLLP!

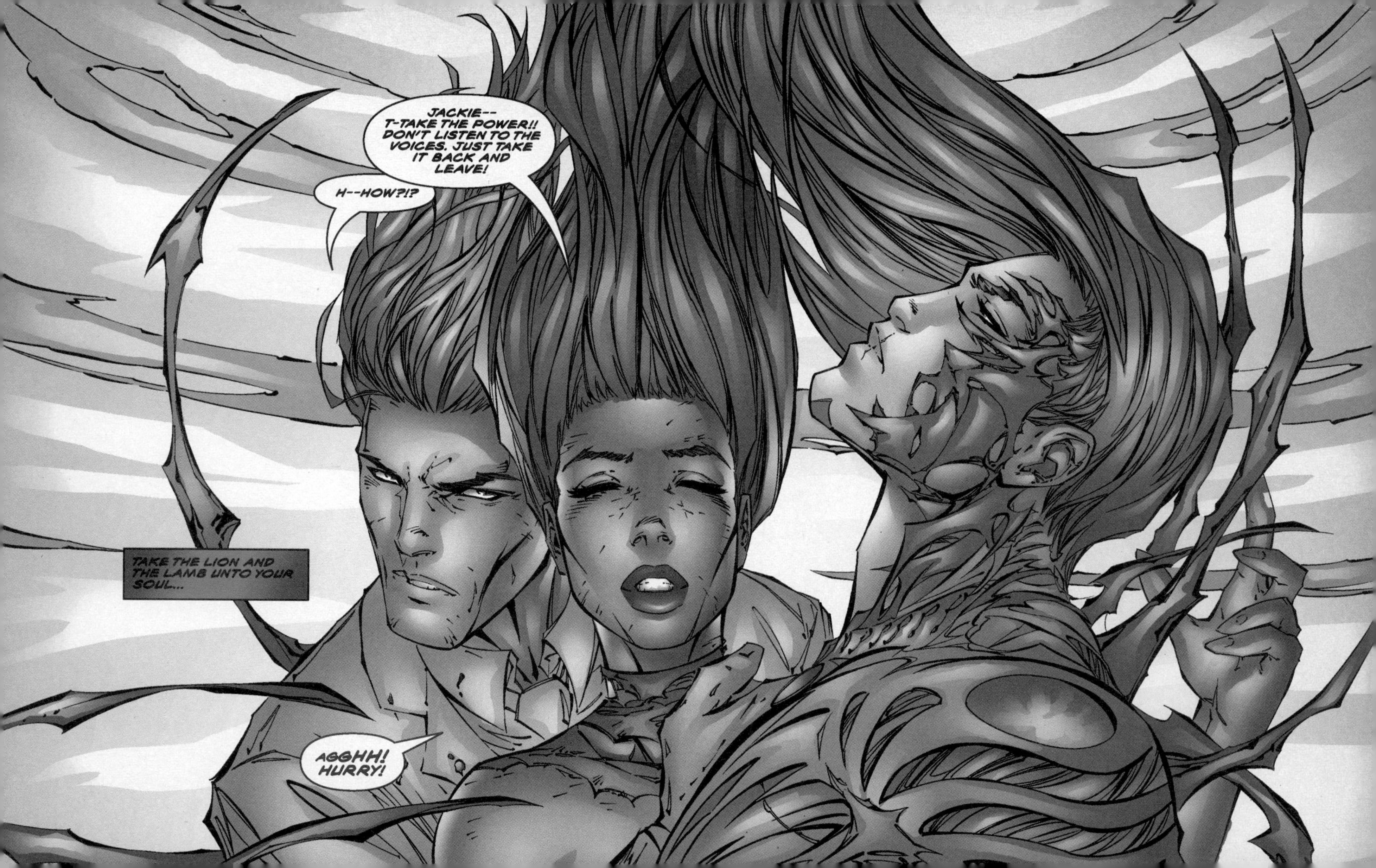
JACKIE-- T-TAKE THE POWER!! DON'T LISTEN TO THE VOICES. JUST TAKE IT BACK AND LEAVE!
H--HOW?!?
TAKE THE LION AND THE LAMB UNTO YOUR SOUL...
AGGHH! HURRY!

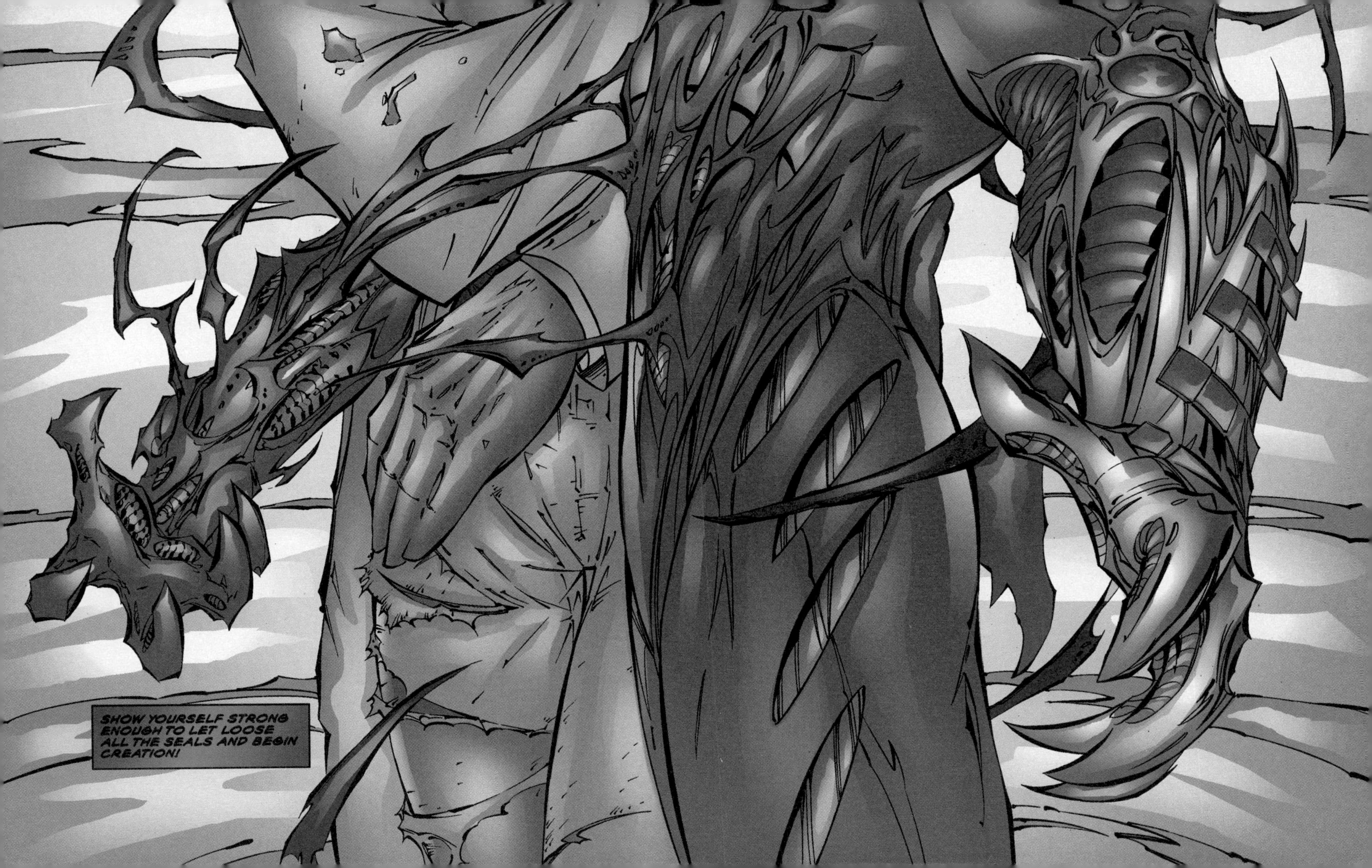
SHOW YOURSELF STRONG ENOUGH TO LET LOOSE ALL THE SEALS AND BEGIN CREATION!

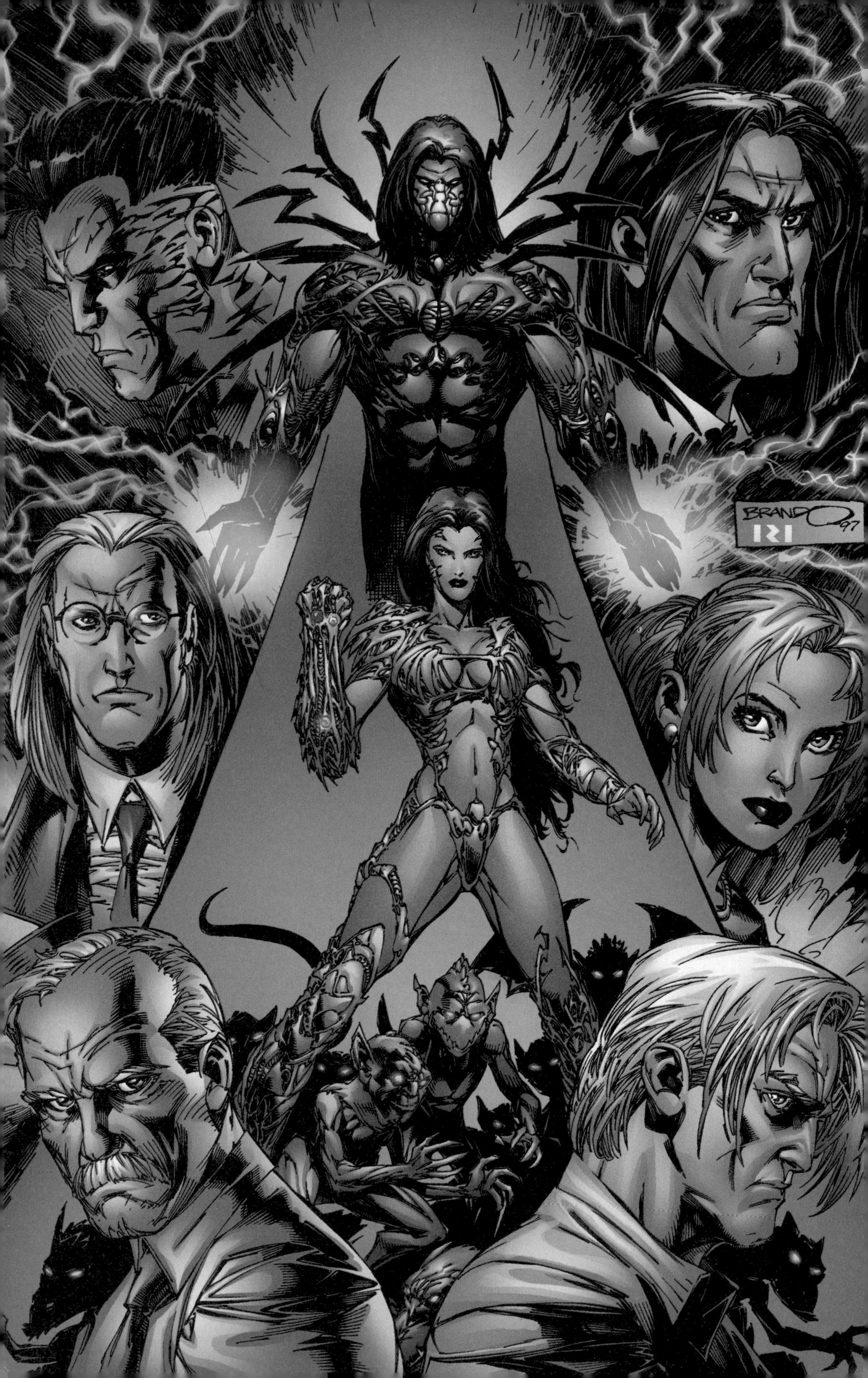

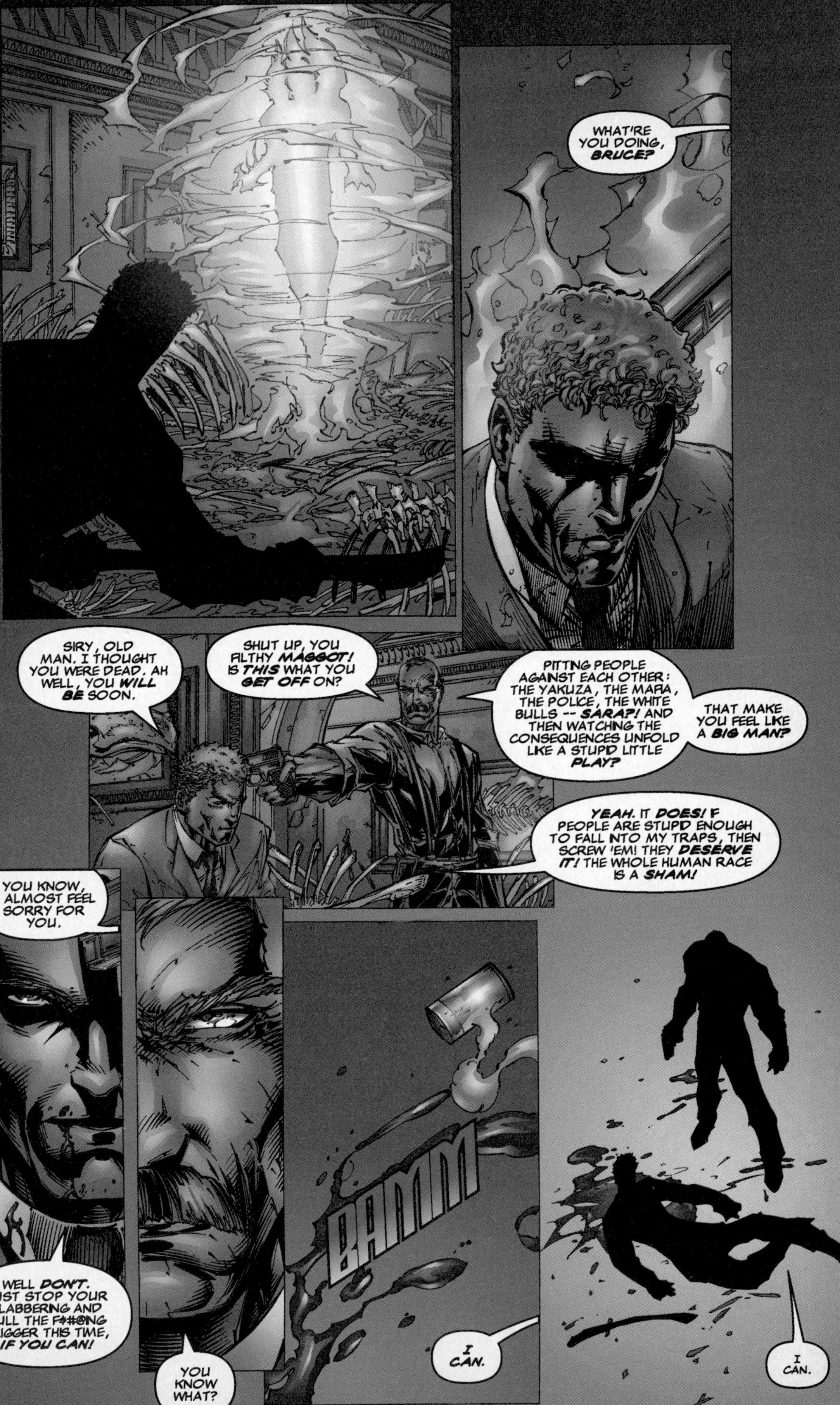
WHAT'RE YOU DOING, BRUCE?
SIRY, OLD MAN. I THOUGHT YOU WERE DEAD. AH WELL, YOU WILL BE SOON.
SHUT UP, YOU FILTHY MAGGOT! IS THIS WHAT YOU GET OFF ON?
PITTING PEOPLE AGANST EACH OTHER: THE YAKUZA, THE MAFIA, THE POLICE, THE WHITE BULLS -- SARA?! AND THEN WATCHING THE CONSEQUENCES UNFOLD LIKE A STUPID LITTLE PLAY?
THAT MAKE YOU FEEL LIKE A BIG MAN?
YEAH. IT DOES! IF PEOPLE ARE STUPID ENOUGH TO FALL INTO MY TRAPS, THEN SCREW 'EM! THEY DESERVE IT! THE WHOLE HUMAN RACE IS A SHAM!
YOU KNOW, I ALMOST FEEL SORRY FOR YOU.
WELL DON'T. JUST STOP YOUR BLABBERING AND PULL THE F#@ING TRIGGER THIS TIME, IF YOU CAN!
YOU KNOW WHAT?
BAMM
I CAN.
I CAN.

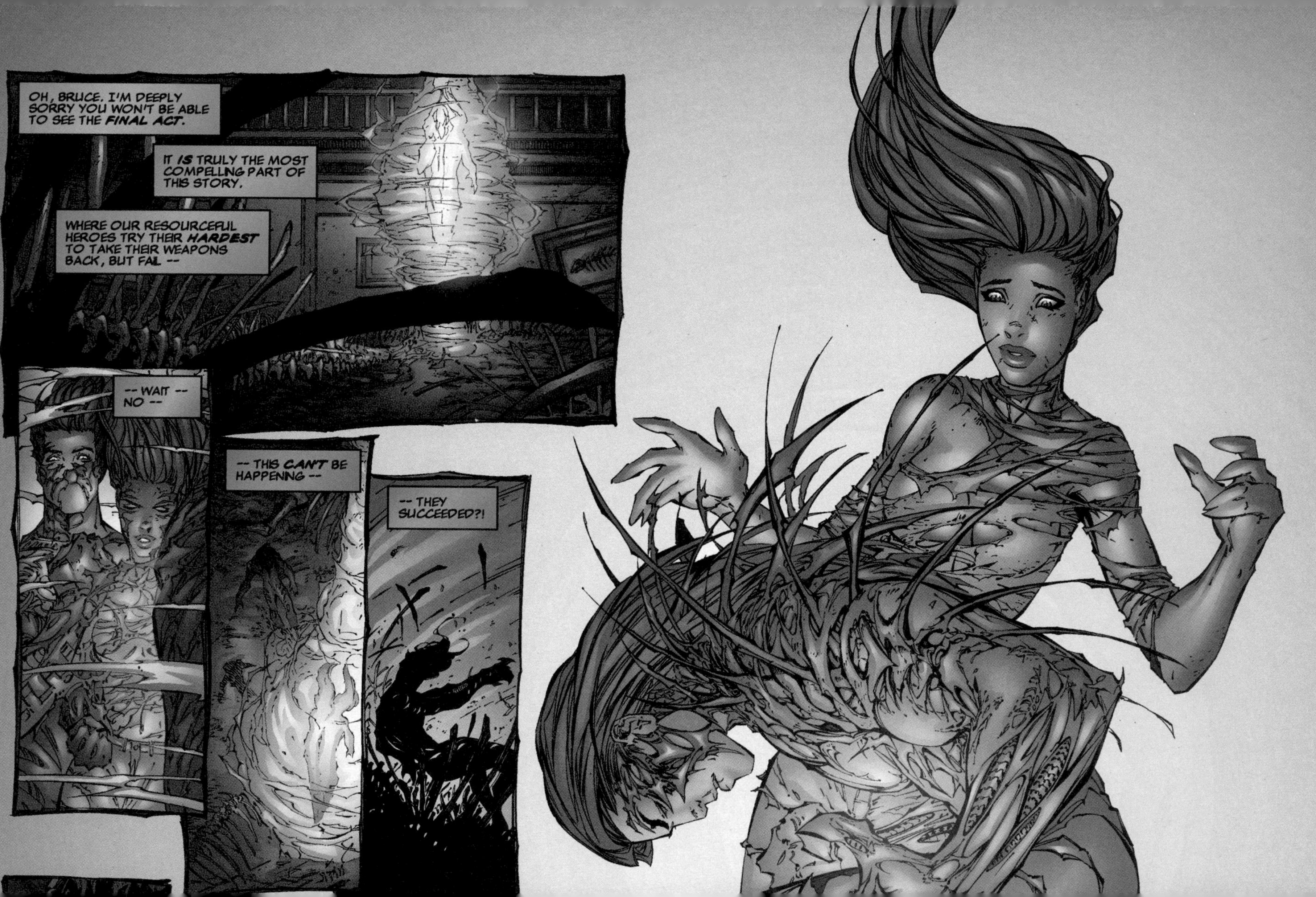
OH, BRUCE. I'M DEEPLY SORRY YOU WON'T BE ABLE TO SEE THE ***FINAL ACT.***
IT ***IS*** TRULY THE MOST COMPELLING PART OF THIS STORY.
WHERE OUR RESOURCEFUL HEROES TRY THEIR ***HARDEST*** TO TAKE THEIR WEAPONS BACK, BUT FAIL --
-- WAIT -- NO --
-- THIS ***CAN'T*** BE HAPPENING --
-- THEY SUCCEEDED?!

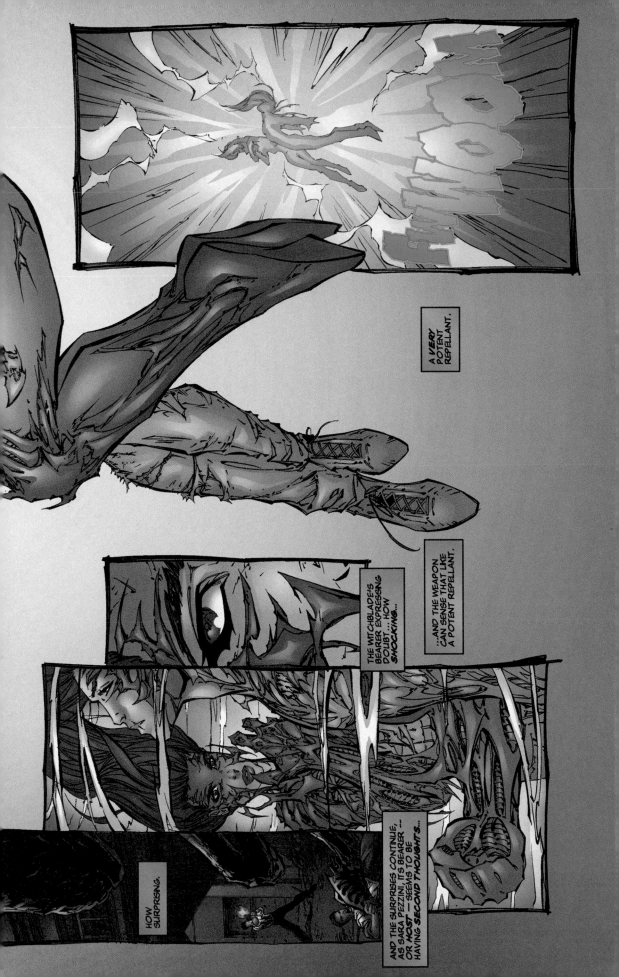

FWOO

A *VERY POTENT* REPELLANT.

THE WITCHBLADE'S BEARER EXPRESSING DOUBT... HOW *SHOCKING*...

...AND THE WEAPON CAN SENSE THAT LIKE A POTENT REPELLANT.

HOW SURPRISING.

AND THE SURPRISES CONTINUE, AS SARA PEZZINI, ITS BEARER — OR *HOST* — SEEMS TO BE HAVING *SECOND THOUGHTS*...

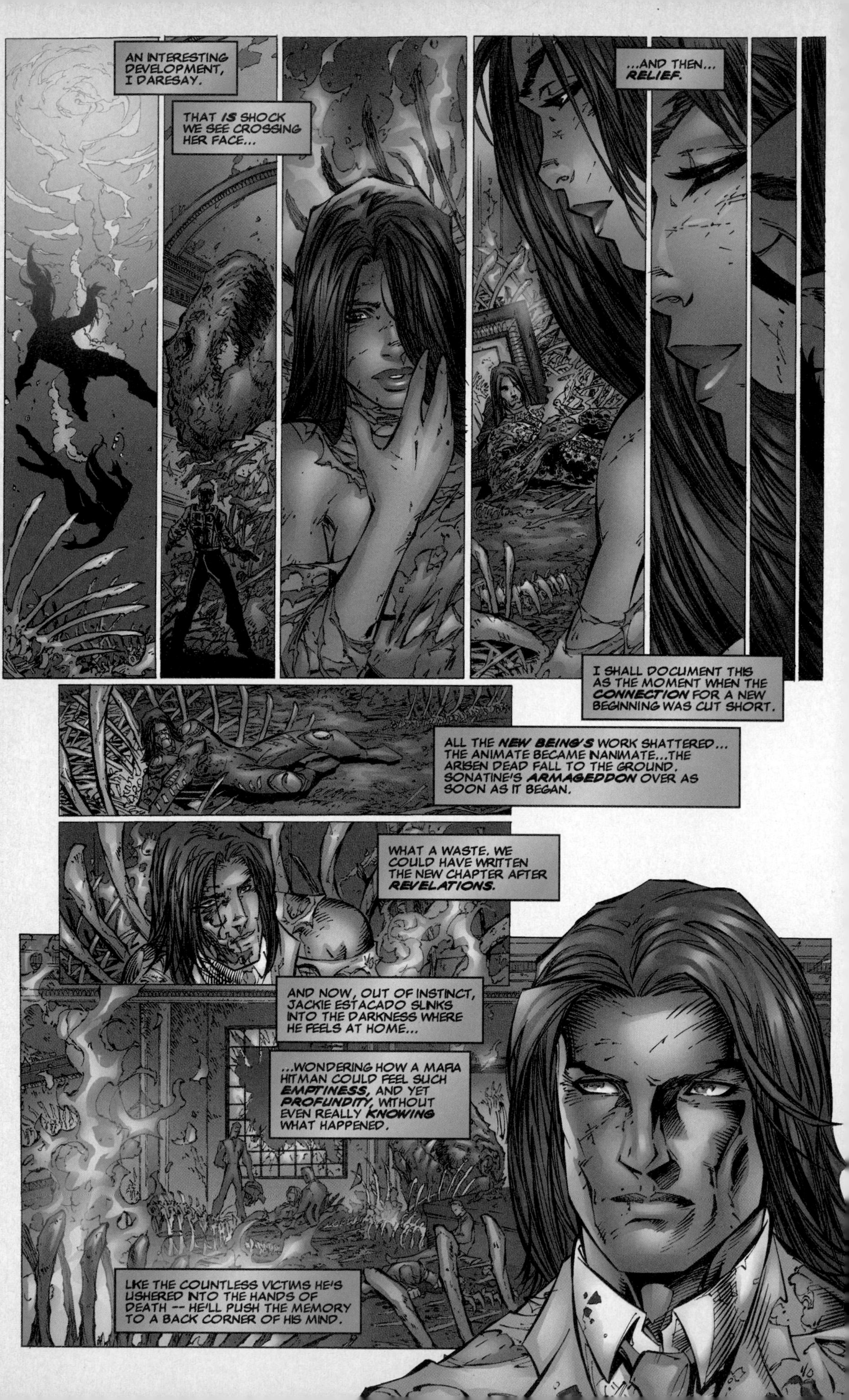
AN INTERESTING DEVELOPMENT, I DARESAY.
THAT *IS* SHOCK WE SEE CROSSING HER FACE...
...AND THEN... *RELIEF.*
I SHALL DOCUMENT THIS AS THE MOMENT WHEN THE *CONNECTION* FOR A NEW BEGINNING WAS CUT SHORT.
ALL THE *NEW BEING'S* WORK SHATTERED... THE ANIMATE BECAME INANIMATE...THE ARISEN DEAD FALL TO THE GROUND. SONATINE'S *ARMAGEDDON* OVER AS SOON AS IT BEGAN.
WHAT A WASTE. WE COULD HAVE WRITTEN THE NEW CHAPTER AFTER *REVELATIONS.*
AND NOW, OUT OF INSTINCT, JACKIE ESTACADO SLINKS INTO THE DARKNESS WHERE HE FEELS AT HOME...
...WONDERING HOW A MAFIA HITMAN COULD FEEL SUCH *EMPTINESS,* AND YET *PROFUNDITY,* WITHOUT EVEN REALLY *KNOWING* WHAT HAPPENED.
LIKE THE COUNTLESS VICTIMS HE'S USHERED INTO THE HANDS OF DEATH -- HE'LL PUSH THE MEMORY TO A BACK CORNER OF HIS MIND.

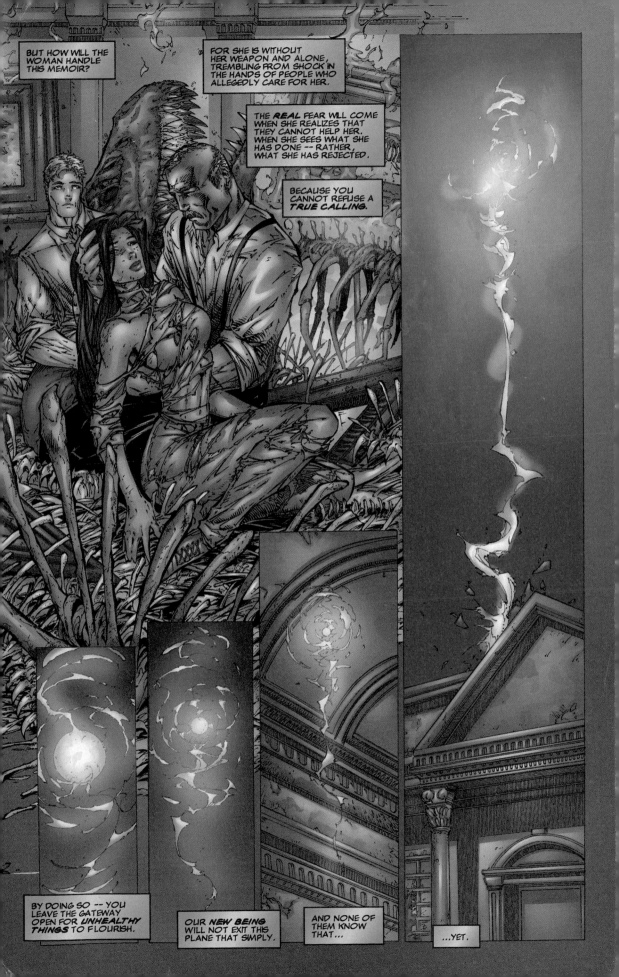

BUT HOW WILL THE WOMAN HANDLE THIS MEMOIR?

FOR SHE IS WITHOUT HER WEAPON AND ALONE, TREMBLING FROM SHOCK IN THE HANDS OF PEOPLE WHO ALLEGEDLY CARE FOR HER.

THE *REAL* FEAR WILL COME WHEN SHE REALIZES THAT THEY CANNOT HELP HER. WHEN SHE SEES WHAT SHE HAS DONE -- RATHER, WHAT SHE HAS REJECTED.

BECAUSE YOU CANNOT REFUSE A *TRUE CALLING.*

BY DOING SO -- YOU LEAVE THE GATEWAY OPEN FOR *UNHEALTHY THINGS* TO FLOURISH.

OUR *NEW BEING* WILL NOT EXIT THIS PLANE THAT SIMPLY.

AND NONE OF THEM KNOW THAT...

...YET.

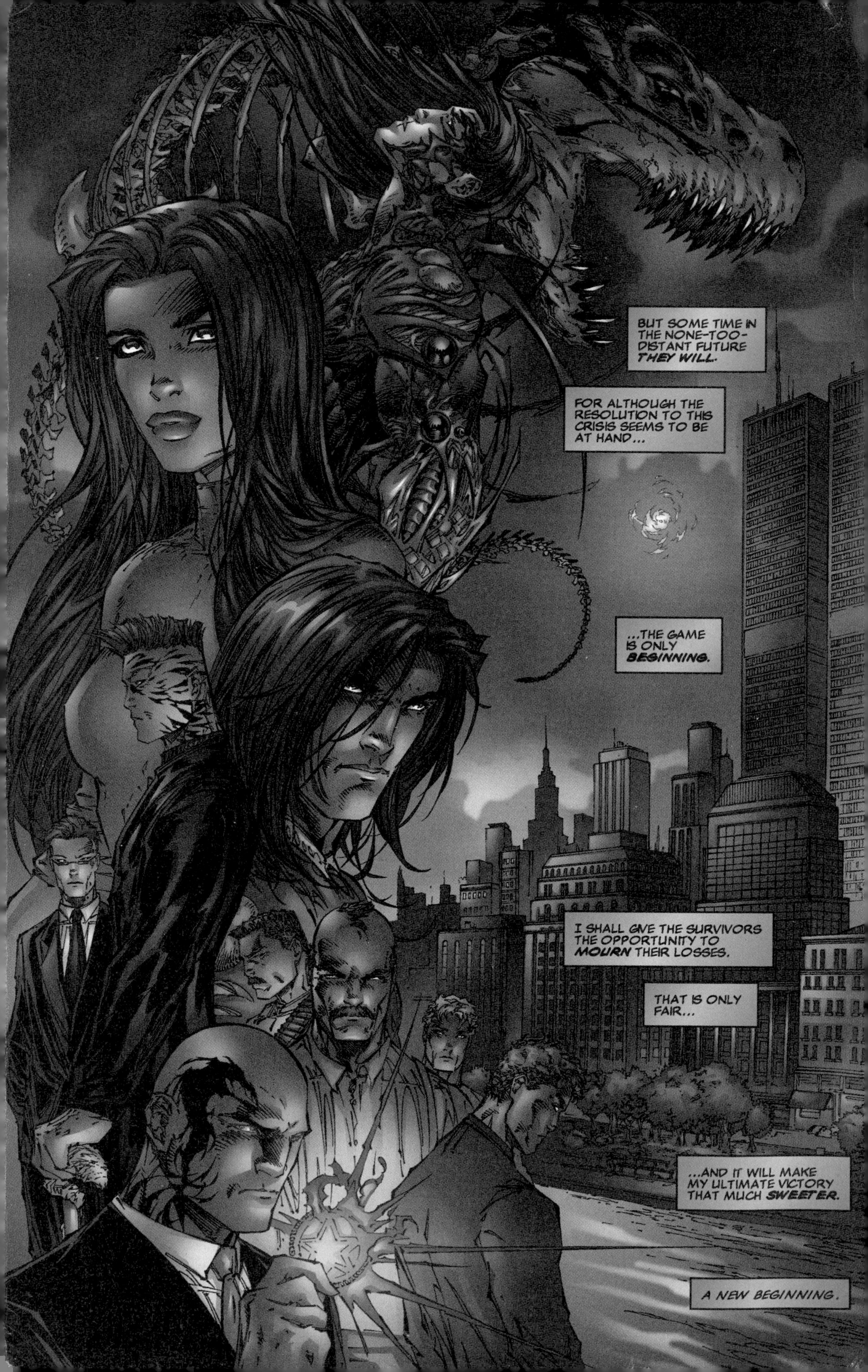
BUT SOME TIME IN THE NONE-TOO-DISTANT FUTURE THEY WILL.
FOR ALTHOUGH THE RESOLUTION TO THIS CRISIS SEEMS TO BE AT HAND...
...THE GAME IS ONLY BEGINNING.
I SHALL GIVE THE SURVIVORS THE OPPORTUNITY TO MOURN THEIR LOSSES.
THAT IS ONLY FAIR...
...AND IT WILL MAKE MY ULTIMATE VICTORY THAT MUCH SWEETER.
A NEW BEGINNING.